CHINESE WOMEN
TRAVERSING DIASPORA

GENDER, CULTURE, AND GLOBAL POLITICS
VOLUME 3
GARLAND REFERENCE LIBRARY OF SOCIAL SCIENCE
VOLUME 1076

GENDER, CULTURE, AND GLOBAL POLITICS
CHANDRA TALPADE MOHANTY, *Series Editor*

CHINESE WOMEN TRAVERSING DIASPORA
MEMOIRS, ESSAYS, AND POETRY

EDITED BY
SHARON K. HOM

GARLAND PUBLISHING, INC.
A MEMBER OF THE TAYLOR & FRANCIS GROUP
NEW YORK AND LONDON
1999

Library of Congress Cataloging-in-Publication Data

Chinese women traversing diaspora : memoirs, essays, and poetry /
    edited by Sharon K. Hom.
            p.   cm. — (Gender, culture, and global politics : v. 3)
(Garland reference library of social science : v. 1076)
    Includes bibliographical references.
    ISBN 0-8153-2162-7 (hardcover)
    ISBN 0-8153-3331-5 (paperback) (alk. paper).
    1. Chinese—Foreign countries.   2. Women immigrants.   I. Hom,
Sharon K.   II. Series.   III. Series: Garland reference library of social
science ; v. 1076.
DS732.C558   1999
909'.4951'0082—dc21   98-39916
                                                                                CIP

Cover art by Mary Ting, "Untitled Landscape," 1983, collage drawing,
Darby Downey Creative Services, New York.

Printed on acid-free, 250-year-life paper
Manufactured in the United States of America

Contents

Series Editor's Foreword

The United Nations Fourth International Conference on Women in Beijing (September 1995) prompts me to think about what feminists have achieved after more than four decades of organizing around issues of social and economic justice for women. I realize that civil rights are not the same as economic justice. While issues such as health, nutrition, reproductive rights, violence, misogyny, and women's poverty and labor struggles have achieved widespread global recognition, women still constitute the world's poor and the majority of the world's refugees. The so-called structural adjustment policies of the International Monetary Fund and the World Bank continue to have a devastating impact on Third World women. Militarization, environmental degradation, heterosexist state practices, religious fundamentalism, and the exploitation of poor women's labor by multinationals all pose profound challenges for feminists as we look toward the twenty-first century.

While feminists across the globe have been variously successful, we inherit a number of challenges our mothers and grandmothers faced. But there are also new challenges as we attempt to make sense of a world indelibly marked by the failure of postcolonial capitalist and communist nation-states to provide for the social, economic, spiritual, and psychic needs of the majority of the world's population. At the end of the twentieth century, globalization has come to represent the interests of corporations and the free market rather than self-determination and freedom from political, cultural, and economic domination for all the world's peoples.

These are some of the challenges addressed by the Garland series Gender, Culture, and Global Politics. It takes as its fundamental premises 1) the need for feminist engagement with global as well as local ideological, economic, and political processes, and 2) the urgency of transnational dialogue in building an ethical culture capable of withstanding and transforming the commodified and exploitative practices of global culture and economics. The series foregrounds the necessity of comparative feminist analysis, and scholarship and seeks to forge direct links between analysis, (self-) reflection, and organizing. Individual volumes in the series provide systematic and challenging interventions into the (still) largely Eurocentric and Western women's studies knowledge base, while simultaneously highlighting the work that can and needs to be done to envision and enact crosscultural, multiracial feminist solidarity.

Chinese Women Traversing Diaspora: Memoirs, Essays, and Poetry, the third volume in the series, is an elegant and creative text that embodies the above premises. It focuses on questions of identity, social location, voice, and the possibilities of feminist solidarity. This text not only complicates our understanding of diasporas, immigrants, refugees, and travelers, but also of the meanings of citizenship, of being U.S. American. Zhang Zhen says in her poem "In America"

> In America all memories about wandering
> Are thrown onto pile of car junks
> Burning in the wasteland
> Learn how to be a mute circle
> Under the boundless clear sky

The writings in this collection cover a wide range of genres, from poetry, memoir, and critical essays, to a roundtable conversation on the Fourth World Conference in Beijing. What holds the writings together is the thoughtful, critical tone naming various migratory histories, and examining in great depth the fraught relationships all immigrants, travelers and settlers to the U.S.A. have to negotiate—between communities of origin and communities of choice. One of the most important contributions of this text is in its mapping of questions of **being** and **becoming** for Chinese women. It is a rare collection, encapsulating in sharp, evocative terms, the diasporic journeys of Chinese women.

As Sharon Hom suggests in her introduction, this collection is a cartography of many points of arrival, and of a "point of no return."

What does it mean to be Chinese? What does it mean to be Chinese American? What does it mean to create alternative paradigms to read history and to dream about a future? What is the place of Chinese women in feminist and racialized communities and discourses, and in citizenship debates? What does it mean to be a part of the Chinese diaspora? How can we build communities of choice which foreground ethico-political agency? These are some of the questions taken up by law professors, journalists, women's studies scholars, literature and film studies professors, choreographers, dancers, tai-chi practitioners, and translators. The writings cross disciplinary, intellectual and spiritual lines.

Chinese Women Traversing Diaspora is a moving and inspiring testament to the radical possibilities embedded in "leaving home." This book illustrates the spirit of comparative feminist praxis that this Garland series is committed to.

Chandra Talpade Mohanty
Ithaca, New York

Acknowledgments

In 1994, while I was attending the annual meeting of the National Women Studies Association, I had the good fortune to discover that I occupied the room next door to Chandra T. Mohanty. Like many other women at the conference, I had read and been inspired by her work, and so I introduced myself. Encouraged by her warmth and intellectual generosity, I mentioned a project on Chinese women that I had been incubating for some time. She later slipped a flyer for this Gender, Culture, and Global Politics series under my door. From that moment of feminist synchronicity, this collection of memoirs, essays, and poetry developed. For this gift of intellectual and political space created by Chandra's vision for the series and faith in this project, I owe my deepest appreciation and thanks. To the contributors who were willing to explore this space with such imagination, honesty, and critical intelligence, I express much love and thanks for their patience, support, and friendship. I also want to thank Bob Lee and Eleanor Yung for access to the Asian American Arts Centre archives where I discovered the wonderful artwork of Mary Ting.

Numerous colleagues and friends have also supported this project. I especially thank my dean, Kristin Booth Glen, for her unfailing encouragement for all my writing projects (even when they did not appear to be directly related to law). I am grateful to Rey Chow, Maggie Chon, and Russell Leong for their generous readings of and invaluable comments on drafts of the entire manuscript; and additionally to Russell Leong for lending his fine poet's ear to brainstorming titles. Thanks also to Penny Andrews, Keith Aoki, Mary Lu Bilek, Sue Bryant, Bob Chang, Kandice Chuh, John Cicero, Pamela Goldberg, Julie Lim, Maureen McCafferty, Paul O'Neil, Ruthann

Robson, Frank Shih, Karen Shimakawa, John Hayakawa-Torok, Eric Yamamoto, Liz Young, and Jean Zorn, for reading various drafts and offering feedback and encouragement over the years. I owe a personal and professional debt to Pat Tynan for years of administrative support; to Lisa Carbone who without missing a beat, stepped in with calm and efficient professionalism over the past two years; and to my research assistant Melissa Fraser for her patience and good humor during the final tedious work of manuscript preparation. I want to also thank my editors at Garland, Claudia Hirsch, Richard Wallis, and Kristi Long for shepherding this project through each stage of development and production.

Finally and always, my gratitude to my parents who made this life possible, and all the "Homs at home" – Mei, Richie, Paul, Kimberly, and Timothy, who keep me grounded with daily noise, chaos, and sense of family. Special thanks and love to my teenage son, James, for his emotional support, love, cool sense of humor, and invaluable computer technical assistance for his low-tech mom.

CHINESE WOMEN
TRAVERSING DIASPORA

Introduction: Points of No Return

Sharon K. Hom

> We are too anxious to become strangers to ourselves
> As though the farther we fare from the starting point, the better
> We forget too many things.
>
> Zhang Zhen, "Too Many Things Forgotten"

In a fading family photo, my five-year-old self, framed by the airplane door, clutching an old doll, steps into that first moment of arrival. I am looking down to avoid falling. In perfectly fluent Cantonese, I disappointedly tell my father, whom I am meeting for the first time, how short he is, not as I had imagined at all. In a lifetime since then, my Cantonese has acquired a northern American accent, and many realities were indeed not as I had imagined. I have also become fluent in the foreign languages of an adopted homeland and a profession of choice. Yet within the destabilizing and contested discourses of the "post,"[1] the politics of location, and identity politics, the matter of "becoming" is clearly neither transparent nor unproblematic. As multiply inscribed subjects, "becoming" as well as being "belongs to the future as much as to the past, subject to the continuous 'play' of history, culture and power. . . . [I]dentities . . . are the names we give to the different ways we are positioned by, and position ourselves within, the narratives of the past"[2]—and, one might add, the transforming narratives of possible alternative futures.

As Chinese women writing and traversing diaspora, the ideological and material inscriptions of race, class, gender, ethnicity, and sexuality are implicated in and problematize our multiple positionings. Yet, we do not suggest that "Chinese women" is a static, coherent, stable subjectivity. One of the working titles for this volume was *Chinese Women in Diaspora*. As the static-ness and false locational stability of the "in" became apparent rather quickly, we searched for a naming that would suggest ambiguity, ongoing process, and the complexity of the various intellectual, artistic, and personal trajectories of these memoirs and essays. Given the inadequacy of existing languages and the impoverishment of terms through formulaic invocations, each effort at naming also implicated other discursive challenges. Settling on *traversing* (a poet friend's suggestion), a verb fluidly inscribed with constructive as well as transgressive possibilities, the present title signals our provisional reconstructions and gestures toward destabilizing movement itself as a locus of being that transcends narratives of linear trajectories or oppositional dichotomies.

In the overdetermined naming of migratory histories, the contributors are immigrants, foreign students, settlers, permanent residents, citizens, and travelers. Originating from Beijing, Shanghai, and Hong Kong, and traversing through Sweden, and Japan, and the United States, with global family networks stretching through China, Canada, Australia, the Caribbean, Latin America, and Europe, our blurred points of arrival and departures span different generations, and different local cultures and dialects. We are geographic inhabitants of various overseas Chinese diaspora communities. We are also figurative inhabitants of imagined heterogeneous and hybrid communities, and we are participants in horizontal alliances. As outsiders and insiders resisting minoritized hyphenated categories, we inhabit shifting centers and peripheries, where the demarcations are increasingly porous. And we share a sense of the difficulty of a return.

As Zhang Zhen asks—already knowing the answer:

> Should I be buried in this foreign land
> or drift back like white rain
> and drop into the lake of my hometown?
> —as if that place would ever let me return.[3]

Mapping intellectual trajectories, artistic explorations, and spiritual journeys, these essays and memoirs excavate the destabilized points of origins, transits, and arrivals. In my own circlings, I often find myself "lost in translation," in Eva Hoffman's words, still cradling" a tenderness for everything that is always lost."[4] Yet, in the face of serious ethico-political challenges presented by a pervasively unjust global (dis)order, it is important to resist the lure of simply romanticizing a reimagined past. The foregrounding of the particular in these personal narratives simultaneously and politically deploys, a "strategic essentialism"[5] that Lisa Lowe has termed an "Asian American necessity." This volume might then be viewed as contributing to the project of "restoring historical and locational specificity to the heterogeneous experiences and struggles of Third World Women" within a transnational circuit.[6] However, instead of projecting "representative" global narratives, these memoirs and essays grounded in, and crossing multiple deterritorialized, yet grounded localities, might be viewed as a type of auto-ethnographies, field reports written by native informants from/to reconfiguring fields.

Through these mappings of the complexities of "becoming" as well of "being" of diasporic experience, the contributors claim overlapping relationships to multiple communities of origin and choice, relationships that do not necessarily privilege race, ethnicity, gender, or any single locus of identity. Many of the themes that surface throughout these essays—border crossings, authenticity, representation, "subjecting" multiple selves and losing one self, agency and constituency, and questions of multiple loyalties and accountability— resonate and often parallel each other. Yet, situated in a localized historicity, invoking global diasporic intersections, and often marked by disciplinary resonances, they do so distinctively in each writer's own voice, including a language of silences. In developing her essay, each contributor has had to also explore a comfort zone for personal narrative that is inflected by disciplinary training, personal style, and professional experiences. This volume connects these personal narratives with a collective reflection project, a Round Table on the Fourth World Conference on Women (Beijing, 1995). In this discussion developed out of a series of E mail exchanges, a group of Chinese women who attended the Beijing NGO Forum present their experiences and reflections on various efforts to negotiate a complex political agency across a transnational terrain.

To introduce and contextualize individual essays and memoirs and the roundtable, I also offer some readings organized under the following subsections: Multiple Selves, Erasure of Selves; Complicating "Chineseness"; Complicating Diaspora; and Elder Half-Sisters, Dragons, and Ethico-Political Agency. Each of the readings might just as easily be reconfigured to fit under any of these sections. As intersectionality analysis underscores, our layered lived experiences and struggles cannot be enclosed within discrete social markers or categories or subjected to hierarchical identity affiliations.[7] We offer these narratives in an effort to enrich collective understandings of the differences embedded in Chinese diaspora and Chinese women's experiences and to complicate current discursive paradigms (in)forming identity politics and difference debates. As many critical race feminists have argued, one problem with identity politics (aside from its rhetorical fatigue) is that its essentialist moves frequently conflate intragroup differences.[8]

For example, Asian American studies since the 1960s has been criticized for its assumption of heterosexuality, its subordination of issues of social class and gender, the normalization of Asian American history as masculine, and its cultural nationalism.[9] Although many of the contributors to this volume resist the domestic frames of Asian American minority discourses and the flattening effect of an Asian American label, this volume's focus on Chinese foreign-born women may contribute productively to current theoretical and political debates within the United States. By offering narratives that complicate and dislodge ethnicity as a master category, these essays and memoirs are reminders of the importance of not allowing diverse experiences to be subsumed, erased, or homogenized into a monolithic Asian American, Asian, or Chinese experience, or by global or masculinist discourses.

In the growing literature of Asian women writing in/from diaspora,[10] this volume also offers an expanded range of interdisciplinary voices. In addition to academics, the contributions in this volume also include the perspectives of practitioners and nonacademics. They include two law professors, a journalist, a historian, poets and writers, women's studies scholars, literature and film scholars, a choreographer, dancers, tai-chi practitioners, and translators. In the face of disciplinary imperatives to label and to enclose work within genres and fields, these essays, memoirs, and the Beijing roundtable might be viewed as belonging to cultural studies, law, performing arts, journalism, literature, women's studies, history, and international human/women's rights.

Except for its sotto voce presence as the nation-state in the wings of immigrant narratives or its predominantly Eurocentric voice in English-language law and literature texts,[11] law is curiously marginal or only a minor disciplinary voice in the current discourses of cultural studies and the theoretical landscapes of the "post." The two law essays in this volume, by Margaret Woo and myself, offer two narratives; both are mediated through a law-trained lens and reflect critical stances to the role of law and legal discourse. In the first essay, "[Un]fracturing

Images: Positioning Chinese Diaspora in Law and Culture," Margaret Woo examines the co-implicated historical interaction of law, racism, and personal re-imagination. She intertwines personal stories with an account of the racism, orientalizing images, and misperceptions of Chinese/Asians reflected in the history and current resurgence of nativism and antiforeign sentiment in the United States. In the discussion of the historical legacy of Asian Americans and of the foreign-born in the United States, she names the complicity of law through Supreme Court cases and state and federal legislation in maintaining the exclusion and discrimination against the early Chinese immigrants.

In my essay, " [Per]forming Law: Deformations and Transformations," I offer an excavation of memory, the always-already-micro-political, to retrace my Hong Kong beginnings, how I get to law, and name some of the micro-aggressions, deformations, and other occupational hazards I encountered along the way. After years of writing in and resisting the language(s) of law, I do not know if it is possible to speak unmediated by law's disciplinary structures and claims of authority and legitimacy.

MULTIPLE SELVES, ERASURE OF SELVES

In her essay, "Self-reinstating and Coming to 'Conscious Aloneness', Ma Yuanxi traces her literal journey to the United States and her figurative journey of an intellectual and emotional search for a "self of one's own," a self that escapes the ideological enclosures of a party-inscribed self. Coming of age under Mao, Ma Yuanxi's essay narrates a micropolitical struggle and names the violence of authoritarian state-enforced regimes of meaning and personhood that create "docile tools." At the core of the demands of Chinese Communist Party doctrine to achieve self-oblivion, self-effacement, and self-abandonment, she locates the ideological prison that results in the dissolution of self. She compares this construction and destruction of self to the Chinese art of crafting dough figures (*nie mianren*), the "self manifested was a self that conformed to the Party's standards. . .that looked 'correct,' in the Party's eye and the public eye." She traces the deterioration of her faith in a contradictory Communist Party ideology that demanded simultaneously a self-effacing individualism and an explicit individual revolutionary heroism. She also explores the "uneasiness" of questions ignored, her struggle to look at "what kind of person" she had become, and her decision to leave behind everything familiar to head out for an alien land. She describes her "ridiculously careful" and fearful interactions at academic and women's conferences in the United States, remembering that in China, "keeping one's mouth shut was certainly the safest way to save one's skin." Finally, in the process of writing her dissertation, and working through the feminist theoretical framework provided by women's studies, Ma Yuanxi begins to write a self and reaches a "conscious aloneness" from which she can gradually find her positionality between "here" and "there."[12]

Eleanor Yung, a dancer, choreographer, and t'aichi practitioner, negotiates silence and words. Her essay, "Moving into Stillness," thus also implicitly complicates dominant Western feminist discourse that tends to stress the importance of breaking silence, speaking out, and articulating a self. In contrast to this focus on asserting an "identity," she invites another trajectory on a spiritual plane. Tracking her journey from making dances and the creation of an Asian American dance theater, to the use of t'aichi practice to heal, to find a core of stillness. Eleanor Yung's essay evokes Buddhist meditation. She questions culturally essentialist notions of identity and the illusions of constructs of individual identity in the material world. She describes a Buddhist practice toward stillness and a transcendental sense of self and being that gestures toward the significance of the life of the spirit.[13]

Grounded in classical Chinese dance, Eleanor Yung's body of choreographic work synthesizes movement vocabularies that draw from multiple cultural and aesthetic traditions, described by one critic as "a strange combination of ancient Chinese and Asian movements with a lucidly clear modern dance technique."[14] Writing about her own dances, Eleanor Yung creates verbal images of movement: crystalline figures at an unmapped end of some distant rainbow; shimmering travelers across centuries of desert trade along the Silk Road; bodies persistently tracing patterns of survival amidst the atrocities of war; paper doll dancers shedding layers of sheer fabric; swirling origami birds swooping in flight; the pounding of bare feet carving out wind tunnels of movement carrying a silent madness induced by cultural dislocations. While designing movement, time, and space on the stage, she also gestures toward the necessary expansion beyond the stage.

In response to authenticity challenges to what is Asian American dance and what is Asian dance, she writes "[i]t can be anything you want it to be. If you ask then does it exist? That would be like asking whether you or I exist, Asian American dance is as real and diverse as you and me. I think asking about what is Asian American dance is really asking about one's identity. Our identities are labels. What I am interested in, is not my identity, but what I am, after I rid myself of all my 'identities'. If we want to identify something in relation to something else, the labeling is only a reaction to something else that needs labeling." With a clear-eyed intention, she is gently shifting the questions. Moving along a spiritual journey toward stillness, Eleanor Yung closes her essay with a meditation exercise, leaving room for "articulate silences."[15]

King-Kwok Cheung has argued that a logocentric privileging of "voice" obscures the many tongues that silence, too, can speak, thus colonizing the very differences we seek to recognize. Cheung warns against a reductive perspective on silence that disregards what happens when voicelessness is induced not only by gender but also by culture and race. And one might add, when silence is full, rich and the product of clear intention. Instead of a distanced "performance" mediated by a proscenium stage, Eleanor Yung is choreographing silence and empty space onto the written page, inviting the reader to enter, to listen to our own breaths, and to open to an awareness of others. Reading her essay, I imagine each of us in a slow dance into healing.

COMPLICATING "CHINESENESS"

One framework currently circulated for expanding the meaning of "being Chinese" is Tu Wei-ming's "cultural China" concept. Within a project to explore the fluidity of "Chineseness" as intertwined with race, territoriality, ethnicity, language, and faith, he suggests an imaginary community of a cultural China composed of the

> continuous interaction of three symbolic universes. The first consists of mainland China, Taiwan, Hong Kong and Singapore—that is, societies populated predominantly by cultural and ethnic Chinese. The second consists of Chinese communities throughout the world. . . . These Chinese estimated to number 36 million, are often referred to by the political authorities in Beijing and Taipei as *huaqiao* (overseas Chinese). More recently, they have tended to define themselves as members of the Chinese "diaspora," meaning those who have settled in scattered communities of Chinese far from their ancestral homeland. . . . The third symbolic universe consists of individual men and women, such as scholars, teachers, journalists, industrialists,

traders, entrepreneurs, and writers, who try to understand China
intellectually and bring their own conceptions of China to their own
linguistic communities.[16]

In the imaginary communities of Tu Wei-ming's symbolic universes,
Chinese women intellectuals, activists, writers, and artists living
"overseas" might be situated on the map as Chinese diaspora. Yet the
"map" is not the territory of lived experiences. In our diaspora
traversings, the referents for one's own linguistic community has been
destabilized by the blurring and repositionings of "home" and the
hybridization of the languages in which we write and dream. Our
"Chineseness" is not only marked by race, territoriality, ethnicity,
language, and faith, but also by class, gender, and sexuality. And not all
of us privilege ethnicity in the complex positionalities and alliances we
claim. At the same time, "being Chinese" is also an "inscribed relation
of persons and groups to forces and processes associated with global
capitalism and its modernities" (Ong and Nonini, 1997:4).

Despite the increasing porousness between the cultural and
political meanings of Asian and Asian American, the relationship of
particular Asian groups to ethnicized minority groups in the United
States—Chinese, for example, to Chinese Americans—needs closer
examination if the differences engendered by diasporic traversings are
not to be erased by a cultural politics enclosed within domestic frames[17]
and a global cultural politics engendered by late twentieth century
capitalism.The essays in this volume track the transnational trajectories
of traveling images and narratives, unpackage their production, and
interrogate these differences and ask why these differences are
necessary and important.

In the disorienting and exhausting transits of layers of being
Chinese, being Chinese in diaspora, and being a Chinese woman in
diaspora and in academe, Margaret Woo claims marginality as a site of
resistance, and a diaspora subjectivity related to but distinct from the
domestically defined and enclosed identity of hyphenated Asian-
Americans. Citing the competing paradigms of loyalty versus
assimilation developed by Ling-chi Wong, Margaret Woo points out
the dangers to Chinese women under both of these paradigms, the
demands of sacrifice in the name of the national interests and
movements under the first and the feminization of women as "the
exotic other" under the second. Moving through layers of community
and self, negotiating the images and tensions of an inside world of

family and an outside world, and negotiating different cultural universes, she attempts to unfracture the contradictory and racist images with which she grew up. Throughout, the sense of being Chinese is for her fed by the competing images of her inside world, the foods eaten, the air breathed, the conversations and stories told at home, and a love of reading Chinese books. As a Chinese legal scholar, she describes coming full circle intellectually and personally to embracing the role of translator and bridge, in her work on the "home" country, to unfracture the images of China and Chinese diaspora for others and for herself from a space of a "third critique," situated between worlds.

Zhong Xueping's essay, "Multiple Readings and Personal Reconfigurations Across the 'Nationalist Grain,'" identifies some of the tensions in reading multilayered projections of "Chineseness," relocates the construction and perception of "foreigness," and explores some of the different ways Chinese Americans (due to domestic struggles) and the dominant American culture (largely due to ignorance) essentializes Chineseness. As a theoretical exercise of a Chinese intellectual reading, she offers a multi-layered reading of the Chinese soap opera series *A Beijing Person in New York*. Her essay is in part a response to the debates in North American academia on the "politics of locality" inspired by postcolonial discourse and the emerging discussions on Chinese diaspora, as well as to the questions posed by her sister about the "realism" of the soap opera portrayals of Chinese in America. In its portrayal of the latest wave of mostly well-educated PRC Chinese, she reads the series as an ambitious "Chinese" representation of the PRC Chinese and as a portrayal of a domesticated Chinese femininity that takes risks for a "real" Chinese man. That is, through its masculinist nationalistic gaze, the series tracks this trajectory of a "westernized" Chinese woman "moving eastward." Yet in discussions of the episodes with her ethnic Chinese students in the United States, she notes what appears to be a historically over-determined refusal to identify with the gaze behind the representation of characters that project to them a "foreign" perception, rooted in Chinese masculinist nationalist discourse. She asks why this representation is rejected as "inauthentic" by Chinese Americans and so positively embraced in China.

Instead of difference as exclusively the perceived-constructed-imposed effect of (an)other and an oppositional space of identity formation, Zhong Xueping names difference here as part of a discursive effort to uproot and dismantle a language of polarity (e.g., white/black, masculine/feminine, hetero/homosexual, East/West, foreign/citizen), and as part of a strategic deployment of difference in an ethico-political project to challenge hierarchical and unjust material structures. This invocation of difference also echoes Lisa Lowe's call both for a recognition of heterogeneity, hybridity, and multiplicity in characterizing Asian Americans and for Spivak's strategic essentialism as an "Asian American necessity—politically, intellectually, and personally—to organize, resist, and theorize *as* Asian Americans."[18]

However, these personal essays and memoirs do not advance an alternative prescriptive agenda nor a counter-theoretical move to these current diaspora paradigms. No single theoretical paradigm can enclose or explain the complexity, tensions, and potentiality of multiply inscribed and negotiated positionalities. As Arif Dirlik has argued in his radical critique of modern Chinese historiography, "[a]lternative paradigms enable us to see the alternative structures that in their contestation reveal the complexity of human activity, and therefore, of history. To bind history to a single paradigm is not merely to subject it to professional and social power but also to exclude investigation that does not accord with the current paradigms."[19] Instead, this modest project seeks to contribute to current theorizing from within and across disciplines by offering some narratives that might engender, complicate, expand, and enrich the dominant theoretical paradigms of Chinese in diaspora. As Chinese intellectuals, activists, artists, and writers, we draw upon these general critical diaspora positionings at the same time that we negotiate the claims of Chinese ethnicity, and dislodge ethnicity from its privileged position.

Dana Takagi has pointed to the "awkward limits of ethnic-based models of identity," particularly reflected in often uncritical notions of identity in Asian American studies. She argues for recognizing nonethnic-based differences such as homosexuality as an "occasion to critique the tendency towards essentialist currents in ethnic-based narratives and disciplines"[20] and for a rejection of the impulse toward a possessiveness of the Asian American experience. She identifies two broad distinctions between being gay and being Asian: the quality of "voluntariness" in being gay/lesbian usually not possible as an Asian American, and the very different political histories and discourses of each group. Critical of a "counting" approach to marginalization and experience, an add-sexuality-and mix-approach, the discourse of "addition" or "inclusion", Takagi warns against assuming that simply "adding gay/lesbian experiences to last week's topics in a course on Asian American contemporary issues, or by including lesbians in a discussion of Asian women, the deed is done." Instead, she suggests that "the task is better thought of as just begun, that the topic of sexualities ought to be envisioned as a means, not an end, to theorizing about Asian American experience." Instead of assuming or, worse, assigning a truth to a subject, she suggests an alternative—to theorize, to uncover in magnificent detail, the "situatedness" of perspectives or identities, to engage in political "conversation *and* argument, between the margins." This political engagement, conversation, and argument between the margins also enables our relationships not only to communities of our "origins" but also to communities we choose.

Vivien Ng's essay in this volume, "Coming to Terms with History," reconstructs her reincarnation both as "an intellectual with a social conscience" and a long process of coming out as a lesbian. Her narrative begins with a reunion call from a classmate, which takes her back to a "pre-history" of a childhood in colonial Hong Kong (a parental choice over the racism of New York City, where the rest of the Ng clan lived). As a child of parents who believed in the greater intellectual value of science over the humanities, Vivien Ng writes, "It was almost preordained" that she would be a scientist, or at least a medical doctor. After all, they gave her a chemistry set and a subscription to *Scientific American* when she was in fifth grade. Nurtured by the rigorous education in the exclusive single-sex environment of Maryknoll Convent school, amidst a six-acre campus exuding an air of prosperity and stability, she lived in a "comfortable cocoon," unconcerned with ethnicity and politics. Chinese history seemed boring, and ethnicity and Chinese culture were just part of family life. With a belief in destiny and chance, Vivien Ng tracks the sharp moments of consciousness shifts, and the ridding of heterosexist baggage and political apathy, that marked her process of "reincarnation," of coming out, into a politically committed life. She traces the catalyst for these transitions to fortuitous course selections and to having had B.J. Miller, an "out" gay, political intellectual with a social conscience," as a mentor in graduate school. In her struggles against her own alienation and the resistance in the field to "out" gays and lesbians, and in negotiating strategies for supporting the gay and lesbian students in hostile homophobic campus environments, she finally decides to overhaul her survival strategies. She puts the Lambda sign on her office door. She concludes that the best way "to maintain a full life was as an 'out' professor fully committed to mentoring students who might need a sympathetic ear during their coming out process, and who would speak out against homophobia. . . . It was the most liberating decision I had ever made in my life." Takagi's article points out that "to be out is really to be in—inside the realm of the visible, the speakable, the culturally intelligible."[21]

In the postscript to her essay, Vivien Ng also gestures towards a temporary peace with ethnic and disciplinary location:

> I have never felt more Chinese or more at peace with being a historian than at this moment in my adult life. I do not know how this came about, but when the first budget crisis hit us, I turned to the *Tao-te ching* (a Taoist classic) for inspiration and solace. When the second and even more serious crisis developed, I told my colleagues with a "straight" face that I would consult the ancient text *The Art of War*. In the classroom and at my office, I find myself telling women's studies students they need to know the history of the subject that they are researching, that they must know the historical contexts. I am now pushing to add more history courses to the women's studies curriculum. I don't know what all this means; perhaps I am finally coming to terms with being a Chinese historian.

COMPLICATING DIASPORA

At this historical juncture of domestic conservatism and the resurgence of nativism in the United States, and with the global circulation of transnational discourses, diaspora perspectives embedded in multiply situated positionings, on the margins yet resisting the polar logic of center margin paradigms, are particularly important for undermining neat categorizations. By exposing the permeability and ideological constructedness of nation-state borders, diaspora perspectives contribute to dislodging nineteenth-century statist assumptions that continue to dominate the geopolitical arena, and to undermining the gate- keeping functions of borders more generally. As Margaret Woo writes in her essay, "It was precisely at the borders that I learned that controls are escapable."

Diaspora perspectives also suggest that instead of a global world order advanced by transnational capitalist discourses, we (once we complicate the "we") are moving toward an increasingly inequitable global disorder. Critical of the discourses of postmodernism, feminists such as Interpal Grewal and Caren Kaplan argue for locating a transnational feminist theory and practice within the structures of transnational economic links and cultural asymmetries.[22] Critical of the discourses of "postcolonialism," Masao Miyoshi has cogently argued that colonialism is more active now than ever in the form of transnational corporations that are "obviously not agents of progress for humanity," as underscored by their complicity in global militarism and destruction of the environment.[23] In their study of the new Chinese transnationalism, Aihwa Ong and Donald Nonini point out that diasporas, like any cultural formation, are not intrinsically or necessarily liberating. They argue for the importance of recognizing internal hegemonies and sytems of inequalities in their call for the humanization and transformation of the so-called global system of late capitalism (1997). In such a neocolonial transnational (dis)order, critical diasporan perspectives and experiences might be helpful in informing local and global strategies of resistance and social transformation.

If, as Victor Li suggests,[24] the sojourner question is "Am I Chinese?" and the settler question is "Am I American?," the diaspora question posed by this collection might be stated as: Who am I and how do I exercise political agency in relationship to my communities of "origin" and of choice? Victor Li optimistically suggests that as those who straddle different cultures, we have a special role as bridges, to help build the new Pacific era and "New World Order," as conveyors of not only goods and services but also knowledge, understanding, and trust, linking two societies and linking the past with the future. Although some of the contributors also invoke this bridge role, some are more critical of the "New World Order" and address some of the tensions and challenges embedded in our problematized positionalities. Like other transnational critiques, diaspora critiques also direct attention to issues of class, inequity, and inequality masked by economic power traveling under more "neutral" banners such as the globalization of capital and labor or marketization (often implicitly tied to assumptions and values of Western-style democracy).

When we locate these pieces within diaspora,[25] we are not referring to what Stuart Hall refers to as "the old, the imperializing, the hegemonising, form of 'ethnicity.'" Instead of this territorially inscribed sense of the term, "diaspora" as inhabited by the contributors of this volume refers to a cultural politics of positioning and of literal and figurative relocations and transformations, to the reimagining of homelands to arrive at heterogeneous and hybrid selves, and to multiple communities of belonging. Instead of the lifelong homeward gaze of a depoliticized diaspora perspective, or the loyalty to a homeland of a nationalist perspective, the perspectives reflected in these diverse essays, memoirs, and the Roundtable remember, resist, and problematize the concept of "home,"[26] while simultaneously negotiating our ethico-political agency and accountability across a globalized and localized terrain.

Zhong Xueping's essay, "Multiple Readings and Personal Reconfigurations Across the "Nationalist Grain," is a self-reflexive account of the tensions in being and reading as a Chinese woman intellectual in diaspora, negotiating one's own positioning with the contestation of one's positionality by others. Zhong Xueping traces her encounter with Western critical theory and feminism and looks back at the political and cultural China-groundings of these encounters. Growing up during the Cultural Revolution, and as the daughter of parents with a deeply entrenched belief in the value of learning, engendered in her "a borderless sense" of what she wanted to learn. Learning English was in retrospect both reaching past borders and a form of resistance. Zhong Xueping also locates her willingness to "see gray," to view questions as more appealing than answers, to resist any form of easy labeling, and above all, to maintain a critical distance to, among other things, "home."

Sau-ling Wong has described a diasporic perspective as transnational, a homeward gaze that could last a lifetime, a lifetime marked by the finality of dislocation.[27] However, Zhong Xueping questions which way is "home." She asks who is constructing this homeward gaze and investigates the overdetermined aspects of these multiple constructions that project simultaneously from/to here/there. Situating herself in-between in an unsettled and unsettling positionality that cannot be assimilated by a single identity, be it counter/margin, the referential point of "home" is destabilized. Zhong Xueping observes that home becomes ". . simultaneously somewhere and elsewhere without definite borders and boundaries. . . . This paradoxical relationship between me and 'home' also conditions my relationship to the place where I currently live (speak and write). It involves constant negotiations of boundaries and borders, as well as efforts trying to find a common ground where even when perceived as an 'outsider' my voice can still be heard." To both places, in this sense, she is, and accepts the status of, a *bianyuanren* or a person on the margins.

When Chinese women in diaspora attempt to speak across demarcated figurative and literal borders, we often face nationalist and nativist challenges to their/our authenticity and legitimacy. Often treated as minors and outsiders in the various fields in which we work in the West, we are simultaneously told by nativist critics that we are no longer "Chinese" as they point to our fluent English and our "contamination" by Western feminism to undermine our critiques of China/Chinese women. Zhong Xueping points out in her essay:

> While the contestation of one's positionality keeps critics like me on constant alert, the question is why minority critics or Third World intellectuals have to constantly sit on their hands trying to behave themselves as "good" minority critics. No matter how vigilant we try to be, we are often held on a seemingly higher moral ground for the totality of challenging Western feminisms and theories. At the same time, it is also a ground that actually commands little authority and power, because, as qualified members of a minority, our positionality is already overdetermined by what Rey Chow refers to as the "center and minor relationship"—that is, at the receiving end of the power relation set by the center. It is a position where those on the margins constantly find their own positioning being undermined, especially when they try to pull away from this center-minor dichotomy. In this sense, unless we localize the postcoloniality itself, our own local histories and historical reference points cannot be taken into serious consideration, and our positioning will always already be done for us with our voices marginalized.

At the same time, our identities and agency are not completely other-defined and reactive. Shaped by historical and ideological processes and structures, the memoirs, essays, and poetry in this volume also reflect self-defined and proactive diasporic positionings. As Arif Dirlik points out, the increasing prominence of diasporas has called into question teleologies informed by nation-state and national cultures and the questions about their historicity makes it possible to imagine the world in terms other than the nation.[28]

Zhang Zhen's poetic memoir, "The Jet Lag of a Migratory Bird: Border Crossings Toward/From 'the land that is not,'" evokes a life of incessant border crossings, geocultural jet lag, and visceral cycles of longing and traversing multiple transit points. Her intensely engaged and (re)imagined memories, reflections, dreams, and poetry resonate an embodied ambivalence of longing and loss, the exhilaration of "leaving" and the "regenerating of amputated limbs" upon each return, the speaking through "the clumsy tongue" necessitated by each crossing, and the blurring of location when the clarity of "home" mists up. The writing is evocative, tactile, and visual and at the edges, one can hear the murmuring of multilingual crossings and the impossibility of return. Living outside the national markings of China, traversings across Sweden, Japan, and the United States, she learns to think and write in languages other than her mother tongue, and comes to ask, "Does one label the nationality of poetry by the language, the place of birth, residence, or simply the color of the passport of the holder?" Disheartened but ultimately relieved of a nationalistic representation burden carried since being a "little red pioneer" (*hong xiao bing*), Zhang Zhen faces the class and authenticity challenges posed by Chinese dissidents and other poets at international meetings, as they point to the privileged materiality and freedom of movement (as a marker of inauthenticity) provided by a foreign passport. In part locating herself freely and with some guilt to the loosely connected poetic "uncountry" of Chinese poets in exile, Zhang Zhen tries to be "useful in small ways," realizing that "being a poet in this epoch is nothing more or less than a very humdrum affair." Yet, this is a poet drawn to the "alchemy of images and imagination," a poet who translated with great love the work of the Swedish poet Edith Södergran (1892–1923) for its expression of a "volcanic intensity and radical iconoclasm" of a woman, who proudly declared, "I have discovered my own dimensions."

Amidst a life of diasporic traversings, Zhang Zhen describes rushing to the Swedish Embassy in Beijing to cast her citizen's ballot for a referendum on Sweden's tie to the European Union. While recognizing that the "fate of the declining welfare state and its place in a larger world" did not depend upon her ballot, she feels compelled to cast her ballot as a gesture of her intention not to be carried away by the "lures of diasapora" Rey Chow warns against. Zhang Zhen writes that this gesture "contradicts neither my lives as a poet writing in Chinese and an academic writing about China in English, nor my emotional and moral responsibility to the people I care deeply about."

In her essay "Growing Up Colonial and Crossing Borders: tales from a Reporter's Notebook," Ying Chan tells her story as she views good journalism: "funny, smart and a little smart alecky" and rejecting sentimentalism as a "luxury" Hong Kong natives cannot afford. With family networks in Brazil, Mauritius, Canada, Taiwan, the Philippines, a member of their own family mini-UN, she locates herself in Chinese diaspora and within a life of crossing borders. A writer whose dreams also "tend to be very verbal," she criticizes the mixed-up language skills of Chinese who learn their own language as a second language, the fate of colonized people to be in a "foreign country" in one's "own country." As a twelve-year-old, when faced with the sudden demand to name herself in English at school, she names herself "Winnie." She is Winnie until in 1972 she leaves Hong Kong and her English name behind for "self-exile" to the United States for graduate study. Hong Kong was "too small and politically and socially suffocating."

From the "ethnic press" to the mainstream press, Ying Chan writes of discovering alliances across gender, race, and ethnicity; bonding on the picket lines, reminding each other to keep their eyes "on the prize— the powerful and the mighty"; collaborating on stories (to "kick ass"); and having fun. In a newsroom culture dominated by men, she writes of the special bond with women reporters, sharing trials and tribulations as women, wives, and working mothers, and celebrating small victories or sharing a hug in weaker moments. She concludes her essay with a funny, tongue-in-cheek list of twenty-five reasons she is a journalist. Reason number one: "You can write about anything you know absolutely nothing about." Reason number 12: "Nothing in your life will go to waste. You can write about your depression, your operation, or with a little bit of foresight, your own death." In describing the often heartbreaking work of the tabloid presses, covering stories of senseless violence, rushing to storefront funeral parlors, city morgues, and hospital emergency rooms, she writes that "I would never say that I have seen it all. The job has taught me to approach each death with respect. For however lowly, each lost life is unique. It is my job to uncover those sparks that have dotted his or her path."

ELDER HALF-SISTERS, DRAGONS, AND ETHICO-POLITICAL AGENCY

In pointing out the contingent and nonmonolithic realities of social categories of analysis, Chandra T. Mohanty writes that "our definitions, descriptions, and interpretations of third world women's engagement with feminism must necessarily be simultaneously historically specific and dynamic, not frozen in time in the form of spectacle."[29] Her call to recognize specificity even as we build global alliances is an important reminder of the importance of daily micro-struggles. In the United States today, there is an increasingly mean, ugly, and dangerous public rhetoric fueling legal and political attacks on poor people, on foreigners," women, children, so-called minorities, and upon the environment. As the twentieth century draws to a close, we enter the next millennium with a global legacy of rampant militarism, environmental degradation, and pervasive social and economic inequality. As the gap between rich and poor widens, the picture of poverty, dislocation, suffering, and inequality also has a woman's face. Despite several world conferences, the adoption of the Nairobi Forward Looking Strategies, and the Convention for the Elimination of All Forms of Discrimination Against Women (CEDAW), women continue to be excluded from access to political and economic decision making, politically persecuted, discriminated against, and battered, terrorized, and killed in widening circles of violence; including "domestic" violence, and rape in war and conflict-torn areas.

In an unjust, gendered, militarized global (dis)order, how do we engage in small-scale work—that is, in Vaclav Havel's words, the "everyday, thankless and never-ending struggle of human beings to live more freely, truthfully, and in quiet dignity?" Rey Chow reminds those of us who are non-Western, but in part are Western trained, that we need to ask ourselves, "How do I speak? In what capacity and with whose proxy?" But how do we speak and act when the very coherency of self and constituency have been destabilized by discursive and material shifts? How can we exploit this very indeterminacy as a potent source for oppositional transformative cultural strategies? In a poststructuralist register in which everything, including our lived experiences, can be read as texts, how can critical theorists avoid the erasure of ethico-political questions through endless interpretative reading strategies and contests? If intellectuals try to avoid the transformative tasks of theorizing and building political strategies, they/we run the risk of engaging in intellectual exploitation of the conditions of our times and the suffering of other human beings. That is, intellectuals run the risk of intellectual vampirism. Yet, situated in complex positionalities, can we and how do we speak or strategize within and beyond existing discourses and disciplining categories of race, gender, nationality, and sexuality? How do we negotiate the strategic deployment of identities to build political alliances at the same time that we try to avoid simply reinscribing these markers?

Rey Chow suggests the importance of a critical awareness of the contradictions of material and invested locations and the legitimacy of the critical postures of diasporic intellectuals situated in the material

West. As Zhang Zhen asks in her essay, "The Jet Lag of a Migratory Bird: Border Crossings Toward/From 'the land that is not'," "How do we justify our privileged lives, of being able to leave when one wants to, to not have to cram into crowded buses, to be able to fly if one misses the train, to go back to running hot water, heated houses, free e-mail and free laser printers?" Rey Chow offers the uncomfortable criticism that "[w]hat academic intellectuals must confront is thus not their 'victimization' by society at large (or their victimization-in-solidarity-with-the-oppressed), but the power, wealth, and privilege that ironically accumulate from their 'oppositional' viewpoint, and the widening gap between the professed content of their words and the upward mobility gained from such words."[30] Yet the subject positionings of intellectuals are not static power positions. In my essay "[Per]forming Law," I invoke "Alice in Wonderland" as a metaphor for the sudden shifts of perceived significance, power, and authority as I "land" in different "rooms", mediated by the ideological operation of gender and race, performing my multiple roles for shifting audiences. Situated as intellectuals, as academics, as inhabitants of materially privileged lives in the West, the contributors in this volume and the roundtable attempt to address our responsibility for the ways we do draw upon the capital of our marginality and privilege to speak. Yet, our speaking is not simply located as marginalized or privileged in light of the shifting discursive and complex political frames within which we work. The Roundtable on the Fourth World Conference on Women explores this complex political agency across transnational terrain, as we grow and shrink in perceived size, power, and authority, landing in different "local and global rooms."

In 1995 China hosted the Fourth World Conference on Women and the NGO Forum '95. This was the first time China had hosted an international meeting of this scope. As many observers have noted, China clearly did not fully understand the full implications of hosting such a meeting when it made its initial bid to host it. In the two years prior to the conference and forum, women all over the world organized and participated in preparatory activities at local, regional, national, and international levels. During this preparatory process, Chinese women living and working on the mainland found themselves in exciting and difficult positions as they negotiated the tensions and opportunities of these international exchanges. During the 1995 FWCW and the NGO Forum '95 meeting in Beijing, governments once again recognized and affirmed their commitment to eradicating gender-based human rights abuses and to acknowledge that violence against women, that is, gender-based discrimination in economic, social, and political life, has disastrous consequences not only for women (more than half of the world's people) but also for the future and possibility of achieving a peaceful, stable, and equitable world.

In the aftermath of the conference and forum, women's rights activists and scholars, women's human rights organizations, and many other individuals and groups that attended have organized numerous debriefings to share experiences and to develop follow-up "bringing Beijing home" strategies. The roundtable discussion brings together several U.S.-based Chinese women who have been active in exchanges with women's groups and Chinese women's studies scholars in China. The participants were asked to discuss their experiences and reflect on the impact of these two international meetings for women in China. For this group, how and where we bring Beijing "home" and our own location in these interventions are complicated by our positions and perspectives as diasporic Chinese women.

Aware of the lures of nostalgia and diaspora, how can we engage the ethico political challenges presented by these shifting material cartographies?[31] Zhong Xueping suggests that to move against the lures of diaspora, "therefore, is to move beyond playing 'balancing' games at the margins, to perceive the margins as entry for intervention or as positions for raising new questions, . . . to resist being repackaged either by nationalistic claims or by any totalizing category, . . . so as to be able to question what is erased and why." In my essay I write memories that connect me to my communities of origin even as I negotiate my communities of choice. I try not to forget even as I try to resist romanticizing memory. I try to remember and write other languages. In the face of law's disciplinary claims of objectivity and rationality, I insert dreams and spirit visitations as other forms of agentiality, as well as poems. I suggest a move away from a politics of authenticity and I borrow cross-dressing and performance metaphors to suggest the possibilities of multiple loyalties and a politics of accountability and commitment through transforming disciplining performances. Yet, in addition to these discursive moves, there are also the urgent challenges posed by a need to engage constructive projects that reimagine our relationships and communities in empowering ways. Although such a transformative project is beyond the theoretical scope of this modest volume, there are many strands of theoretical, cultural, and activist movements across various fields that might be woven into a critical diasporan agency.

In referencing ethnic, gay, immigrant, subaltern, and other multiple realities, Radhakrishnan calls for a dialogic cartographic imaginary. He states: "These realities need to imagine their own discursive homes—homes that are not yet real in history. These spaces need to be 'imagined' in excess of and in advance of (avant garde in this sense) actual history in the name of experiences that are real, but lacking in legitimacy—Each of these lived realities . . . needs to imagine its own discursive epistemic space as a form of openness to one another's persuasion."[32] In this transformative act of engaging a dialogic imaginary, the cross-cultural tensions and experiences of feminist scholars and activists provide some insights into the difficulties and opportunities of imagining our "own discursive homes." What "languages" and theoretical resources can we deploy to imagine ourselves and our relationships to each other?

Women of color have criticized the racism and tokenism reflected in traditional feminist scholarship and the false universalism of "women" as a norm that centers white, middle class women. bell hooks and other Black feminists have criticized the term "sisterhood" for its erasure of class, race, culture, and other differences among women, and suggest the terms "solidarity" and "political solidarity" as the main feminist agenda.[33] Women of color feminists suggest the challenges of taking this heterogeneity seriously while trying to build consensus, political coalitions, and alliances across differences.[34] Maivân Clech Lâm has coined the term "elder half-sister" for facilitating alternative visions of more mutually respectful relationships among feminists. Drawing on Vietnamese language and cultural values, she suggests that "elder half-sister" would suggest both a respect for distance and differences and an acknowledgment of each other as a potential source of wisdom.[35]

In addition to a dialogic relationship that positions us as elder half-sisters (and elder half-brothers), I close with a dragon story. Although the dragon as a symbol of China's stagnant imperial past has been much maligned in recent antinationalistic critiques of Chinese culture, I want to rehabilitate and reappropriate this mythical beast through my reading of the following story behind the Chinese expression Ye Gong Hao Long (Lord Yegong's Love of Dragons). The story is appropriately recorded in the "Xin Xu," *New Discourses by Liu Xiang* (77–6 BC).

> Lord Yegong was known for his love of dragons. He had them painted
> on the walls and carved on the pillars of his palace. His robes were
> embroidered with dragons and his hat was decorated with dragons.
> When a real dragon in the sky heard of Lord Yegong's love of
> dragons, it flew to his house. The dragon put its head into the southern
> window of the house and its tail into the northern window. When Lord
> Yegong saw the dragon, he trembled with fear and hurriedly hid
> himself. What Lord Yegong loved were the fake dragons he had
> constructed.[36]

The expression that the story gives birth to, Ye Gong Hao Long, has
come to refer critically to someone who professes love and admiration
for what he or she really fears. In current U.S. debates around diversity,
multiculturalism, immigration policy, and implicitly, competing visions
of social justice, I have often thought of this story for its insights into
the importance of recognizing false welcomes to the halls of power, for
its reminder of the need to continue sticking our heads into the halls of
power that have excluded us in the past, and to resist the false
constructions of us within those halls. For each of us situated in our
relative positions of power to others, the challenge is also how to resist
engaging in false constructions of each other, and the violence of
reducing others to the sum of identity or intersectionality labels—race,
ethnicity, gender, sexuality, or class.

I also reread this story in the light of the dragon's significance in
Chinese mythology as the noblest, the most powerful, because
ultimately all things come to the dragon within whom all things already
reside. As we form multiple alliances and strategic coalitions, based not
on exclusionary or territorialized differences but upon multiple loyalties
to communities that choose us and that we choose, the ethico-political
challenge facing us includes this call to recognize and honor the spirit
and power of the dragon in each other, and to approach each life and
each death we encounter with respect.

NOTES

1. For example, I am referring to the discourses of postcolonialism,
postmodernism, and poststructuralism.

2. Stuart Hall, "Cultural Identity and Diaspora," in *Discourse and Post-
Colonial Theory: A Reader*, edited by Patrick Williams and Laura Chrisman
(New York: Columbia University Press, 1994), p. 394

3. Zhang Zhen, "Deep into Småland". See page 101 of this volume.

4. Eva Hoffman, *Lost in Translation: A Life in a New Language* (New York: Penguin, 1989), p. 274.

5. Gayatri Chakravorty Spivak, *In Other Worlds: Essays in Cultural Politics* (New York: Methuen, 1987).

6. Bishnupriya Ghosh and Brinda Bose, eds., *Interventions: Feminist Dialogues on Third World Women's Literature and Film* (New York: Garland, 1997).

7. For a current collection of perspectives on race, gender, power, and law, see Adrienne Katherine Wing, ed., *Critical Race Feminism* (New York: New York University Press, 1997).

8. See, for example, Kimberle Williams Crenshaw, "Demarginalizing the Intersection of Race and Sex: A Black Feminist Critique of Antidiscrimination Doctrine, Feminist Theory, and Antiracist Politics," in *University of Chicago Legal Forum: Feminism in the Law: Theory, Practice, and Criticism* (Chicago: University of Chicago Press, 1989), pp. 139–167.

9. The following publications provide more information about Asian-American studies since the 1960s: Yen Le Espiritu, *Asian American Women and Men: Labor, Laws, and Love* (London: Sage, 1997); Shirley Hune, "Rethinking Race: Paradigms and Policy Formation," *Amerasia Journal* 21 (1995):29–40; Gary Y. Okihiro, *Margins and Mainstreams: Asians in American History and Culture* (Seattle: University of Washington Press, 1994).

10. In addition to the influential theoretical work of Rey Chow and Chandra Mohanty cited by many of the contributors of this volume, see, also Meena Alexander, *Fault Lines: A Memoir* (New York: The Feminist Press, 1993) and Shirley Geok-Lin Lim, *Among the White Moon Faces: An Asian American Memoir of Homelands* (New York: The Feminist Press, 1996).

11. See, for example, Peter Brooks and Paul Gewirth, eds., *Law's Stories: Narrative and Rhetoric in the Law* (New Haven: Yale University Press, 1996).

12. Ma Yuanxi's essay needs to be read in the context of the dominant trope of self-introspection in political discourse in the 1980s in China and theoretical calls for the rehabilitation of the "human" as a theoretical and transformative political category. See, also Jing Wang, "'Who Am I?'– Questions of Voluntarism in the Paradigm of 'Socialist Alienation,'" *positions: east asia cultures critique* 3 (1995): 448–480. Jing Wang calls for a theory of subjectivity and a dealienated subjectivity that has the potential for resistant, emancipatory, and transformative action because it bears a diacritical and disidentificatory relationship to the state, the collective, and the Party. Jing Wang, "'Who Am I?" - Questions of Voluntarism in the Paradigm of 'Socialist Alienation,'" *positions: east asia cultures critique* 3 (1995): 448-480.

13. Because Asian American studies neglects religious traditions, movements, and institutions as "sites of power" and as guiding forces in Asian American communities, it is important to examine connections of "being" both a racial subject and a religious spirit in America. See Russell Leong, "Racial Spirits: Religion & Race in Asian American Communities," *Amerasia Journal* 22 (1996): viii.

14. Bill Moore, "An Asian Balm," *Otherstages* (April 21, 1983).

15. King-Kwok Cheung, *Articulate Silences: Hisaye Yamamoto, Maxine Hong Kingston, Joy Kogawa* (Ithaca: Cornell University Press, 1993).

16. Tu Wei-ming, "Cultural China: The Periphery as Center," in *The Living Tree: The Changing Meaning of Being Chinese Today,* edited by Tu Wei-Ming (Stanford: Stanford University Press, 1994), pp. 13–14.

17. As a result of major changes to the immigration law system in the U.S. in 1965, the demographics of Asian Americans changed drastically in numbers, in diversity of national origin, economic class. According to the 1990 U.S. Census, Asian or Pacific Islanders constituted 2.9 percent of the population, and Chinese constituted 0.7 percent. Bill Ong Hing, *Remaking Asian America Through Immigration Policy, 1850–1990* (Stanford: Stanford University Press, 1993), p. 4.

18. Lisa Lowe, "Heterogeneity, Hybridity, Multiplicity: Making Asian American Differences," *Diaspora* 1 (Spring 1991): 22–44, p. 28.

19. Arif Dirlik, "Reversals, Ironies, Hegemonies: Notes on the Contemporary Historiography of Modern China," *Modern China* 22 (July 1996): 243–284, p. 246.

20. Dana Y. Takagi, "Maiden Voyage: Excursion into Sexuality and Identity Politics in Asian America," *Amerasia Journal* 20 (1994): 1–17. Takagi defines sexuality as "that variety of practices and identities that range from homoerotic to heterosexual desire." In her article, she focuses on "homosexual desire and the question of what happens when we try to locate homosexual identities in Asian American history" (p. 3).

21. Diana Fuss quoted in Dana Y. Takagi, "Maiden Voyage: Excursion into Sexuality and Identity Politics in Asian America," *Amerasia Journal* 20 (1994): 8.

22. Interpal Grewal and Caren Kaplan, eds., *Scattered Hegemonies: Postmodernity and Transnational Feminist Practices* (Minneapolis: University of Minnesota Press, 1994).

23. Masao Miyoshi, "A Borderless World? From Colonialism to Transnationalism and the Decline of the Nation-State," *Critical Inquiry* 19 (Summer 1993): 726–751. Situating his analysis in a narrative of

decolonialization, Miyoshi is also critical of the preoccupation of academics with the discourses of "postcoloniality" and multiculturalism.

24. Victor Hao Li, "From Qiao to Qiao," in Tu Wei-ming, "Cultural China: The Periphery as Center," in *The Living Tree: The Changing Meaning of Being Chinese Today,* edited by Tu Wei-ming (Stanford: Stanford University Press, 1994), p. 220.

25. In its historical meaning, the term "diaspora" evokes exile and a myth of "homeland," and suggests a historical, cultural continuity with the homeland and, at the same time, the discontinuities of transplantation on "foreign" soil. The creation of historical diasporas may result from dispersal that includes forced exile, voluntary sojourning, migration, and dislocations due to ethnic strife, economic exigencies, and other pressures. See William Safran, "Diasporas in Modern Society: Myths of Homeland and Return," *Diaspora* 1 (Spring 1991): 83–99.

26. Sau-ling C. Wong, "Denationalization Reconsidered: Asian American Cultural Criticism at a Theoretical Crossroads," *Amerasia* 21 (1995): 1–27.

27. Sau-ling Wong, "Denationalization Reconsidered: Asian American Cultural Criticism at a Theoretical Crossroads," *Amerasia* 21 (1995): 10.

28. Arif Dirlik, " Reversals, Ironies, Hegemonies: Notes on the Contemporary Historiography of Modern China," *Modern China* 22 (July 1996): 243–284.

29. Chandra Talpade Mohanty, "Introduction," in *Third World Women and the Politics of Feminism,* edited by Chandra Talpade Mohanty, Ann Russo, and Lourdes Torres (Bloomington: Indiana University Press, 1991), 6.

30. Rey Chow,*Writing Diaspora: Tactics of Intervention in Contemporary Cultural Studies* (Bloomington: Indiana University Press, 1993), p. 17.

31. I expand upon this reference to ethico political challenges in "Cross-Discipline Trafficking: What's Justice Got to Do With It?" in *Disciplining Asia: Theorizing Studies in the Asian Diaspora* edited by Kandice Chuh and Karen Shimakawa (Durham: Duke University Press, forthcoming).

32. R. Radhakrishnan, "Postmodernism and the Rest of the World," *The International Journal of Organizational Analysis* 1 (1994): 328.

33. bell hooks, *Ain't I a Woman: Black Women and Feminism* (Boston: South End Press, 1981).

34. See Bishnupriya Ghosh and Brinda Bose, eds., *Interventions: Feminist Dialogues on Third World Women's Literature and Film* (New York: Garland, 1997).

35. Maivân Clech Lâm, "Feeling Foreign in Feminism," *SIGNS: Journal of Women in Culture and Society* 19 (Summer 1994): 865–893.

36. *Best Chinese Idioms* (Hong Kong: Hai Feng Publishing Company, 1989), pp. 237–238.

In America

Zhang Zhen

In America
Car windows open onto the wasteland of history
Where waves of rocks clang
I arrive at our new home: it has no kitchen
In America, I think of those Japanese cats
Tailless, as if castrated
Playing hide and seek with pilgrims
In the temples, up and down the mountains
In America I will become a cat
A cat with a tail, but it cannot meow
Roaming about in hollow white buildings
Not wanting to return to my kitchenless home
In America all memories about wandering
Are thrown onto piles of car junks
    Burning in the wasteland
Learn how to be a mute circle
Under the boundless clear sky

[Un]Fracturing Images: Positioning Chinese Diaspora in Law and Culture*

Margaret Y.K. Woo

The most recent portrayal of the mysterious Oriental appeared on the cover of the *New York Times Magazine*. Under the heading "The 21st Century Starts Here: China Booms: The World Holds Its Breath" was a picture of an ominous-looking Chinese man complete with close-cropped hair, oval sunglasses, and a cigarette in hand. The inside story continued with, 'Do you like dog?' Li asks. McCune freezes, his chopsticks in midair. It takes a moment before he regains his composure and politely tries the dish. 'It tastes a bit tough, he says, not unlike scrawny beef.'[1] It was and still is unclear to me how eating dogs could add to the understanding of the latest economic developments in China.

A similarly unflattering portrayal came in a past Republican presidential debate, when the conservative candidate Patrick Buchanan pounced on the importance of protecting the United States from

* I would like to thank Sharon Hom, the editor, for her constructive suggestions and for providing the space for all of us to speak. I also thank Deborah Kaufman and the participants of the Matthews Distinguished Professor Seminar series for their comments on a presentation of this chapter, and to Maggie Chon for her constructive comments and for her scholarship, which points out the importance of the narrative voice. See Margaret (H.R.) Chon, "On the Need for Asian American Natives in Law: Ethnic Specimens, Native Informants, Storytelling and Silences," *USLA Asian Pacific American Law Journal* 4 (Fall 1995):4–32.

"Chinese Communist" goods. The message underlying the phrase "Chinese Communist" was clear—it was a McCarthyite warning to the American public of the dangers of "Chinese Communism." Rather than referring to goods from the People's Republic, Buchanan was trying to reinvoke images of the "Orient" as the evil empire, a fractured image that was so clearly present when I was growing up in America, as a first-generation immigrant.

I shook my head at both these portrayals—in disbelief and also in recognition. The cold war was over, along with the images of "yellow peril," or so I thought. Yet, the images reflect the resurgence of nativism in America, a movement not new to American history and one that has taken tangible form not only in the rhetoric of presidential contenders such as Patrick Buchanan, but also in anti-immigrant legislation, and the growing wave of English-only laws enacted in various states.[2]

Upon reflection, I realize that these images reaffirmed for me some of the reasons for doing what I am doing—researching, teaching, and writing on the legal system of the People's Republic of China. The images crystallized for me my journey from settler in a foreign land to serving as bridge between my adopted home and the land of my birth.

According to Tu Wei-ming, three symbolic universes marked the imagined homeland that is "cultural China"—societies populated predominately by cultural and ethnic Chinese; the overseas Chinese communities throughout the world; and individual men and women, such as scholars, teachers, journalists, and writers, who try to understand China intellectually and who bring their own conceptions of China to their own linguistic communities. Yet, it is the third universe that has shaped international discourse on cultural China more than the first two combined.[3] It is important, then, that the Chinese diaspora partake in the third symbolic universe. I have for the past seven years taken on the path of negotiating my identity within these universes, facing the tensions at the points of intersection.

I am a foreign-born immigrant woman from Hong Kong, now a professor of law in a private East Coast university. I say this in the face of anti-Chinese sentiment, when a candidate like Pat Buchanan, who would like to see the United States be returned to European Americans, can win the New Hampshire primary and be, in some eyes, a viable candidate for the presidency.[4] I say this in the face of strong anti-immigrant sentiment, a time when the United States Congress is debating immigration reforms that will close the doors on immigration and deny needed benefits to legal immigrants.[5]

My parents and I immigrated to the United States in 1964 when I was seven-years-old. We came during a window of immigration reform after a century of exclusion. We came to join my grandfather and grandmother. My grandfather arrived in the 1920s and thereafter spent the bulk of his life arranging for our immigration. My grandmother came pursuant to a special bill in the 1950s. She came with a suitcase of fancy Chinese gowns (*qipo*) of colorful silks. In her vision of the United States and of herself, such clothes were necessary. Upon arrival to the United States, she never opened the suitcase, but instead, donned a chef's apron and worked silently in my grandfather's restaurant for the next twenty years.

Multiple images of ourselves surrounded us and our arrival. We were the first immigrant family in Boston to be given a quota of eight. According to my grandfather, the news of such a large quota had excited the Boston Chinatown community. Thus, when we arrived, the local newspaper came to do a human interest story on our journey to America. After all, my father and my grandfather had not seen each other in over forty years. In the mind of the reporter, we were a quixotic family, representative of the hope that America supposedly offers to all. We had waited a lifetime to come, and now America had given us the grace to land on its shores. Today, I still have on my desk a reproduction of that news photograph of me, posed with my father and my grandparents, looking slightly lost in the new country.

I had few preconceived notions of America. My image of this country came from the tins of biscuits and cookies that my grandfather would periodically send to us from America. In my young mind, then, America was associated with the sweet crunchiness and aromatic excitement that accompanied the arrival of each box. My imagined America were silhouettes of gracious ladies in bonnets, bearded men with tall hats, prancing horses and carriages, figures that decorated the cover of these biscuit tins. Nothing prepared my family and me for the vast isolation that struck us as we rode down Highway 28 to our roadside restaurant home. Nothing prepared us for the loneliness that came from being a community of one in a small blue-collar town, a loneliness that marked our early years in this country and lingers with us today.

Like most Asian immigrant children, I grew up in a dichotomous world—a world divided by language, culture, and emotion. There was an "inside" world and an "outside" world, and between the two was a porous boundary allowing for jarring interventions. The times when the two worlds touched were often times of misperception and fractured images.

In the "outside" world, it was a fractured image that my family and I faced. In the decade of my immigration, the media images of Asians were of *The Seven Faces of Dr. Lao, The Castle of Fu Manchu, The World of Suzy Wong*—all of which portrayed the East as mystical, exotic, seductive, and evil. The questionable, benign stereotype of Asian Americans as "model minority" was yet to come. In my "inside" world, my family and I were, to my eyes, quite ordinary, boring, and anything but evil.

In my "inside" world, memories and traditions from the "old country" sustained and centered me, even though I was a child when I left. In traversing each day between the "inside" and "outside" worlds, I found myself often in the position of explaining my "inside" world to friendly ears. Unbeknownst to me, then, my self-journey began—first as a small child who had to explain that "Chinese people eat rice, not lice," later as an academic who seeks to understand and explain her comprehension of Chinese America to mainstream America and of the Chinese legal system to the U.S. legal system.

My focus and my work, now as it was then, is to unfracture images of China, and in the process, also unfracture images for the Chinese diaspora. My forays into comparative law are as much a self-journey as an extension of what I have done most of my life. It is an intellectual path chosen because of my continuing interest in the broader inquiry of the relationship between law and society. On an emotional and political front, my work is meaningful to me because it also translates and positions China and Chinese America in the landscape of law and culture.

ON BEING "CHINESE"[6]

For Asian Americans, what happened to us in the "old country" continues to haunt us. As Robert Chang has so aptly pointed out, mainstream America placed a "figurative border" around Asian Americans.[7] In the late nineteenth and early twentieth centuries, Chinese immigrants, in stark contrast to European immigrants, were viewed as being unassimilable; the Chinese were perceived as foreign and exotic.

Mainstream American culture reinforced these images of China, and by extension the Chinese diaspora, as exotic through "altruistic anthropological desires."[8] Thus, Chinese racial representations were considered appropriate for museum or freak-show displays and caricatures in literary writings, from Barnum & Bailey's circus to Bret Harte and Mark Twain's Asian character in Ah Sin (1877). It was this concept of "foreignness" that led to the exclusion and the invisibility of Chinese Americans in the American landscape.

These images of Chinese immigrants were even given legal sanction. Thus, in *People v. Hall* (1854), the California Supreme Court upheld a reading of the Civil Practice Act to prohibit Chinese from testifying as witnesses against whites. In so doing, the court justified its decision on the grounds of the

> anomalous spectacle of a distinct people, living in our community, recognizing no laws of this State, except through necessity, bringing with them their prejudices and national feuds, in which they indulge in open violation of law; whose mendacity is proverbial; a race of people whom nature has marked as inferior, and who are incapable of progress or intellectual development beyond a certain point, as their history has shown; differing in language, opinions, color, and physical conformation; between whom and ourselves nature has placed an impassable difference.[9]

At a time when most immigration policies were left to the states, California, where most Chinese immigrants landed, greeted its immigrants by enacting the following anti-Chinese legislation: "An Act to Discourage the Immigration to This State of Persons Who Cannot Become Citizens," "An Act to Prevent the Further Immigration of Chinese or Mongolians to This State," "An Act to Protect Free White Labor Against Competition with Chinese Coolie Labor," the Foreign Miner's License Tax, and even a constitutional amendment with a number of anti-Chinese clauses.[10]

Federal law was no better. The Chinese Exclusion Act of 1882 denied entry and admittance for naturalization to a specific ethnic group for the first time, and erected a number of statutory racial barriers to naturalization. And in the 1898 United States Supreme Court case of *U.S. v. Wong Kim Ark* (169 U.S. 649, 731), which dealt with whether children born within U.S. territory of noncitizen parents were U.S.

citizens, Chief Justice Melville Fuller in writing for the dissent quoted from an earlier 1893 decision which complained that

> large numbers of Chinese laborers, of a distinct race and religion, remaining strangers in the land, residing apart by themselves, tenaciously adhering to the customs and usages of their own country, unfamiliar with our institutions, and apparently incapable of assimilating with our people, might endanger good order, and be injurious to the public interest.[11]

The concept of "foreignness" made it easier to deny Chinese immigration, citizenship, employment, or even the right to purchase land.[12] The identity that the American public created for and enforced upon the Chinese was repeated in the laws, which in turn legislated the Chinese out of existence. As James Moy has so aptly pointed out, "a good Chinaman came to be defined as one who made no impact," and a "'Chinamen's chance' was to have no chance at all."[13]

It was with these images of Asians—exotic, evil, weak—that I struggled and grew up. It was not until much later that social scientists and journalists generated a new image of the successful Asian American measured by educational achievement, occupational status, and income. The new image of the "model minority" is one that nevertheless still classifies Asians Americans as passive, submissive, and, by the inevitable association with the East, still the exotic "outsider."[14]

To combat these "outsider" misperceptions as I grew up, I had assistance and ammunition—other images that were similarly unspoken, but that existed in the foods I ate, in the air I breathed, in the conversations I overheard, and in the stories I was told in the "inside" world. I would overhear arguments between my father and his father on the merits of communism for China. I was told stories of my father's father as a young student protesting Japanese goods, or as an entrepreneur raising war bonds for the nationalist government. I would also hear my mother talk about her father, a minor warlord in Wuhan during a time when warlords ruled China.

But my image of China and, later, of Chinese diaspora took its most tangible form in the pages of the Chinese novels that I devoured in the summer months, and in the long hours after school and after homework was done. My mother, while not formally schooled beyond the sixth grade, loved to read. As an only child with parents who gave her little time, attention, or thought, she educated herself through the books that she borrowed or bought. When it came time to move herself and her family to a new land, unsure of what to bring, my mother did know to bring suitcases of Chinese books—ones that she loved and from which she will never be parted, and also children's books for fear that there would be none in her new home.

I was taught to read and to write Chinese by my mother in the summer months, and it was through the vehicle of written Chinese that I built my own images of China. I began with Chinese comic books and movie magazines, which my mother later mail-ordered from San Francisco. My mother did not care what I read, so long as it was in Chinese. Her theory, which has proven to be so very true in my case, was to give me absolute freedom in choosing what I wanted to read, in order to instill in me the joy of reading and of reading Chinese. As I grew older, I worked my way up to novels, many of which were historical, and even some of the classics.

It must have been in those years and through those readings that the roots of being Chinese, of being a Chinese in diaspora as an element of "Asian-America," took hold in me. Those years of reading gave me a sense of continuity, from my origin to my present, and helped me to reject a strictly domestic perspective of being an "Asian American"— that of an ethnic/racial minority within the national boundaries of the United States, separated from her cultural and immigration past.[15]

It was also those years of reading that instilled in me a belief in the beauty and power of the written word, which has led me to a life of scholarly pursuits—of reading, writing, and thinking. As someone who has combated the misperceptions of being linked to my "home country," I have returned full circle to define myself intellectually and personally through my work on the "home country." As Tu Wei-ming has written, "the meaning of being Chinese is intertwined with China as a geopolitical concept and Chinese culture as a lived reality."[16]

ON BEING CHINESE IN DIASPORA

The era of my immigration was the beginning of a movement by overseas Chinese to emigrate with the deliberate intention of permanent settlement. In the 1940s, the civil war on the mainland had stranded overseas Chinese, who expected to be able to escape the inhospitability of their temporary homes. This was true for my family as well, being unwillingly "diasporaed" to take root in a new land. When my parents first left China, they had no intention to make the departure a permanent one. They became Chinese diaspora with the onset of the Chinese civil war, first transiting temporarily to Hong Kong, and then permanently to the United States.

When the communists moved into southern China, my father was in Hong Kong on business, joined by my mother and my second eldest brother. A month later, my grandmother and my eldest brother followed with the intention of waiting in Hong Kong until things calmed down and the family could return home.

As the boat carrying my grandmother and my then three-year-old brother entered Hong Kong waters, my brother, exhausted from the long boat ride, pleaded with my grandmother "to turn back and go home." My grandmother consoled him. She said, "Let's stay and see what fun things there are in Hong Kong for a few days."

It was evening when the boat entered Hong Kong harbor, and my brother, fascinated by the glittering lights of the city so unlike the darkness of the village homes, cried out, "Look at all the lights. Will we return home when there are no more lights in Hong Kong? Will we return home then?" My grandmother absentmindedly replied, "Yes, we will return home when there are no lights in Hong Kong." In retrospect, my grandmother realized how very prophetic my brother's remark turned out to be. The lights in Hong Kong never went out, and there was no "returning home" to the village for my family. Our stay in Hong Kong lasted fourteen years.

According to L. Ling-Chi Wang, the Chinese diaspora is caught between two opposite paradigms—the assimilationist paradigm of the United States, the country where she has settled, and the "loyalty" paradigm of China, the country of her origin.[17] While the assimilationist paradigm poses an impenetrable barrier of exclusion by characterizing the overseas Chinese as unassimilable, the loyalty paradigm commands the overseas Chinese to remain loyal to their imagined homeland, be it the native villages, Chinese culture, or the nation-state. Particularly for the unwillingly displaced, the loyalty paradigm has resulted in an assumption of China-oriented nationalist sentiments.[18]

A settled but perhaps vivid example of the China-oriented society existing in the United States can be heard in conversations by overseas Chinese about Anglo-Americans. I have constantly marveled at the insistent reference by my parents and their friends to Anglo Americans as "*weiguoren,*" or "foreigners." In their China-centered minds, Anglo

Americans who live in America are foreigners just as, at the same time, my parents who live in America are "foreigners" to Anglo Americans.

On a more substantial level, loyalty can mean that China's national sovereignty and honor had to be defended. This sense of loyalty was heightened when China (like the Chinese in diaspora) was rendered weak and invisible by the imperial West. To the Chinese who made their way overseas around the turn of the century, many attributed their mistreatment abroad to China's weakness. As one poem carved into the walls of the Angel Island detention center in San Francisco Bay, which held the majority of approximately 175,000 Chinese immigrants who came to America between 1910 and 1940, lamented:

> For what reason must I sit in jail?
> It is only because my country is weak and my family poor
> My parents wait at the door but there is no news
> My wife and child wrap themselves in quilt,
> sighing with loneliness.[19]

Law was one major vehicle through which the West asserted dominance over the East. Much as Chinese Americans were not given voice in American law, the Chinese state was deemed voiceless as Western powers came to view the Chinese legal system as beyond the norms of the legal landscape. This perception of the Chinese legal system was epitomized by sociologist Max Weber's conclusion that the Chinese courts performed what he calls "khadi justice," which "knows no rational rules of decision."[20]

On the basis of the "backward" Chinese legal system, Western powers extracted territorial rights from China and, indeed, even established foreign courts on Chinese soil. Between 1840 and 1880, foreigners set up fourteen consular courts and two "mixed" courts (presided over by a "mixed" panel of Chinese and foreign judges) in Shanghai. The United States Congress even founded a federal district court in Shanghai, stretching its jurisdiction across the Pacific into the borders of China. These courts adjudicated cases brought by foreigners against local Chinese, and in the case of the "mixed" courts, even cases involving solely Chinese litigants.[21]

For many decades, even the discipline of Chinese law was largely neglected or the impact of law on China was mischaracterized. Only a handful of scholars wrote on the topic of Chinese legal history, and fewer still in the area of contemporary Chinese law.[22] When China was to have a presence in Western legal discourse, it was often presented as the "other" by which the United States can define itself. As William Alford so aptly observed about Western studies of China, "law is typically treated as an afterthought, if at all, with little, if any, effort to integrate observations about it into the more general picture being offered of Chinese intellectual, social, political or economic life."[23]

For many overseas Chinese, then, the desire to see China restored as a major power proved strong. Yet, the loyalty paradigm had and has its dangers, including operating to blind, honest critiques of China. In the years following the pro-democracy movement of 1989, China enhanced its patriotic education of students, promoting nationalism as a measure to win back legitimacy as well as the hearts of Chinese youths. It was an attempt to silence critiques by redirecting all critiques outward.[24]

Similarly, overseas Chinese have been and are called upon to uphold Chinese values and frequently to condone or understand problems as being "uniquely Chinese." Hence, the Chinese government justified some of the most blatant violations of human rights by rapidly evoking "Asian values" and some Chinese conceptions of human rights. Until recently, the Chinese government has vigorously resisted the idea of universal human rights, arguing instead that these rights are relative, contingent on culture and the level of economic development. While human rights with Asian values could mean the opportunity for "a soul-searching exercise for Asians to have a broader historical study of Asian traditions for values consistent with democratic, political, and civil rights,"[25] it has more often been invoked by the Chinese state to silence critiques.

For me, the loyalty pull also exists, a "yearning, if you will, for a more historically, culturally, and racially more complete home."[26] Hence, in 1987, I, like so many overseas Chinese, made my way to China, as a form of *xungun* or "searching for my roots." More importantly, I wanted to be in a place where I would not have to explain myself, where I thought I would belong. I lived for almost a year in Wuhan at the South Central Institute of Politics and Law, as a "foreign expert" in American law. Sojourned to "home," classified as "foreign," I was in transit in the land of my origin.

Wuhan, or more specifically, Hankou (now merged with Hanyang, Wuchang into the city of Wuhan) was a special place in my mind. It was where my mother was born, where she grew up, and where she later met and married my father. I had heard about Hankou from her, and through the web of memory and romance, I saw China as it was. I walked the city looking for traces of my mother's memories, each recognition validating that this was the "homeland China." I would write long letters home detailing life to my parents, happy when the details were confirmed in some fashion. Yes, people brought bowls with them to buy tofu, as they did then. Yes, the same department store was still the largest department store in Wuhan.

But inevitably there were differences. For one, I was never completely certain that I found my mother's old home. With streets renamed and buildings rebuilt after the wars, the city had so changed that it took several tries before I identified a house that came closest to my mother's description. The house, now inhabited by several families, bore the burden of the years and a new guardian who chased me away with hostile questions, making sure that I know I do not now, if ever I did, belong.

It was with this sense of "returning" and yet not "arriving," "foreign" and yet not so "foreign," that I found myself being asked yet again to condone and to understand. It was in China, feeling not completely Chinese, categorized as "foreign," that I realized I was not "Chinese" but "Chinese in diaspora." While in many instances coming from a similar cultural tradition does make it easier to understand, there were also many other instances where I did not. At the same time, it was precisely my position in diaspora that gave me more liberty to critique. It was in that position that I was able to raise concerns not otherwise within reach of my Chinese colleagues. It was precisely at the borders that I learned that controls are escapable.

ON BEING A CHINESE WOMAN IN DIASPORA

It may be ironic or perhaps representative that in the weeks during which I was writing the "woman" portion of this chapter, my children had a succession of colds, flus, and other viruses. I stayed up night after night, not with thoughts of what it meant to be a "woman," but with my lived reality (socially constructed or otherwise) of what it is to be a "woman." It was then that the Chinese novella *At Middle Age* by Shen Rong rang with special resonance.

At Middle Age is a story of a middle-aged Chinese woman doctor who collapses under the pressures of work and family. In the novella, the doctor confesses her guilt: "I am a selfish woman, who thinks only about her work," her voice quivering. "I have a home but I've paid it little attention. Even when I'm not at work, my mind is preoccupied with my patients. I have not been a good wife or mother."[27] This refrain was to be repeated in *The Second Shift* by Arlie Hochschild, published in the United States two years later, which documented a second shift of work awaiting American women at home after a full day on the job.[28]

Persistent cultural demands placed on women, such as those of femininity and self-sacrifice, require the women to play the roles of virtuous wife and good mother in the service of society and the nation-state. It is in this form that nationalism under both the "loyalty" and "assimilationist" paradigms poses particular dangers to women. Indeed, the relationship between women and the nation-state has never been simple.[29] Because "the imagined community of nationalism is authorized as the most authentic unit or form of collectively . . . the women's question is constrained to take on a nationalist expression as a prerequisite for being considered political."[30]

Under the "loyalty" paradigm, nationalistic expression calls upon women to sacrifice their equality on behalf of national interests and movements.[31] Thus, in China, the goal of gender equality has historically been subordinated to higher national goals and interests. As national interests change with each new economic and political campaign, Chinese women's role also changes in self-sacrifice to serve nationalist interests—from the "socialist mother" of liberation to the "iron woman" of the Cultural Revolution and back to the "mother" role implicit in the "return home" policy of present-day economic reforms.[32]

Under the "assimilationist" paradigm, meanwhile, nationalism in the Western context manipulates the category of woman to feminize the East, thereby further subjugating the East as the unassimilable "exotic Other." Placing East and West at either ends of a spectrum, Western catalogues define the East as weak, passive, and feminine, while the West is defined as dominant, active, and male. And by extension, the Chinese diaspora is treated as weak and submissive.

Indeed, there is an international dimension and gendered dimension imposed on any issues dealing with Asian Americans, one of which is America's perception of countries in Asia as "feminine." Perceptions of China were especially linked to the historic relationship the United States had with China originating in the nineteenth century—a time of national definition obtained through colonialism as the imperial West descended on China to extract land, treaty ports, and trade concessions. Aside from portrayals of China as exotic, then, there was a portrayal of the East as feminine, and by definition, weak and submissive.

One of the most vivid indictments of this "feminine" imagery of the Orient is captured in *M. Butterfly*, a play written by Henry David Hwang.[33] In *M. Butterfly*, Huang depicts a man, Rene Gilliard, who falls in love with a Beijing opera star, who turns out to be a spy and a man. As summarized by Song Liling, the Beijing opera star who encompasses Gilliard's fantasy of collapsing the Orient and the self-sacrificing woman:

> the west has a sort of international rape mentality—the west thinks of itself as masculine—big guns, big industry, big money—so the East is feminine—weak, delicate, poor, but good at art, and full of inscrutable wisdom—the feminine mystique.

For Chinese women in diaspora, then, the imposition of femininity on the Orient renders our images even more fractured. Using one category to subjugate another doubly cripples the voices of Chinese women.[34]

Being "Chinese," being "in diaspora," and being "woman" are all layers of identities that coexist within me, along with those of class and status. I transit to each layer depending on the moment and circumstance. Elaine Kim once wrote optimistically that "we can 'have it all' by claiming an infinity of layers of self and community.[35] Yet, it is precisely this constant transit between worlds and identities that can become so exhausting. This transit, like all transits and journeys, can be at times disorienting, at times exhilarating, and, at those moments when worlds intersect, so fractious.

ON BEING A CHINESE WOMAN IN DIASPORA AND ACADEME

My grandfather had wanted to be a scholar. When his father died unexpectedly, and the family was in debt, my grandfather left school to sojourn to the United States, not as a scholar but as a businessman. My grandmother had wanted to be teacher. When she turned eighteen, her parents told her that an arranged marriage, not teaching, was in her future. She cried all that night and many others. Growing up in the back of my grandfather's restaurant, I had not thought of being either a scholar or a teacher. That status and privilege came much later, as I moved beyond the restaurant to elite schools and professions. Yet, I remain in the margins as I struggle with the knowledge that privilege did not come easy and that privilege pulls one to leave others behind.

"You are looking for a couch?" asked the saleswoman. "Yes, for my office." I answered. "What do you do?" she inquired. "I teach," I replied simply. "Oh, what grade?" she questioned. "No, I teach at the college level," I responded, a little frustrated at the all-too-familiar exchange. Could it be that astonishing that I am a professor? Afterall, we were in Cambridge, Massachusetts, a haven for academics and would-be academics. "What do you teach—physics or math?" the saleswoman naively persisted.

I remain in the margins even as I work, live, and produce in the center. The reality is that today Asian Americans are still underrepresented on U.S. law faculties (there are only about eighty Asian American law professors in the United States, of whom a smaller number still are Chinese Americans). As I grow older, however, I hope this positionality may increasingly be by choice. As bell hooks has written, "I make a definite distinction between that marginality which is imposed by oppressive structures and that marginality one chooses as site of resistance—as location of radical openness and possibility.... We are transformed, individually, collectively, as we make radical creative space which affirms and sustains our subjectivity, which gives us a new location from which to articulate our sense of the world."[36]

This site of resistance is certainly necessary as misconceptions of China as "foreign" continue to rage. Global issues follow the Chinese diaspora, and images of Chinese diaspora are still defined by misperceptions associated with events thousands of miles away. When trade talks between the United States and Japan suffered, images of Japanese Americans also suffered. So too has the recent cooling of relations between China and the United States revitalized negative images of the exotic Orient, resulting , at the extreme, in increased racial violence against Asian Americans.

Repetitious of history, immigration exclusion accompanies exotic images of Asians. I do not know whether myths drive legislation or legislation drives myths.[37] But most certainly, they go hand in hand. Thus, we see today immigration reform legislation that seeks to shut off immigration, with the biggest impact on Asians and, in particular, Chinese diaspora.[38] California, still the portal for Asian immigration, led the way with Proposition 187, and federal law is following closely behind. Recent federal immigration reform proposals will again close the door to Chinese immigrants, to effectively build a wall around the

United States—a scenario that China has once implemented and then rejected in the imperial past.

For the Chinese diaspora or Chinese Americans, a link to China is important as a form of history and context for Chinese Americans, who occupy a unique space of both Chinese and American culture.[39] The identity of Chinese Americans does not begin with their immigration to the United States, devoid of their cultural and historical roots. More importantly, definitions of Chinese Americans should not be defined by misconceptions of "cultural China."

Clifford Geertz once wrote on the liberalizing experience of confronting radical otherness. As one who would like to engage in serious comparative studies, I am caught between worlds. How do I avoid the pitfalls of characterizing China as a radical other? How do I negotiate my identity as part of the Chinese diaspora with my identity as a scholar? How do I maneuver against the preconceived notion that I belong to one group and not to the other, and against scholars who would see me as an overseas Chinese whose knowledge is limited to my background? How do I respond to the Chinese diaspora who call on my identity not to criticize, and on my nationalism?

I have no answers, but as an Asian-born academic, I believe my outlook and research activities may be different. As I write in the area of Chinese law, I want, as Rey Chow once stated, to present a "third critique of China, one that is neither east nor west, but from a unique position of transit."[40] It is the position of studying and being studied, of the ethnic spectator as it is called by Chow, and the "marginal (wo)man," as it is called by others.[41] The term "marginal man" was coined by anthropologists to refer to the informant who knows both native culture and the vocabulary of the investigator, and the anthropologist himself who will become a "marginal man" if he or she has successfully penetrated and participated in the life of the investigated. It is this marginality that is empowering, and that I hope will remain.

NOTES

1. Ian Buruma, Seth Faison, and Fareed Zakaria, "The 21st Century Starts Here: China Booms: The World Holds Its Breath," *New York Times Magazine* (February 18, 1996). For a thoughtful article on images of Asian Americans and the law, see Keith Aoki, "Foreignness and Asian American Identities: Yellowface, Propaganda and Bifurcated Racial Stereotypes and World War II

Propaganda," *ULCA Asian Pacific American Law Journal* 4 (forthcoming 1998).

2. See Illegal Immigration Reform and Immigrant Responsibility Act, Pub. L. No. 104-208, 110 Stat. 3009; Personal Responsibility and Work Opportunity Reconciliation Act of 1996, Pub. L. No. 104-193, 110 Stat. 2105. At last count, close to half of the states in the United States had passed English-only legislation making English the exclusive language for public documents and proceedings. In addition, several pieces of federal legislation were introduced in 1996 by Congress that would make English the official language. See S. 356, the Language of Government Act, introduced by Senator Richard Shelby of Alabama, and H.R. 351, the Bilingual Voting Requirements Repeal Act, introduced by Representative John Porter of Illinois. See also Linda Greenhouse, "Justice to Review Arizona's Law Making English Its Official Language," *New York Times* (March 26, 1996): A10.

3. Tu Wei-ming, "Cultural China: The Periphery as Center," in Tu Wei-ming, ed., The Living Tree: The Changing Meaning of Being Chinese Today, (Stanford: Stanford University Press, 1994), pp. 13–14.

4. For example, Buchanan was quoted as saying, "There is nothing wrong with us sitting down and arguing the issue that we are a European country." Les Payne, "What Buchanan Really Means," *Newsday* (December 22, 1991):46.

5. See Illegal Immigration Reform and Immigrant Responsibility Act, Pub. L. No. 104-208, 110 Stat. 3009 ()September 30, 1996); Personal Responsibility and Work Opportunity Reconciliation Act of 1996, Pub. L. No. 104-193, 110 Stat. 2105.

6. My use of quotations around certain terms is deliberate. It is to recognize that there are differences within certain categories and to indicate that I am not defining what is essentially Chinese or diaspora or woman, in this essay. Rather, I am simply giving voice to my experiences within the dominant understanding of these socially created categories.

7. According to Chang, foreignness is inscribed upon Asian Americans much like a figurative border, which in addition to confirming the belongingness of the "real" Americans, marks Asian Americans as targets of nativistic racism. See Robert Chang, "A Meditation on Borders," in Juan Perea ed., *Immigrants Out! The New Nativism and the Anti-Immigrant Impulse in the United States* (New York: New York University Press, 1997).

8. James S. Moy, *Marginal Sights: Staging the Chinese in America* (Iowa City: Iowa University Press, 1993), p. 8.

9. *People v. Hall*, 4 Cal. 399, 409 (Oct. 1854).

10. Images and media intertwined. According to a study by James Moy, shortly after Harte and Twain's play *Ah Sin* opened in New York, the California

State Senate submitted "An Address to the People of the United States Upon the Evils of Chinese Immigration" (August 13, 1877). James S. Moy, *Marginal Sights: Staging the Chinese in America* (Iowa City: Iowa University Press, 1993), p. 27.

11. *United States v. Wong Kim Ark*, 169 U.S. 649, 731 (1898), quoting *Fong Yue Ting v. United States*, 149 U.S. 698, 717 (1893).

12. Neil Gotanda argued that the United States Supreme Court has created for Asian Americans the dual identities of "alien" and "racial minority" such that "Other non-Whites" have been entitled to much more deferential judicial review with far less favorable results than "non-Whites." Neil Gotanda, "Asian American Rights and the 'Miss Saigon Syndrome,'" in Hyung-chan, Kim ed., *Asian Americans and the Supreme Court: A Documentary History* (Seattle: University of Washington Press, 1992), p. 1096.

13. James S. Moy, *Marginal Sights: Staging the Chinese in America* (Iowa City: University of Iowa Press, 1993), p. 34.

14. Neil Gotanda, "Asian American Rights and the 'Miss Saigon Syndrome,'" in Hyung-chan Kim, ed., *Asian Americans and the Supreme Court: A Documentary History* (Seattle: University of Washington Press, 1992), p. 1096.

15. Albeit the line between "Asian" and Asian American" is blurring as Asia ascends as an economic power and as the postmodern world rejects the boundaries of nation-state. As aptly pointed out by Sau-Ling C. Wong, this is also reflected in the relaxation of distinction between Asian-American studies and Asian studies. Sau-Ling C. Wong, "Denationalization Reconsidered: Asian American Cultural Criticism at a Theoretical Crossroad," in "Thinking Theory in Asian American Studies," *Amerasia Journal* 21, nos. 1 & 2 (1995): 1–29.

16. Tu Wei-ming, "Cultural China: The Periphery as the Center," in Tu Wei-ming, ed., *The Living Tree: The Changing Meaning of Being Chinese Today* (Stanford: Stanford University Press, 1994), p. 1.

17. L. Ling-Chi Wang, "The Structure of Dual Domination: Towards a Paradigm for the Study of the Chinese Diaspora in the United States," *Amerasia Journal* 21, nos. 1 & 2: (1995):149–169.

18. The claim to loyalty in part is attributable to the traditional thinking of the Chinese people and state that overseas Chinese (regardless of racial mixture) remain Chinese in the fullest sense as long as they are able to claim a Chinese male ancestor, a homeplace in China from which this ancestor supposedly emigrated, and observe some manner of cultural practices. David Yen-ho Wu, "Chinese and Non-Chinese Identities," in Tu Wei-ming, ed., *The Living Tree: The Changing Meaning of Being Chinese Today* (Stanford: Stanford University Press, 1994), p. 152.

19. Him Mark Lai, Genny Lim, and Judy Yung, eds., Island: Poetry and History of Chinese Immigrants on Angel Island 1910–1940 (Seattle: University of Washington Press, 1980), p. 84, (Poem no. 34).

20. Max Weber, G. Roth, and P. Wittich, eds., *Economy and Society*, vol. 3 (New York: Bedminster Press, 1968), p. 976.

21. For a good discussion of how the "mixed" courts served foreigners to gain greater access to the Chinese economy, see Tahirih Lee, "Risky Business: Courts, Culture and the Marketplace," *University of Miami Law Review* 47 (1993): 1335; see also, Thomas B. Stephens, *Order and Discipline in China: The Shanghai Mixed Court, 1911--927* (Seattle: University of Washington Press, 1992).

22. Stanley Lubman, "Studying Contemporary Chinese Law: Limits, Possibilities and Strategy," *American Journal of Comparative Law* 39 (1991): 293–341.

23. William P. Alford, "Law, Law, What Law? Why Western Scholars of Chinese History and Society Have not Had More to Say about Its Law," *Modern China* 21, no. 4 (October 1997):398–419.

24. Under the guise of nationalism, China has sought to characterize the U.S. government's threats to impose trade sanctions on China for copyright piracy, and its pressures on human rights, and its objections to China's entry into the World Trade Organization, as a strategy to prevent China's rise as a major Asian power. Patrick E. Tyler, "China's Campus Model for the 90's: Earnest Patriot," *New York Times* (April 23, 1996): A4.

25. Joseph Chan, "The Task for Asians: To Discover Their Own Political Morality for Human Rights," *Human Rights Dialogue* 4 (March 6, 1996): 5.

26. Victor Hao Li, "From Qiao to Qiao," in Tu Wei-ming, ed., *The Living Tree: The Changing Meaning of Being Chinese Today* (Cambridge: Harvard University Press, 1994), p. 219.

27. Shen Rong, *At Middle Age* (Beijing: Foreign Languages Press, 1987), p. 45.

28. Arlie Hochschild, *The Second Shift: Working Parents and the Revolution at the Home* (New York: Viking Press, 1989).

29. For articles questioning why nationalism invariably entails the subordination of women, see Hilary Charlesworth et al., "Feminist Approaches to International Law," *American Journal of International Law* 85 (1991): 620; R. Radhakrishnan, "Nationalism, Gender, and the Narrative of Identity," in Andrew Parker et al., eds., *Nationality and Sexualities* (New York: Routledge, 1992), p. 77.

30. Partha Chatterjee, "The Nationalist Resolution of the Women's Question," in Kumkum Sangari and Sudesh Vaid, eds., *Recasting Women:*

Essays in Colonial History (New Brunswick, N.J.: Rutgers University Press, 1990)

31. Joanna de Groot, "Conceptions and Misconceptions: The Historical and Cultural Context of Discussion on Women and Development," in Haleh Afshar, ed., *Women, Development and Survival in the Third World* (New York: Longman Press, 1991), p. 107.

32. In times of labor surplus, as in the First Five Year Plan from 1953 to 1957, women were encouraged to stay home and contribute to the socialist cause through their housework. In times of mass mobilization or revolutionary zeal, as in the Great Leap Forward or the Cultural Revolution, women were called back out of the home and into the labor force. Today, with economic reforms and concomitant greater unemployment, women are again asked to "return home." At each juncture of nation-building, then, Chinese women have been asked to sacrifice for the state. See Margaret Y.K. Woo, "Chinese Women Workers: A Delicate Balance Between Biology and Equality," in C. Gilmartin et al., eds., *Engendering China* (Cambridge: Harvard University Press, 1994).

33. For a good discussion of America's representation of Asia as seen through Henry David Hwang's *M. Butterfly*, see James S. Moy, *Marginal Sights: Staging the Chinese in America* (Iowa City: University of Iowa Press, 1993), pp. 115–124.

34. Chinese women were refused permission to land in California by the commissioner of immigration, who was authorized to remove "debauched women."

35. Sau-ling Wong, citing to Elaine Kim, "Foreword," xvi, "Denationalization Reconsidered: Asian American Cultural Criticism at a Theoretical Crossroads," in *Amerasia Journal* 21, nos. 1 & 2 (1995): 19.

36. bell hooks, "Choosing the Margin as a Space of Radical Openness," from *Yearning: Race, Gender and Cultural Politics* (Boston: South End Press, 1990), p. 153.

37. The myths accompanying recent immigration reforms include those reflected in a 1993 poll in which 70 percent of Americans agreed with the view that today's immigrants are not as well educated as native-born Americans; immigrants put people out of work; immigrants are overloading state prisons; and immigrants use more welfare than the native-born. For a good analysis of the myths surrounding immigration, see Michael Fix and Jeffrey S. Passel, "Perspective on Immigration," *Los Angeles Times,* August 1, 1994, Metro, part B, p. 97, col. 1; "Amid Myths and Misconceptions of Immigration," *The Houston Chronicle,* August 14, 1994, p. 1; "Public Attitudes about Immigration Shaped Largely by Myth and Emotions," *The Columbia* (Vancouver, WA), August 24, 1994, p. A13.

38. See Illegal Immigration Reform and Immigration Responsibility Act, Pub. L. No. 104-208, 110 Stat. 3009.

39. Thus, Asian studies and Asian American studies may be moving together, because we should not "[draw] boundaries and [isolate] the immigrant's history and culture of the homeland under the rubric of Asian studies, and focusing only on [their] existence after arrival in the United States as shaped by the American context. 'America' could not be understood independently of 'Asia' or vice versa." See Sucheta Mazumdar, "Asian American Studies and Asian Studies: Rethinking Roots," in Shirley Hume et al., eds., *Asian Americans: Comparative and Global Perspectives* (Pullman: Washington State University Press, 1991), pp. 40–41.

40. Rey Chow, keynote address at a conference on "Sex, Gender and Public Space in Contemporary China," Tufts University, Medford, Mass., April 5, 1996. Chow has written on the role for ethnic spectators and the non-Western, but Westernized, context, in "Seeing Modern China," in Rey Chow, *Woman and Chinese Modernity: The Politics of Reading Between East and West* (Minneapolis: University of Minnesota Press, 1991), pp. 32–33.

41. Cho-yun Hsu, "A Reflection on Marginality," in Tu Wei-ming, ed., *The Living Tree: The Changing Meaning of Being Chinese Today* (Stanford: Stanford University Press, 1994), pp. 239–241.

The Jet Lag of a Migratory Bird: Border Crossings Toward/From 'the land that is not'

*Zhang Zhen**

TRAVELOGUES

tongues and limbs

Summer is perhaps the quintessential time of arrival and leave-taking in the modern calendar, characterized by school recesses, tourist exodus, and retreats to the countryside and nature, which are supposedly untarnished by smog and city noise. Doubtless complicit in many ways with this programmed notion of summertime, I have treated my various summer sojourns as intensely personal, especially since I left China in the summer of 1983 as a hopeful and anxious young immigrant to Sweden. Summertime travel has not simply meant for me departures, reunions, temporary suspension of routines, and sometimes adventures, they have been, more than anything else, spatial and linguistic events that involve perspectival shifts and cultural transpositions between different places, faces, and tongues.

Yet, prior to any intellectual reflection on the rewards that language courses, summer research projects, or ethnographic travels

*I wish to thank Norma Field for the conversations we had about travel and border crossings, and for her helpful suggestions for the revision of this essay. Helon Koh read an early draft of this essay with meticulous care. I am also grateful to Sharon Hom for her encouraging comments and editorial assistance, and for her decision to include my poems in this volume.

will bring, moving across borders and continents in sweltering summers is above all a visceral experience. Entrusting one's body to a trans-Atlantic or -Pacific plane is a serious business. It means a literal uprootedness above the clouds for a considerable duration, a dehydrating and claustrophobic space with artificial oxygen that is never adequate, as in a movie theater (which most transcontinental aircrafts in a sense *are*). That's not all. The worst begins when the flight ends. Jet lag often leaves the excited yet exhausted traveler in a state of dream-walk for days, the length of which, according to some folk wisdom, is proportionate to the number of hours one has "lost" when frivolously crossing those lines "marked" on the globe as longitudes. No wonder my mother would confidently repeat her favorite proverb: "A night without sleep, ten days to wake up" (*yiye bushui, shiri buxing*). Adjusting the biological clock to ticking in tune with local time often entails headaches, mouth sores, bloodshot eyes, stomach upset, and an overall feeling of awkwardness and disorientation.

To some, there will also be a potential sensation of aphasia, sometimes momentary and sometimes persisting through the entire stay: In which language should I speak to the immigration officer? What should I say to my folks whom I haven't seen and talked with for so long? Do I know all the updated local slang? Will there be joyous shouts or just shyly murmured greetings? On a couple of occasions, upon arrival at the Hongqiao International Airport in Shanghai or the Malmö terminal in southern Sweden, I suddenly had a sensation of a swelling and clumsy tongue. The relatives are waving behind the glass doors, and you try so hard to match these familiar yet strange figures with the fading photographic images in your memory. But the distance between the customs control counters and the exit seemed endlessly long. You smile and smile, finally you are pushing the luggage cart forward as if toward an unfathomable cliff. Any word would seem too light and trivial compared to the weight of the suitcases that contain carefully chosen gifts, and the books you planned to read but know that you will most likely bring back unopened.

When my mother gave birth to her first child on a sleepless muggy summer night, Shanghai was being besieged by a severe shortage of food and overshadowed by international insulation in the early 1960s (China had recently broken its brotherly tie with the former Soviet Union). My mother did not envision a life of incessant border crossings for me. Nor could she have any idea that she and my father would frequent the airport and the train station to meet me arriving from all sorts of directions. I have seen her aging through the exit doors, above which hangs the huge "Arrivals" sign. But she has treated me as the girl embarking the trans-Siberian train to cross the vast Euro-Asian continent nearly thirteen years ago. She always comments on my weight and my "face color" (*mianse*, which Chinese believe shows one's state of health) as soon as she grabs my hand, while my father meticulously makes sure I have the right number of luggage pieces with me and excitedly suggests the easiest and least expensive means to get home. This scenario is always the standard but ever-so-intimate prelude to a drama called "homecoming." Carefully placing my tired feet, half-numbed by the long hours of motionless sitting, on the ground of a familiar city, I would remind myself that this time would be just as transitory as previous ones. I would think of a passage in Norma Field's eloquent book on an unusual sabbatical year spent in her mother country, Japan, which captures the poignancy of this state of mind and body:

> I remind myself that this is necessarily an artificial homecoming. I must become, again, daughter, granddaughter, and even niece, *a process akin to regenerating amputated limbs*. I know that I will have to shed these same limbs at the end of the year, when my resuscitated capacity to lunch with family while conversing amiably about the noonday women's show and reporting on the obligatory reception attended the previous evening will be superfluous. (My emphasis)[1]

I cannot seem to remember anymore how many times that I felt as soon as my "amputated limbs" were reconnected, then it was time to pay the farewell visits to relatives and friends. Usually there was not enough time for all of them. Hurriedly packing one more gift into the exploding suitcase, I realize that the room is going to be emptier tomorrow after I have left. At some point "home" simply ceased to signify a permanent shelter for me. My parental home has became one of the pivotal points from which most of my journeys start and end. In the process, I have given my family a number of mailing addresses. As my life away from Shanghai began to exceed a decade, and especially since my parents moved away from my childhood home and neighborhood a few years ago, homecoming appears to be more and more like a long transit in a major airport, where you always find yourself eventually walking toward different gates of departure after some sightseeing and shopping. But still, being "stranded" in a native city for days or weeks has an emotional dimension that demands commitment, care, and eventually acceptance of the inevitable sense of loss, or "amputation," when it is time to return to other transitory homes, and thus begin another cycle of longing and traversing.

a tale of rails

There is a point in one's youth that one time and again singles out as the most revealing moment, a moment of surprise and ecstasy, or indeed, as an epiphany of sorts. For me that crucial moment literally penetrated my unconscious while I was dreaming on the train to Moscow—my first journey abroad. It was as though something invisibly slashed your skin but not until much later that you found a scar, a souvenir, of that experience so profound it almost amounted to a paradigm shift.

My tracks shifted, literally, at that strange point (if my memory does not fail me) called Dzamïn Uüd on the border between China and the Republic of Mongolia on a chilly August night in 1983. After having "passed" the Great Wall, and after hours of staring into the vast Gobi Desert and then the grassland of Inner Mongolia, the crowded and steaming streets in Shanghai and Beijing had at last receded into a haphazard background, and began to take the shape of a past.

This was not the first time I had traveled by train to a place far away from the bustling and overpopulated metropolis Shanghai. This northern nomadic landscape reminded me of my big adventure at age eighteen when I, with two friends, sat on a hard bench on a train to Xinjiang in the northwestern corner of China. It took us three days and three nights to reach Urumqi, the other end of the longest domestic rail route. We then hitchhiked almost all the way to the border of what is now Kazakhstan and visited Yili, the legendary oasis at the end of the desert where many disgraced Chinese literati, officials, and dissidents through all ages have been sent into exile. We went even farther toward the border area, which had such a terrifying and tempting power, like that of a magnetic field. As a lover of geography in elementary school, I always wondered how the actual borderline was drawn where there was no *natural* division such as a river: Was there some line drawn by chalk, as we usually used to divide our desks at school? How long would the distance be between every armed guard?

It was such a thrill to be near the national border in a time when it was the iron-wrought limit of our existence. Going abroad had never occurred to me as a realistic idea; in fact I always felt dizzy whenever I tried to think concretely about "the world out there"—it was meant to be an illusion, a myth, an unfathomable horizon. As someone from the coastal metropolis in southeastern China, Yili was the farthest inland border area I could get to. Although I had devoured enough Russian literature in translation as a teenager, I knew, looking into the sky beyond the border, that the road to Moscow and Leningrad did not start here, as there was simply no railway. From the local people we heard terrifying stories about how trespassers were punished. One young man had one of his legs broken by the Russian guards after he had managed to cross the border, only to have the other one broken by the Chinese when he was promptly sent "home." I was speechless.

After returning to Shanghai in time for my sophomore year at the university, I wrote to friends in Yili for a long time. All the while I felt a little uneasy and guilty for having the privilege of living in a city that was materially more like the West for them. But I told them that the polluted air and demographic density could be suffocating, and that there was less and less breathing space for me. Finally I told them that I was going to hit the rails again, this time across the entire expanse of Siberia. And I was not going to get my legs broken and sent "home." I hardly knew the difference between a passport and visa in my preparation for the longest rail journey in my life. In my case I got the latter before the authorities, after a long delay, finally granted me a passport, the legible token of freedom, but also a seal of fate in China. To get a passport, I had to relinquish my residency in Shanghai and my civil rights as a whole, which had entitled me to food and clothing rations and, above all, my right as a social subject within the borders of China.

Worn out by fatigue, excitement, and a mixed sense of loss and guilt that had dominated my life weeks prior to this grand journey of "going abroad" (*chuguo*), I could not even continue writing the first few pages of a brand new diary. When night fell, the unfolding film of the exotic landscape also receded, vanishing behind the compartment window. The rhythm produced by the powerful but monotonous friction between the wheels and the rails finally sent me to sleep—this time I had a second-class berth. The week-long railway journey was only beginning, and I needed to recuperate my energy.

First I heard whispering in English—no doubt from the British couple who were in the same compartment—then a mixture of languages in the corridor, among which I, to my comfort, discerned

Chinese (the train had a Chinese crew)—the only language I could understand without difficulty at that point. Then, I heard a rather loud voice in Russian, but I could not understand it. The two years of Russian I had learned in elementary school had dissipated long ago, since China readjusted the tracks of its development after Mao's death in 1976, and massively reorganized the national curriculum so that most schoolchildren learned English, the language of modernization, rather than the outdated and estranged Russian. I was told that the train would be stopping for a few hours to have the wheels changed. Change the wheels? I thought I had heard wrong.

Yes. It's the rails.

Rails? What's wrong with the rails?

To the people living in this border town between China and the Republic of Mongolia, and especially to the workers who did the wheel-shifting job twice a week, my ingenuousness must have seemed laughable. But I had seen many foreign trains in films, and their wheels all seemed to me fundamentally the same as those of Chinese trains. Of course, it never occurred to me that they would be different depending on the width of the rails! I was flabbergasted. I speculated on possible and sensible explanations for this bewildering reality. The only thing I could come up with was a strategic hence political imperative that was required to demarcate the ideological difference between China and the Soviet bloc. But it was unclear to me whether or not the railway(s) were built after the self-estrangement of China from the Soviet bloc. That seemed unlikely.

Watching the train being lifted from the Chinese railway and then eventually put down onto a different pair of rails (the Republic of Mongolia and the former Soviet Union have the same standard), I paced the dimly lit platform, awed by the immensity of the metamorphosis, the foregrounded materiality of the train, and the nakedness of the rails underneath. I felt that something was crumbling in me, that something had irretrievably changed my vision. In retrospect, it is no exaggeration to say that this was a veritable disjuncture in my life. The train left the Chinese rails behind, as if leaving behind a pair of amputated limbs that stretched all the way back to Shanghai. When things seemed to be back to normal on the train, I was told that the Chinese restaurant car was also left behind at the border. From the morning after, the passengers would be served Russian food in the newly hooked up restaurant car. I would not know how and what to order.

I was unable to sleep. Never in my life had I been so concerned about the mechanical structure of a train, or for that matter, the railway system worldwide. Lying in my narrow berth, I listened to the rhythm of the new wheels and worried over whether they really matched the new rails.

DOMAINS OF WRITING

layers of a body

It has almost become a ritual. When the last line of the last poem of your reading is still lingering in the air of intense concentration, awaiting a distant echo, you will be asked which poets have influenced you most profoundly. You have to shift gears, to assume a cool-headed comparatist position and adopt the prose of criticism to measure (against) your own writing. You have to be humble to the masters, bowing to their invisible presence. You suddenly feel as though you had been asked to strip, to pluck out your feathers and bare your limbs.

The trouble is that I have changed my wardrobe too many times since I began to want to write and always picked up incongruous items duty-free at airports, funky vintage stores, and dusty flea markets in the cities I inhabited or transited, in addition to underwear bought at department stores targeting mass consumers. I have inherited some old Chinese garments from my mother and a knee-length white shirt from a deceased Swedish peasant. I kept giving away clothes, and swapped some with friends.

So how should I begin "stripping"? Occasionally I would resort to a culinary metaphor coined by the well-known contemporary Chinese woman poet Shu Ting: "Since I was born I have been fed with too many kinds of food—rice, noodles, bread, or what have you, and their combination has made me what I am. And the same is the case with my poetry."[2] But this circumvention, clever as it is, would not satisfy people. In a world inflated with names and signs, people need reassuring anchoring in canonical continuity. I would then name Li Bo, the quintessential icon of Chinese masculine classicism. No matter how my later training in literary criticism taught me to question canonicity and male hegemony, I could not deny that in my hunger for literary works during my early teens in the long shadow of the Cultural Revolution, I was by accident exposed to his poetry first. In a time when poetry was nothing but propagandist slogans, the image of this ancient man, always drunk and roaming among valleys and rivers in the heyday of the Tang Dynasty, producing poems charged with audacious imagery and emotional contagion, was irresistible. I hand-copied his poems reverently, as years later I would do the same with the underground "Misty-poetry" by a group of young literary and social outcasts in Beijing. Seeing him as more than a poetic genius, I identified with him primarily as a reckless traveler, always on the road, venturing into formidable landscapes. When I later journeyed to northwestern China, where Li Bo was born of a racially mixed couple and spent much of his life in exile, I was partly trying to live up to my teenage dream of experiencing those landscapes in person.

Later, I was also enthralled by a number of other Chinese and non-Chinese poets. I was drawn to the esoteric Li Shangying of the late Tang and the woman poet Li Qingzhao of the Song Dynasty. During my self-imposed apprenticeship with these poets of the past, I imitated them in the classical forms of their times until I found the indulgence too removed from the austerity and crudity of my daily experience. After voracious readings of Pushkin and the German and English Romantic poets in translation, I also discovered modern Chinese poets who first experimented with the vernacular language and free verse in the early decades of the twentieth century. Budding puberty inclined me to the vast body of love poetry. But inhibited by a mixture of the puritanical socialist sexual ideology and persistent, though latent, Confucian doctrines on sexual segregation, I found myself addressing my first lyrical poems to some intimate girlfriends. In our fanciful world of writing as romantic bonding, we would switch genders as if playing in a traditional opera, or vicariously living out the roles in the classical novel *The Dream of the Red Chamber*.

It was also during that time that I found in the most secret drawer in our home, which my mother forgot to lock one day, a strange black-and- white studio photo of a "couple" from the 1950s: my premarital mother dressed up in a double-breasted suit, complete with a wide tie and a soft-felt Bogart hat covering up her hair, and next to her was a sweet young woman wearing a chiffon scarf. They smiled wistfully at the camera. It was apparently a fad among the young women in those days to play with their gender in a photo studio. But such decadence was totally, at least officially, wiped out during the Cultural Revolution. I didn't tell my mother I saw the picture. But secretly I felt empowered by this quaint photo of masquerade. I learned to ride my father's motorcycle, one of the products of his idle years during the Cultural Revolution. As the oldest child, I also fought, like a big brother on behalf of my vulnerable little sister and brother. I thought that was the only way to be strong, at least on the surface. After all, my parents, as most Chinese still do to this day, wanted a boy so badly that my mother risked her health and her reputation to bear a precious son at age thirty-nine.

Throughout my years of apprenticeship I did not come across a woman poet I truly idolized, partly due to a lack of access to literature (and libraries). I was not sure what it meant to be a woman poet rather than a poet pure and simple. Shu Ting's poetry had great impact on my transition to a more experimental style, but her subsequent canonization by the state literary apparatus and the overly dramatized "feminine" quality of her poetry made me wonder about ties between the state and the efficacy of female voices. It was becoming apparent to me that if I wanted to continue to publish and establish myself as a significant woman poet (*nüshiren*), I was to write a sort of poetry with a Shu Ting touch plus a trendy, if not opportunistic, attitude about reform and modernization. I felt I needed a drastic retreat. However, little did I know that it not only meant a retreat from the literary scene in China, but also the beginning of a two year period of solitary writing in a strange country and climate.

In my long and anxious wait first for permission to marry a foreigner and then for my passport, my future Swedish husband and I passionately translated the work of the Finno-Swedish poetess Edith Södergran (1892–1923) into Chinese. That was also my first serious lesson in a language that was to become part of my life. I was captivated, possessed by this idiosyncratic woman who lived her short life around the threshold of the twentieth century in a little border village in Finland called Raivola. Encountering poems like this one called "Virge Moderne" (Modern virgin) was an electrifying experience:

> I am no woman, I am a neuter.
> I am a child, a page and a bold resolve,
> I am a laughing stripe of a scarlet sun . . .
> I am a net for all greedy fish,
> I am a skoal to the glory of all women,
> I am a step towards hazard and ruin,
> I am a leap into freedom, and self . . .
> I am the soul's ague, the longing and refusal of the flesh,
> I am an entrance sign to new paradises.

I am a flame, searching and brazen,
I am water, deep but daring up to the knee,
I am fire and water in free and loyal union . . .[3]

Born in St. Petersburg to a Finno-Swedish couple, Södergran went to a German school in the tsar's capital, where she also wrote her first poems in German, Russian, Swedish, and French. After being diagnosed for tuberculosis in 1908 (probably from her diseased father), she spent years in sanitaria both in Finland and Switzerland. Her first book of poems, *Dikter* (*Poems*, 1916), was published in Swedish with a style and subject matter that shocked the provincial literary establishment of Finland. She was even accused of blasphemy. After the 1917 Russian Revolution, Raivola became an even more isolated outpost, affected directly by the war in Russia. Far from the centers of European modernism but also Helsinki and Stockholm, Södergran published her second book, *Septemberlyran* (The September lyre), in 1918, despite her disease and poverty. Her stance against the verse of classicism scandalized the established literary critics in Stockholm and Helsinki. They simply could not swallow her kind of volcanic intensity and radical iconoclasm of the woman, who proudly declared: "I have discovered my own dimensions."[4]

That is how I have come to mention her as one of my key influences, a cherished part of my wardrobe. Of course hardly anyone knows about her. So when I utter her name with the strange Swedish vowel with the umlaut, silence usually follows.

At the end of my trans-Siberian journey in Moscow, I boarded a train for Helsinki, and then a ferry over the Baltic sea to Stockholm. I heard the peculiar Finno-Swedish for the first time; I heard Södergran. My acquaintance with her poetry was preparation for this major move in my life, as it calmed my anxiety as a newcomer considerably. I felt I was already in some way related to this part of the world, and not a complete stranger to the Nordic landscape clothed with dense pine and birch forests.

"the land that is not"

Södergran's posthumous collection is titled after a poem she wrote shortly before her death, "Landet som Icke Är" (The land that is not). Aside from an intense utopian longing for a country that neither has a name nor exists in the usual sense, I was from the very beginning intrigued by this semantically nonsensical and grammatically odd title. As a Swedish descendent living in a peripheral Finnish village, what kind of relationship did she have with her "mother country?" Does one label the nationality of poetry by the language, the place of birth, residence, or simply the color of the passport of the author?

The longer I live outside the borders—those "markings" on the globe—of China, the more embarrassment and uneasiness seem to seep into the moments when I have to be presented, by others or myself, in terms of those national "markings." Some years ago, long before the violent events in Beijing forced, directly or indirectly, many contemporary poets to go into exile, some Chinese poets gathered at an international poetry festival in a European city. I was not an official guest of the festival, and I was the only one among the Chinese group who paid my ticket there, on my way to visit my Swedish relatives. My seeming "freedom" somehow became a marker of my inauthenticity as a Chinese poet, as such an individual should be politically persecuted, not know Western languages, and be financially at the mercy of the Western patrons. I found myself gradually becoming an interpreter or tour guide for my famous fellow countrymen. I enjoyed doing that because I truly respected their work and moral stature in China. But when a poet said he would probably have recommended me to the festival organizer as a future guest, were I not a Chinese who had officially moved abroad, I did not know what to say. I could only blame myself for not looking and sounding "native" anymore, although at that time I was actually living in Beijing. It was a disheartening realization that I could not represent China in any formal capacity anymore, but somehow I also felt relieved of an invisible burden that I had to bear ever since I was a "little red pioneer" (*hong xiao bing*). I went to a disco in my miniskirt, mingled with the local teens, danced to the deafening rock 'n' roll, and forgot that I was a Chinese poet.

Years later, in rereading Södergran, I was once again struck by the poignancy and ambiguity of the phrase "the land that is not." I also came across the French woman poet and critic Hélène Cixous' trenchant words on border crossing, in writing as well as in life: "I want the word *dépays* (uncountry); I'm sorry we don't have it, since the *uncountry* is not supposed to exist. Only *pays* and *dépaysement* exist. I like beings who belong to removal (*dépaysement*) . . . [the] inhabitants of the uncountry, of the incountry, of the country hidden in the country, or lost in the country, of the other country, the country below, the country underneath." On the art of crossing borders, she wrote:

How do we cross borders? It can be done in a completely indifferent and apathetic fashion, although the person who crosses borders in an indifferent fashion never crosses borders. The person who doesn't tremble while crossing a border doesn't know there is a border and doesn't cast a doubt on their own definition. The person who trembles while crossing a border casts doubt on their own definition, not only on their passport, not only on their driver's license but also on every aspect and form of their definition; from the definition of age, which we talk about very little, to the definition that concerns us the whole time and which is, at the same time, the one we can't or won't reply to, that of sexual definition. What nature are we? What "species" are we?[5]

I came to understand that "land that is not" for Södergran is not some disembodied dimension in her feverish tuberculosis-induced state of mind. It is a *dépays* that cannot be easily circumscribed by any markings on the globe (Cixous describes them as "incredible as unicorns"). Raivola was virtually a non-entity in a war-torn cartography at the dawn of this century; in fact one cannot find it on an ordinary world map. The tiny border village was, however, the gateway to a country within the countries, a country underneath: where her family house stood, where she wrote "I am a neuter" while coughing out blood, and where her body was eventually buried. Bedridden for the most part, she was on the brink of starvation and death. No one asked her to attend any festivals (there simply was not anything like that yet), representing anything or anyone, as many writers do today, with their plastic badges loudly flashing their names and countries (called geopolitical identities). Had she lived longer, Södergran still would have had nothing to do with the Nobel Prize blessed by the Swedish royal family, either. She would have been too eccentric for that, not geographically and politically representative at all.

1989 . . .

The Chinese poetic landscape was dramatically reconfigured after the events of 1989. Many poets who were considered threatening, or who considered themselves to be antagonistic, to the established ideological order suddenly found themselves in the literal "land that is not" of one kind or another. Prior to that, I had also left Beijing to live in Tokyo. There I began to receive letters and phone calls from this group of friends, now spread thin over the whole globe (but of course mostly in the Western countries that could afford to patronize and shelter them, at least for a while). Always in the struggle for the next visa from a new country, or a new grant from a different foundation or university, they envied me for holding a foreign passport in spite of the fact that I did not have a permanent address in that country, or anywhere else. They made me feel guilty again, although no foundations would grant me money to devote myself to writing, as I simply would not be qualified as a Chinese poet in exile.

I was nevertheless grateful for being included in this loosely connected poetic community in exile. At least it gave me a sense of belonging. Encouraged by the emergence of a new readership, limited as it was, created by the post-1989 diaspora reality, I wrote more diligently. I also tried to be useful to the new cause in small ways, such as helping to find contributors for a new literary journal. Once I rode the subway to Ikebukuro, spending hours in the labyrinth of the business district looking for a small independent press that had published a collection of modern Chinese poetry in Japanese translation. I knocked at the door, introduced myself as one of the poets included in the book, and bought several copies of the book to send to friends in Shanghai. On the train back home, staring at the billboards for instant noodles, it dawned on me that being a poet in this epoch is nothing more and nothing less than a very humdrum daily affair. Yes, the O.L. (Office Lady) turned Haiku poets who wrote about instant noodles and love hotels into media celebrities (a phenomenon I would like to understand, too), but the days of reciting poetry for hundreds of people at a university auditorium or at Tiananmen Square were history.

When the terrible news of Gu Cheng's suicide after murdering his wife on a small island in New Zealand reached me in Chicago on a beautiful autumn Sunday in 1993, I was cooking a Chinese dish. At first I was unable to react to the news. Waving the stir-fry ladle in the air, I laughed because I thought it must be a joke. Hours later, when I began to accept the fact that the tragedy had actually happened, the feeling of guilt and anger surged simultaneously in me, this time in an explosive proportion. I could have corresponded with the couple more often than I did. I could also have tried harder to reach them while they were on a reading tour in the United States, months before the frightful finality. At least I could have showed my care, my friendship for the last time . . .

The last time we met was in Stockholm back in the summer of 1987, after they had recently left China. Xie Ye had unexpectedly become pregnant, and decided not to have an abortion partly because the fees were too high in Sweden for a transient visitor like her. But I felt she wanted to have that child from the bottom of her heart. Gu Cheng was reluctant and noncommittal on the issue, although he carefully asked whether Sweden was one of those countries that practiced citizenship by birth. That child whose presence I felt only in his second month has grown up with a Maori family on a tiny island in the South Pacific. But the mother who carried him first in Europe and then in their new-found home in New Zealand was slain by his father, who could not face the ruins of his collapsed fantasy world built in his self-imposed exile in the wilderness. Edward Said was deadly serious when he tried to demythologize exile: "To think of exile as beneficial, as spur to humanism or to creativity, is to belittle its mutilations. Modern exile is irremediably secular and unbearably historical."[6] In this case, the pain of mutilation far exceeded any rhetorical force, and was irremediably inflicted upon the body of the wife of an exile who had already sacrificed too much.

I remember we went to an art museum in Stockholm together, then a concert in the Royal Palace. We also spent one day together in the same house they were staying. We cooked and chatted. They said they wanted to stay abroad. There was no life waiting for them to go back to in China. The night before we parted, when I complained that my suitcase was too small for all the books and clothes I had acquired on the trip, they insisted on exchanging their big and hard Chinese black trunk with my little red suitcase. They said they wanted to travel light. We promised each other that we would reexchange when we met again. I brought their trunk to Beijing, but they carried my suitcase all the way to that island. They died before we could complete the circle of this exchange. In the morning before our parting, we found a crack on the ceiling of the living room. Water was leaking down from the bathroom above. We panicked. We called the owner of the house on his vacation in the country, and then the insurance company, which promptly sent two men over to take photographs as evidence. I now wonder if that crack and leak were actually among the ominous portents of their shattered future.

For many weeks, after I turned off lights before going to bed, I would see the glitter of an ax and blood in front me. I cried and screamed. I did not know how to mourn properly for the abhorrent death of people with whom I made dumplings and played language games. Like many, I too would have prayed for Xie Ye's survival if it could have helped. She was beautiful, generous, and talented. She herself was a poet. But next to her famous husband, she was always seen as a secretary, a helpmate. I wish I had communicated with her more as a woman to another woman. I wish we had gone shopping together in Stockholm without her husband, who would not let her leave him even one meter apart. In my agitated mourning, I found I had unconsciously wished life for her in a poem I wrote while I was still in Japan, long before the tragic outcome. It was partly based on a dream about them. In a nightmare I dreamed of Gu Cheng's suicide. I saw the "beautiful widow" with the child appearing in front of me, informing me about the tragedy. But reality is always cruder than our dreams; my nightmare did not turn out to be a complete premonition. Only the child survived. In the magnitude of the tragedy, I felt the impotence of my poetic fantasy. I stopped writing for a long time.

SCHOOLS AND FILMS

the republic of schools

For most Chinese young people who left China in the 1980s, a good part of our sojourn overseas is bound to schools. Schools help us get visas, sometimes give scholarships, provide cheap housing, and provide free e-mail service. Schools are surrogate homes for many of us who live on campus. Our attachment to schools has become an obsession, an inertia, and sometimes it almost feels like a parasitic existence. Schools are our addresses, our identities. Our résumés are strung together with the schools we have attended, withdrawn from, transferred to, and with the degrees we have collected or aborted along the way. It is a tortuous journey, full of surprising turns and chance encounters. We are constantly on the road, riding Greyhound, Amtrak, U-Haul, if not our own or friends' second-hand cars. We move to/from our schools, always packing and unpacking. The number of boxes increases after every move: more books and furniture accumulated, more photos taken, more letters received, more papers written, and more computer disks filled.

What parallels this frenzied journey of schooling is the process of our learning to think and write in languages other than our mother tongue. Our skill in handling a personal computer matures as we develop simultaneously better (but never completely comfortable) linguistic control of a language other than our own. We are grateful for the spell-check feature in our software. We practice our presentations in the mirror, correcting the movement of our lips. When we began to understand most (but never all) of the jokes in the classroom, we think we have finally been admitted. There have been countless forms filled out with our unpronounceable names, while our transcripts keep churning out more universally accepted A's and B's.

I am one of the fortunate ones who has so much schooling that most of my countrymen and women would see it as an extravagant feast, and perhaps also waste, for a woman. I have attended six schools in China (not including nursery homes and kindergartens), five universities, and nine short or long language programs in different parts of the world. A friend once joked with me, "Whenever I get a postcard from you, you are in a school somewhere!" Yet all my schooling turned pale when I realized one day that I could not write in any of the languages I knew to my illiterate grandmother, who lives alone in the country on the mouth of the Qiantang River, famous for its spectacular lunar tides. Usually I would write either to my father in Shanghai or to my uncle who lives in another village in the same county, asking them to forward to her my greetings and my sketches of my life abroad. In her simple mud-floored house there is a twelve-inch black-and-white television that used to belong to my uncle. She does not have a phone (in fact I believe she has never talked on a phone). Even if she had one, I don't know how we could communicate, as it takes great effort for me to understand her dialect even face-to-face. When my father called one night last spring to tell me that she had been hospitalized and was in unstable condition, I was desperate to communicate with her. But with all the modern apparati for instantaneous transmission—telephone, fax, e-mail—that I had access to, I was unable to write or speak to her. She was in a coma for a long time, while I was trying so hard to remember the details of a precious part of my childhood spent in my grandparents' old house. I was fluent in the dialect then. I often slept in her wood carved canopy bed, falling asleep listening to her rambling on about an evasive past or humdrum daily affairs.

The time when my grandmother lingered on the brink of death, and eventually won her life back, also happened to be a trying period in my school life. I had just emerged from a dark winter quarter that had tested my strength of survival as a Chinese woman trying to assert herself in an alien social environment. I was sick. I wished I were with my grandmother instead, as during those seemingly endless summers far away from schools in the city. We could lie in the same bed together just as before, recovering our bodies and souls amid the moist and tender fragrance of an embalming spring in the "land of fish and rice" (*yumi zhi xiang*). That was only fantasy, of course. But my grandmother's struggle with death in an under equipped rural hospital helped me put things in perspective. It made me wonder if I had really gone a long way from the earthen-floored house in which my grandmother totters around in her bound feet. What would she, devout Buddhist who was born in the first decade of this century but who never uses the Western calendar to organize her memory, think of her oldest granddaughter, who had to strive for her existence in a foreign land and in a foreign tongue at the end of the century? One sunny late spring afternoon in the library, I wrote a poem (the first in a long time) for her, wishing her to live to cross the threshold of the next century with me. I suddenly realized that I had been going to so many schools vicariously for her, and that I had to go on.

celluloid dreams

I spent a good part of 1995 traversing the globe in pursuit of Chinese silent films: to trace their existence, to view them, to experience their historical palpability, and to brood over and eventually to write about what they might have meant and still mean for Chinese modernity and Chinese women. On top of that, I was thrilled by the idea of excavating out of the remaining celluloids and archival materials an evasive and repressed part of Shanghai, the city that supplied and reproduced those tantalizing and broken modern dreams in the early decades of this century. And these old dreams are now being relived and faced with crushing new realities in the *fin de siècle* metropolis swept up in a frenzied race for wealth, power, and glamour.

My school life was always intimately bound with a passion for cinema. Without that celluloid world of fluid dreams and multiple identifications, my long journey in and out of school gates would have been more arduous and much less rewarding. Growing up in a neighborhood within a stone's throw of the Shanghai No. 1 Department Store in the heart of the city, I was a frequent visitor to those old movie theaters ever since I was a child. There were not many films to choose from in those days, but I watched everything, including seven obligatory "model operas" (*yangbanxi*, film adaptations of revolutionary Peking operas and ballet plays) produced under the aegis of Mao's wife, Jiang Qing, who was an actress in the 1930s. When I went to an intensive boarding high school in Pudong (the east bank of the Huangpu River, now a fast-developing economic zone), I longed eagerly for the weekends when I could take the ferry back home and go to the cinema to see a matinee with a cheap student ticket. It was still an age without television in China, at least not at home. Enveloped in the comforting darkness, I was enthralled by the shimmering shadows and images produced by the light beams coming from behind me in the theater. I was then becoming quite nearsighted, so I would always sit in the front rows (they were cheapest, too), submitting myself to the huge screen. I would momentarily forget my high school, which was rather like a military camp, and the pressure to eventually pass the university entrance examination and get admitted to an elite university.

In the cinema, many strange and fascinating worlds unfolded in front of my eyes. I was ecstatic when a film really struck me. I found myself learning lessons of romance and family, geography, and ethnography, aside from class struggle and revolutionary sacrifice that dominated the national curriculum. I saw some "harmless" (after a lot of editing, of course) foreign films (but dubbed in Chinese) such as *Jane Eyre*, *Rebecca*, *The Idiot* (Kurosawa's Japanese adaptation), and quite a lot of contemporary Chinese films by old and new filmmakers who were trying to resuscitate the Chinese film industry after the hiatus created by the Cultural Revolution. Some films made in the 1930s and 1940s by progressive filmmakers who were persecuted during the Cultural Revolution were reexhibited. I was surprised to see the old Shanghai in those films, so familiar yet seeming light years away. That was my parents' world. They told me about other films not shown, about other stars long passed away, and I wondered what happened to them.

I also could not have survived without cinema the two years I lived in Sweden. In fact, going to the cinema and writing poetry became the two central activities in my life there as a newly-arrived immigrant, still without a permanent residence card. I often wonder if I would have become the poet I am now without films—especially those of Tarkovsky, Buñuel, Fellini, and Duras. Not able to express myself freely in Swedish nor in the pathetically little English I knew, I found cinema the best and safest place to learn new languages, without the kind of embarrassment I felt in my rigorous language classes. So I joined a university student cinema club, and watched all those films that I had dreamed of seeing. It was a feverish experience. I tried so hard to read the Swedish subtitles while listening to dialogues in English or French that my eyes and ears hurt. Emerging from the cinema, I was exhausted but ecstatic, although I usually had understood only half of the plot. But the images would stay with me for a long time, mingling with the images in my dreams and daily life. In my poems then I would write about the offshoots of these processes of alchemy, the alchemy of images and imagination. From film to poetry—it was a fulfilling circle amid the dizzying anxieties and frustrations I was experiencing in a new climate.

I was so mesmerized by cinematic power, that I decided to study film. After attending a course in film history, I went on to do a course in film and video making in an art school in Stockholm. To support myself, I traveled, with a tattered city map in hand, all over the city by subway to various schools, ranging from kindergartens to vocational schools, to teach immigrant children and teenagers how to speak, read and write in Chinese.[7] Some weekends I also worked at a hospital nursing bedridden old people, comforting them in my broken Swedish with a southern accent, and telling them what was in the news. Zigzagging by subway between these different worlds set apart by age and language, I sometimes found myself lost, not in the beautiful, always rather chilly city on the Baltic Sea, but in a montage world of past and present, here and elsewhere.

I entitled my twenty-minute project on super 8-mm for the film course "Mellanrum," a peculiar Swedish word meaning "space/room in between." I drafted the script, and my camerawoman, an aspiring young photographer from a working-class family, helped to find a coffee shop for our on-location shooting. I asked a Taiwanese girl to star in the film. My chopped-off long braid was a key part of the *mise-en-scène*. It was a typical amateur film, a collage of footage from downtown Stockholm and still images from China, with a sound track mixed with voices in Swedish dialogue and poetic monologue in Chinese, highway noise, and distant Chinese music. The course, however, ended with a collective project on a commercial.

I never got to see the finished product, or for that matter, commodity, because I had already left Stockholm to live in Beijing. It was an ironic coincidence that I soon found myself mingling with a production team from Shanghai Film Studio that was shooting *Action Across the Border*, a detective/espionage film. The acclaimed Chinese woman director Huang Shuqing (*Woman, Demon, Human*), wanted to try her hand at the male dominant action genre, and she agreed to take me as an apprentice. Besides helping the casting director to find some Westerners as extras, I was also asked to fill a scene filmed in the opulent Maxim's nightclub in Beijing, appearing as a lone Chinese woman with a Western style (i.e., smoking and drinking). I never saw the film in the theater, but my mother hurried to see it and told me that I looked ridiculous in that heavy makeup and the shoulder-baring evening dress I had found in a vintage clothing store in the subway station near my art school in Stockholm. We both laughed. That was the verdict on my acting venture in the fictive "action across the border," but it was by no means the end of my more mundane border crossings in real life.

Revisiting Shanghai and Beijing this past summer with my dissertation research project on Chinese early cinema, I experienced for the first time in ten years a more tangible yet all the more unsettling sensation (not reality) of "homecoming." I squeezed my body and my luggage into my parents' small apartment. Equipped with a notebook, a paper fan, and a bottle of water, I rode the bus and the new subway line to visit libraries and archives during the heat-waves. My family also enthusiastically participated in my project, at least emotionally. My parents probably felt they were regaining the daughter who had embarked on that trans-Siberian train such a long time ago. That seemingly endless journey of schooling eventually led me homeward and into the world of their childhood. On the weekends we would go to various movie theaters to see contemporary Chinese and foreign hits (including *Forrest Gump*). On our walk home we chatted about the films and the history of the theaters where they had seen those films in Shanghai "before the liberation" (*jiefang qian*),[8] which I was researching. I felt the compression of time and space; it was as though my parents' lives and mine were in a flux of mutual superimposition.

One sweltering afternoon, I once again ascended the tower of the Shanghai Library to work in the modern Chinese history reading room. I was struck by the uncanny incongruity and simultaneity between the view of central Shanghai with new skyscrapers and elevated expressway on the one hand, and the dusty, ravaged, yellowed printed materials with pictures of the same area on my desk on the other. The famous Grand Theater (*Da guangming*), the most luxurious movie theater in the city, and the No. 1 Department Store still looked the same as in those faded pictures, but in between them, a gigantic tall commercial center under construction was soaring above, on the same ground where once stood the popular entertainment center the New World (*Xinshijie*), which opened in the first decade of this century. The revolutionary slogans once hung on the shop fronts on Nanjing Road had long been replaced by neon signs and electronic screens for commercials. Young women strolled past the shop windows in the latest fashions that could also be found in Tokyo, Seoul, and Hong Kong.

The days when the political instructor of our class at the university I attended ordered me out of the classroom to tell me that I should zip up my jacket are definitely over. But reports about the hair-raising working conditions in which cheap female labor from impoverished rural areas make the fashionable garments and bags in those "joint (ad)venture" assembling factories, and the sight of country women begging with their infants on the street, are disturbing. They make me wonder if Chinese women attracted to the cities and the dreams of a better life are really not once again forced to mimic the tragic heroines in those celluloid shadows projected from the past. Traversing between the adjacent regions of the past and the present, there is little room for nostalgia.

EPILOGUE

Half-unconsciously and half-deliberately, I planned to have part of my stay in Beijing researching at the film archive coincide with the Fourth World Conference on Women that took place there (or rather, for the NGOs, outside of the capital, in Huairou). I was not attending the conference officially, but I wanted to know how it felt to be living in the ambiance of the festive and serious gathering of women from all over the world. How would it affect the ordinary Chinese life on a daily basis? To what extent would Chinese women such as my grandmother, my mother, my sister, and those begging women on the street be represented? I was not hoping to get any statistical answers to these questions by going to Beijing. I did not have a mission, but I thought at least I would have something to tell my mother and sister, who had an interest in the event but thought it too far away from their burning concerns.

My friends took me to Huairou for sightseeing on our excursion to the countryside just days before the opening of the NGO Forum. Driving through the empty streets and the yet-to-be-finished building blocks, I envisioned the cheerful crowds of women of all colors making themselves heard in all languages through modern media. But I also wondered whether the distance between this quiet resort town not far from the Great Wall and the sweatshops and the deprived villages was too long to transmit the messages from Huairou and get echoed in time.

During the days of the conference, I carried on with my routine. During the morning rush hour I maneuvered my way through the crowded subway stations, catching crowded trains to go to the archive. During lunch break, I ate at small eateries on the street, and took a break in a friend's dormitory room nearby. On my way "home" I picked up some vegetables at a market for supper. In the evenings I met with friends, some of them from America (or living there) who were attending or reporting on the conference, others living in Beijing with hardly anything to do with the event, but were not reluctant to pass on to me local rumors and heresies about it. I wasn't sure whom I should believe, and what to believe. In the free market, the vendors were all too happy to have so many delegates as customers. The conference helped them to get rid of overstocked silk lingerie. I also went to a gathering of Chinese poets. We read our poems out loud, but the women poets and critics I met there did not know how they should relate themselves to the ongoing event in meaningful ways.

The most intimate experience I had during those days, however, was at a party of a few women poets on a rainy muggy evening in a cramped apartment in east Beijing. There we were: one of us lives in Japan and was on her way back to her home in Tokyo after an emotional visit with her parents in northern China; another was studying at an American graduate school, while her son and husband lived in Beijing; another woman, a beautiful and gregarious woman from Sichuan, was a migrant artist *cum* entrepreneur living in Beijing; and our hostess, originally from Jiangsu, was a mature feminist critic and poet who taught literature at a college. The husband of the hostess, a prominent poetry critic, volunteered to cook for us. "For the sake of the Women's Conference," he said. We started with sweet osmanthus wine, and then as our chatting about our dispersed lives flowed, we shifted to strong Chinese spirits and toasted to women and writing.

I didn't stay through the end of the official part of the international meeting of women. On my last day in Beijing, after bidding farewell to my friend who had lent me that dorm room for lunch-break naps and hosted our heart-warming mini-conference, I hurried to the Swedish embassy to cast my citizen's ballot in the referendum on Sweden's tie to the European Union. The fate of the declining welfare state and its place in a larger world of course did not depend on my ballot as a naturalized citizen and now an expatriate. But somehow I felt compelled to do so, not simply because it was for an adopted country for which I can exercise the basic civil right of voting. It was more a gesture of my intention not to be carried away by what Rey Chow calls the "lures of diaspora," that has served, more often than not, as cause for intellectual cynicism.[9] And this gesture, I believe, contradicts neither my lives as a poet writing in Chinese and an academic writing about China in English, nor my emotional and moral responsibility to the people I care deeply about.

Once again, I left Beijing, my onetime home, and the home of the last grand union of women in this century. But this departure proved far more trying. Amid the pouring rain, I rushed to the Beijing Railway Station to catch the night train for Shanghai. I thought I had enough time to make it to the platform, but the whole station was packed tight by mostly migrant workers who had swarmed in from the open square for shelter. My friends who were seeing me off tried their best to follow me in the fight through the human walls. I panicked. It was much worse than Nanjing Road. There at least the crowds moved with an illusory or real delight in consumption. The air was moist and stuffy. Babies were screaming, women crying, men cursing aloud. At one point I felt I was simply carried back and forth by the bodies around me, and my feet left the ground. My arms, too, were in the air, raising up my bags. Just one hour ago I was discoursing about the Women's Conference and Hillary Clinton's speech at the dinner table with some American friends, and here I was, drowning in the teeming masses from rural China who wanted their small share of urban modernization, hard-earned with sweat and sometimes injuries. When I finally made it to the platform, the train was already moving out, and the conductors sternly warned me not to jump on. I missed my train, for which a friend had made great effort to secure a ticket for a berth, a sought-after commodity. The next day, I had to reorganize my small budget in order to buy an air ticket ten times more expensive at the air-conditioned office in the International Trade Center. There the new urban white-collar workers sat in front of their computers in tidy suits. Smiles, sofas, and flowers decorated the high-tech modern interior. I was obliged to buy air insurance for my life. Walking out of the far too spacious building lobby, I wondered whether trying to ride a train was not any less precarious than flying in a speedy and comfortable plane.

On my long flight back to Chicago, I was unable to concentrate on the in-flight movies. For three months, I resuscitated my limbs and tongues (Shanghai dialect, Mandarin, and even a little Haining dialect in which I talked to my grandmother), and the ability to bargain at the free markets and to navigate through the crowds on Nanjing Road or railway stations. I was not sure if, at the end of the journey, on the other side of the Pacific shore, I would be able to recover smoothly from my geocultural jet lag. How quickly or slowly can I throw myself back in the race for academic progress and intellectual attainment on the "island" of Hyde Park, in a racially highly segregated city? I also thought about the "limbs" I had to shed behind, how I could possibly justify my privileged life in diaspora when my grandmother had never traveled by train farther than Shanghai and didn't even know about the Women's Conference, and when my mother had never flown once in her life? I can always leave when I want. I don't have to endure the crowded bus, as my mother has all her working life. I can fly after I have missed a train. Yes, it is sad to leave the kindred ones, to leave the women poets who share the language in which I write poetry and talk about life. But I am also taking leave from those simple but awkward daily discomforts—I am going back to running hot water, heated housing, free e-mail, and free laser printing.

When the plane stopped briefly in Seattle on a beautiful early autumn afternoon, while loitering in the clean lounge, I also thought about Bharati Mukherjee's *Jasmine*, about a more shadowy kind of migrating experience through the transnational atmosphere, "through wars, through plagues." Entrusting their lives to those unlisted cheap airlines, which serve no food and no beverages, the refugees, the mercenaries, and the guest workers were portaged through unknown cities and disused airfields. They are Jasmine's fellow travelers, and I have seen them during those discount flights.

> We are the outcasts and deportees, strange pilgrims visiting outlandish shores, . . . We are dressed in shreds of national costumes, out of season, the wilted plumage of intercontinental vagabondage. We ask only one thing: to be allowed to land; to pass through; to continue. . . .[10]

I got home safely. With suitcase full of new books and xeroxed copies, I seem to have also transplanted my trips to those dusty archives to the shores of Lake Michigan. But I knew it would take a very long time for me to really understand the meaning of this transplantation. Soaking in my bathtub to cleanse myself of the dust from the journey, I felt as though I was in a steamship sailing across a vast ocean. My limbs are lithe as sea grass, but my vision is blurred by the thick steam.

NOTES

1. Norma Field, *In the Realm of a Dying Emperor: A Portrait of Japan at the Century's End* (New York: Pantheon Books, 1991), pp. 8-9.

2. I learned this from the poet Yang Lian, at a poetry reading in Chicago in 1992.

3. Edith Södergran, *Samlade Dikter* (Stockholm: Wahlström and Widstrand, 1977), p. 15. The translation is from *Complete Poems: Edith Södergran,* trans. David McDuff (London: Bloodaxe, 1984), p. 59.

4. *Complete Poems,* McDuff's introduction, p. 32.

5. Hélène Cixous, *Three Steps on the Ladder of Writing*, trans. Sarah Cornell and Susan Sellers (New York: Columbia University Press, 1993), pp. 130–131.

6. Edward W. Said, "The Mind of Winter: Reflections on Life in Exile," *Harper's Magazine* 269 (1984): 50.

7. The Swedish immigration laws and education system entitle them to free lessons in their mother tongue. But I have learned that this is changing now, as the welfare system is showing signs of failure and xenophobic sentiments are rising.

8. Even today, many Chinese people refer to the Republican period ruled by the Nationalists (now in Taiwan) as the "old society" or "before the liberation," that is, before the communist takeover in 1949.

9. Rey Chow, "Against the Lures of Diaspora: Minority Discourse, Chinese Women, and Intellectual Hegemony," in Rey Chow, *Writing Diaspora: Tactics of Intervention in Contemporary Cultural Studies* (Bloomington: Indiana University Press, 1993).

10. Bharati Mukherjee, *Jasmine* (New York: Fawcett Crest, 1989), pp. 90–91.

Self-reinstating and Coming to "Conscious Aloneness"

Ma Yuanxi

In the middle of an autumn night in the mid-1980s, I stepped onto this alien land—the United States. A mysterious and elusive nightfall covered everything. Under the dim street lights and through flashes of neon lights, I vaguely saw houses, buildings, and stores alongside streets and avenues on the way from New York's JFK Airport to my American friend's apartment. My two American friends, both of whom I got to know in China, were the only people I knew in New York.

In this strange city, I found some resemblance to Shanghai, my birthplace, but there were immediate differences: Surrounded by cars in front, back, and around our car, I had never seen so many cars, yet so very few pedestrians. Perhaps it was too late, I thought. Unconsciously, I was comparing things between this country and my own, the only two countries I knew. Since then, I have been comparing similarities and differences of the two lands, peoples, and cultures, sometimes consciously but most of the time unconsciously.

An unknown future lay ahead of me filled with uncertainty and no definite destination. Since I did not obtain my visa to the United States until school had started, the university that had accepted me postponed my enrollment to the spring semester and my teaching assistantship was given to somebody else. Thanks to the help of some American friends in China, I finally got my visa, but classes had already been in session for three weeks. Nevertheless, I came anyway, for many of my friends advised me, using a Chinese saying, "a long night is fraught with dreams" (*ye chang meng duo*) meaning "you'd better get over there before any other trouble comes in your way." Some people asked me whether I had ever thought of the problems and difficulties I might encounter here in a strange place surrounded by strangers. Not really, I responded, and I could not clearly explain why. At the time I thought of "The Road Not Taken," a poem by Robert Frost[1], especially these lines:

> Two roads diverged in a wood, and I—
> I took the one less traveled by,
> And that has made all the difference.

and the last stanza of a Chinese poem, "Leaving Behind" by Xu Zhimu, a Chinese poet and writer:

> Leaving behind, this and that, leaving behind I am!
> Standing in front is the peak piercing into the sky;
> Leaving behind, everything, leaving behind I am!
> Stretching out in front is the infinite infinity![2]

The lines of both poems gave me encouragement, and I felt a strong desire urging me to move beyond the old boundaries, the limitations of time and space, and break through conformity. It seemed that a faith in "knowing how way leads on to way"[3] strengthened my determination to embark on the unknown and uncertain—the road of darkness[4] and infinity.

COMING OF AGE UNDER MAO

When I was coming of age in China, the "great leader Chairman Mao Zedong" and the Chinese Communist Party reigned over my motherland. The cultural instructions and propaganda, and the moral values and correct conduct education I received was shaped by the doctrines of the Chinese Communist Party and the spirit of communism, a combination of Marxism, Mao's ideas (or Mao Zedong Thought[5]) and a large portion of Confucianism tainted with some spirit of Christianity (especially, the spirit of self-sacrifice). The core of this education was to achieve self-oblivion, self-effacement, and self-abandonment—"dissolution of self."[6] In the long term, this was presented as a lofty ideal and a noble cause we were taught to believe in, and, in the short term, the tasks I was presently assigned to accomplish and the purpose was always "in the service of the people." Mao's essay "Serve the People"[7] was the motto.

When I entered college in the 1950s, we held a "criticism and self-criticism"[8] meeting in groups of six or seven o'clock every Sunday evening. It was a rule of the university that students must return to school by seven for the meeting. The meeting marked a summary of the previous week and the start of the new week. Each person first gave a speech criticizing whatever he or she had done during the past week that violated socialist or communist ethics or principles, and then the other participants would praise or criticize what good deeds or bad behavior he or she had performed. One comrade was criticized for forgetting to lend his notes for the course the "History of the Chinese Communist Party" to another; the accusation was that he had no concern for his comrade-in-arms. A girl made self-criticism of her going home to see her sick mother instead of attending an important report on the world situation by a leader from the Ministry of Foreign Affairs. Tears of remorse could not stop as she reproached herself for placing personal interest above the political fate of the country and the world. Another student was criticized for not cleaning the classroom when he was "on duty"[9] to do that. His negligence to such public responsibility would lead him astray, he was told. These are just some of the examples I can remember about the meetings. Were they trivial? Different standards or perspectives would perhaps suggest different answers. At that time for us, these examples were just the opposite of trivial. In the end every fault was analyzed, traced or tracked down to its class root—"individualism"[10] of the bourgeois and petty-bourgeois classes. The condemnation of individualism was the order of the day.

I had criticized myself and been criticized for three months for the unwillingness and reluctance I openly showed in accepting the teaching job assigned to me when I had studied only two semesters at my university. I wanted to go on studying, and I had never thought of becoming a teacher. However, in those days it was out of the question and unthinkable to refuse any assignment given by the Communist Party. One may be ousted from school or at least would be disgraced as a "backward element"[11] for not obeying the Party. A person without a unit or who had been labeled a "backward element" would forever have a hard time no matter where he or she was. I was not courageous enough to have had the capability to defy such an oppressive reality. I began teaching and worked very hard in my job.

The Party secretary of my department and my colleagues often came to talk to me to help me see the grave nature of my mistake: my unwilling acceptance of the teaching job. The rationale they presented to me was that if people in the revolutionary rank[12] did not obey the decision of the Party unconditionally, it would be reduced to a state of disunity like a sheet of loose sand, and then there would be no revolution. When the Party made any decision, it had the interest of the whole nation in mind. It was not enough that I took the job. I was still supposed to work hard to find out why I had let my individualism take the upper hand and reacted unwillingly to assume the Party's task. I was also supposed to try to understand the responsibility the Party had bestowed on me so that I would really like the job of being a teacher and strive to be an excellent teacher. I was told to read Chairman Mao's article "Serve the People" again and again to understand the essence of it. One comrade mentioned to me the song we sang whenever somebody was assigned a new job or had to leave for some task, "Wherever the People Want Us to Go, We Are Ready to Go There." He said to me, "Why don't you sing the song to yourself every night? That'll remind you of your life mission." So I exerted my efforts to dig into the "deepest of my soul"[13] and the class origin from which such bad thoughts of individualism stemmed. I spent a great deal of my time and energy doing this, as I was convinced that I was wrong and was sincere in my attempt to mend my way. The criticism and self-criticism finally stopped when I said I had started to enjoy being a teacher. And I truly did. It was rewarding to see the progress students made in their studies. Several years later I was awarded the title of "Excellent Teacher" of the city of Beijing.

Individualism, as we were taught, meant any thought or act for oneself and one's family and their interest. One's self should dissolve and merge with the great masses of the working people, and one's individual interests should yield to that of the collective, the state and Party. Individualism was the equivalent, or synonym, of selfishness. The lofty ideal of communism elevated me, the bustling atmosphere of the continuous political movements excited me, and the exposure to the horrible sufferings of the laboring people caused by the exploitation and oppression of the wealthy class cultivated in me a new understanding of the evils of the old society and the way of life and thinking of a different kind of people—workers, peasants, soldiers, and revolutionary cadres with whom I should be one.[14] I took in everything in earnest at its face value and believed in the whole Marxist theory (which, in fact, was mostly paraphrased for us, since we read little of Marx's original works). I made honest and sincere efforts to think and act in compliance with the Party's guiding principles and to fit into its norm.

In 1957 the Party launched the Anti-Rightist Movement[15] to attack those who made complaints about or criticized the Party's shortcomings or mistakes and put forward suggestions in answer to the call of the Party to help with its Rectification Movement in the previous year. Many of my colleagues and students were labeled "rightists," and I could not figure out how they could have become "enemies of the people" overnight and had to be so severely punished.[16] This Anti Rightist Movement was a heavy, intimidating blow to many of the intellectuals. Some had kept silent and said only what was "proper" or "correct" ever since. People started to distrust each other, as everyone was called on to expose oneself and others of any anti-Party and anti-socialist words or actions.

Not long afterward the Party organized its members to study Liu Shaoqi's book *On the Cultivation of a Communist*.[17] The central idea of Liu's theory was that a communist should be a "docile tool of the Party" (*zuodang de xunfu gongju*). A campaign of "Striving to Be a Docile Tool of the Party" was carried out throughout the country. The word "docile" explained it all. A sense of uneasiness and sometimes dissatisfaction, vague and hard to pin down, would seize me now and then. At the back of my mind a feeling of doubt sometimes haunted me. I questioned how one could really exercise one's full initiative if one's self was entirely subdued or effaced. Absolute obedience to the Party and state, complete subservience to the collective, total surrender to the cause all seemed so passive an attitude. But every time these thoughts emerged I pushed them aside instantly; besides, it was not the time nor the atmosphere for deep thinking. Independent thinking was dangerous; it was not encouraged and was even denounced, as it went directly against the Party's instructions.

Another contradiction concerning individualism, again vague and unclear, puzzled me. While directing people to condemn and eliminate individualism, the Chinese communist doctrine also cherished "revolutionary heroism" in a person. We were told that "revolutionary heroism," was "a world apart from 'individualistic heroism,'" and that it should be cultivated and developed in a person and displayed when a proper opportunity arose. So on the one hand one should try very hard to bury one's own self in docility, and on the other hand one should also try very hard to find ways to present or even show off oneself as a "selfless revolutionary ready to sacrifice for the communist goal and for other people's interest." While one was supposed to put work and other people above oneself, all the teaching about remolding oneself made one more conscious of oneself and anxious to show how one had improved and what good one had done. "Am I behaving in the right way? Am I doing the correct thing? Have I said anything that I shouldn't have said?" These were questions that constantly dwelt in many people's minds as well as mine. We paid such careful attention to how the Party and others thought of us.

There were two types of role models set up by the Party in those days: One was a revolutionary hero like Huang Jiguang, who ran up to the enemy's stronghold with explosives and sacrificed his own life in the explosion to pave the way for his army to occupy a plateau. This was a conscious display of explicit revolutionary heroism. The other role model was Lei Feng, who was called an "unknown hero" and who was made a known hero after his death by propaganda for the purpose of establishing him as an example of serving the people wholeheartedly. Lei Feng worked from morning till night, and on weekends he did extra jobs helping other people and units, without compensation, of course. With his money, time, and energy, he offered assistance to others wherever and whenever the occasion arose. There was a campaign launched by Mao calling on the whole country "to learn from Comrade Lei Feng." After all, heroes like Huang Jiguang, the first type, and occasions for such people to display their revolutionary heroism did not occur every day, but Lei Feng was an ordinary person like most of us and lived and worked under similar circumstances to ours. The image of Lei Feng was much more approachable, and his example was worthy of imitation. Therefore, people tried to learn from Lei Feng to be "unknown heroes" in order to become known.

In actual reality, I discovered people, consciously and unconsciously, competing for the attention of and leaving a good impression of themselves with the Party leadership or, to put it more crudely, to curry favor from the Party by showing off themselves or making themselves prominent through doing "good deeds" and constantly "improving" themselves to get closer to the models set forth for them. For quite some time, I could not comprehend this contradiction: self-effacing versus self-displaying and trying to forget the self versus becoming more aware of the self. Then I found myself gradually engaging in the same behavior, trying very hard to suppress the "self of individualism" (*geren zhuyi de ziwo*): self-interest, wishes, desire, doubts—anything that supposedly benefited the individual self and went against the Party guidelines. At the same time I worked hard to "remold" this self of mine to become the Party-inscribed self in order to obtain recognition and praise.

My hard work enabled me to make contributions through my teaching job, and I tried to help others when I could. In negotiating the tension between the "interest" of my individual self and that of the Party-inscribed self, however, I gradually lost track of my own true thinking. I seemed to have fewer and fewer questions and doubts because of my own discarding or suppression of them. The more ideological and political education I received and the more political movements that took place, the more my original self (*yuanlai de ziwo*)[18] shrank or withdrew or the deeper it hid itself. The self manifested was the self that conformed to the Party's standards, the self that looked correct in the Party's eye and the public eye. It was the other self (*ling yige ziwo*)[19] in the same person displayed for certain circumstances. It was like the Chinese handicraft—dough figure making (*nie mianren*),[20] making stereotyped figures out of dough. This other self was created not only for mere survival in the given environment but also for a better existence (as it is ironic that human nature has the instinctive desire to constantly crave a better life in any circumstance). It was certainly also a way to protect oneself from being a target of criticism or political repudiation. Perhaps this is genuine individualism, at least part of it, if individualism is to be understood as thinking of and protecting personal interest as the Communist Party had always taught us.

I found at critical moments, such as during severe political movements, especially during the Cultural Revolution, when one had to choose immediately which side one was to be on, on the side of the

Party and revolution or on the side of a close friend or a family member, this other self grew larger and displayed an even stronger individualism, disguised by revolutionary language. While the individualism that was criticized in the 1950s and early 1960s manifested itself mostly in trivial forms or events that were mainly limited to personal affairs, this disguised individualism could be dangerous and evil. It led to and was responsible for dishonesty, deceit, hypocrisy, distrust, betrayal, and mutual destruction.

The term "original" or "true" self thus becomes really problematic as one's self is strongly conditioned by economic, political, social, and interpersonal factors and relations. In the course of the struggle to survive the political confrontations, and for some people, to strive for upward mobility to a position of power and control, are the personality, feelings, and emotions one reveals derived from one's original self or from some other self that had gradually developed and become dominant, eventually replacing the original self. Sometimes one self could not even distinguish between the true or original self and (an)other self. One forgot what one's true self was like. One's way of thinking and behavior had changed.

BLIND TO GENDER DIFFERENCES

In my almost thirty years of living and working under the communist rule as a Chinese woman, I was never aware of my sex. I had always believed in Mao's words, Chinese "women hold up half the sky, whatever men can do, women can do too,"[21] and in the articles of the Chinese Constitution that guaranteed equal rights between men and women. At least based upon my life and work in the university, I thought I was equal to any man with whom I worked. I taught and did whatever other work I was assigned to as conscientiously and as well as men, if not better, and I was no less enthusiastic in participating in political movements and social activities. My mind never dwelt even for a moment on whether there might be any difference or discrimination in the political, economic, or social aspects between the sexes. Lacking any gender consciousness, I took no heed of such things, as I was so engrossed in my belief of the equality between men and women and in trying to transform myself to meet the norms, socialist or traditional, that I became more and more insensitive and unquestioning.

It was not until a small incident that occurred toward the end of the Cultural Revolution that I started seriously thinking about women's position in Chinese society. One day a meeting was to be held in the Great Hall of the People that was supposedly very important, as most of the top state and Party leaders would be present. A limited number of tickets were issued to each unit. My university announced that for couples, tickets would be given only to the husbands who could well represent the husband and wife. The meeting itself did not really interest me. The way things were handled puzzled me at first, and then upset me. I suddenly realized that because I was a woman and a wife, I was placed second. So there was a difference in the treatment of male and female after all.

Actually, ever since the Cultural Revolution was launched, many things had puzzled me. Though I was still bound by the same ideological and political framework, questions and doubts surfaced almost daily. For instance, I couldn't understand why all of a sudden the past seventeen years seemed to have been dominated by a black line that had created my generation of "revisionists," (*xiuzheng zhuyi fengzi*)[22] and we in turn had led our students astray, that is, onto a "bourgeois and revisionist path." I could not accept the idea that nothing good but wrongdoing had come out of our sincere and hard work. Yet, my old obedient attitude died hard. I again tried assiduously to criticize myself and follow the new trends of Mao Zedong Thought.

That ticket incident took place when my mind was in a state of confusion and doubt. I had worked as hard as any man and made no less contribution in any respect. Why should I be treated differently just because of my gender? Then I began to observe and notice things and people around me from a new perspective. Phenomena, happenings, and events I had not taken any notice of before became significant. Wasn't it always the case that only one-third of the total enrollment of my university was allotted for women students? Why did so few people question the fact that most working places were reluctant to accept women college graduates and bargained with the university authorities about the male/female ratio being assigned to them? Why should women have to score higher than men in the college and graduate school matriculation exams and in job applications? Things I had not given any previous thought to and had taken for granted now seemed problematic.

Following the end of the Cultural Revolution, the country gradually opened up to the outside world, and the outside world lost no time displaying its multifarious facets to and making its way into and exerting its influence on an ancient and isolated country. With the termination of daily struggle meetings (*douzheng hui*)[23] and the fading of the slogan and practice of "putting politics in command,"[24] a much freer and more relaxed atmosphere prevailed. People, especially writers, artists, and scholars, began to raise questions and doubts and to rethink what had happened to the country and to themselves over the past few decades. For many people, the focus of attention in the ideological and theoretical sphere soon seemed to shift to the individual, to the self. For a period of time, terms such as "self re-discovery," "self re-analysis," "search for self-identity," "exploration of self value" and "restoration of self-dignity and integrity" appeared in abundance in discussions, publications, and conferences.

"LEAVING BEHIND, THIS AND THAT"

One of my greatest shortcomings (a "strong point" in the Mao years) was the lack of independent thinking. However, with the changing atmosphere and ambiance after the Cultural Revolution, I could not help examining myself, the life I had gone through, and all that I had experienced under the circumstances and the outside influences on my life. What kind of person had I become after all these years? What kind of woman am I? Where and what is my own self, the true self? Is there such an identity as a true self when everything seems to be conditioned by political, economic, and social factors? Have I ever had a life of my own choice? But what kind of life do I want? What is a life of one's own choice? I could answer none of these questions.

Over the past few decades I was so used to brushing aside doubts that now I had to really make myself think. However, I did have a desire to think things through and longed to find answers. I wanted to have a change of environment. Somehow I felt that in order to answer or just to think through those questions and more, I needed to have a fresh start, to be in a totally different and new setting, to throw myself among strangers. I sensed that I would not be able to think straight and soberly in the too familiar milieu. The old way of thinking, the force of habit, apprehension, and lingering fear would constantly be in the way. I needed to break through the old temporal and spatial boundaries to entirely let myself loose. Besides, I had always dreamed of obtaining an opportunity to study full-time, as I had only two semesters of studies at college before I was assigned to teach. Though I had taken some graduate courses while teaching, my theoretical, literary, and linguistic knowledge was scattered, limited, and narrow in scope. I had never received any systematic professional learning nor any rigorous training in methodology. After a period of four years of crossing one hurdle after another and overcoming all kinds of obstacles, I finally landed in the United States in pursuit of my graduate studies and in quest of a "true self" (*yige zhenzheng de ziwo*) in an attempt to establish genuine independence in mind and heart.

It is a decade now since I first arrived in this country. Perhaps I could divide my life and experience of these ten years into several phases.

The first phase would be the period of my studies and working as a teaching assistant. As I was already late for school, I plunged into my studies and teaching responsibilities and tried to catch up as soon as I settled down in the new city. I was overwhelmed by the readings I had to cover for my own courses and those I assigned to my students for the courses I taught. My exposure to the new literary, philosophical, and feminist theories, British and American women writers and their works, and the varied ideas expressed and discussed at seminars fascinated me and opened up new vistas. However, for a person who had been educated in mainly Marxist and Maoist theory, it naturally took me quite a while to understand all the new perspectives I tried to absorb and digest.

A few things impressed me deeply during the course of my studies and teaching. With the exposure to different theories, instead of a single "correct" approach, I realized there were different approaches and angles to view a phenomenon, an event, a person, or anything. One day a professor said to me, "You seem to always agree with me or with what most people say." I said, "I'm trying to understand all these new theories and ways of thinking." "But at the same time you should think from your own knowledge and experience and raise questions," he tried to encourage me. It dawned on me that the core of my past learning and way of looking at and judging things was *conformity*, and that the habit of not questioning anything had been very much internalized. The approach I was so used to was to accept what was said in the books, taught by the leaders or teachers without questioning, without even any thorough understanding. The most important thing was to repeat what was offered to me in my words and apply it in my deeds. Anything else was immaterial. Now I began to see why a stubborn adherence to one theory could result in dogmatism and rigidity or ossification in one's knowledge, thinking, and learning attitude if one did not try to at least understand what other theories expounded. Like the Chinese proverb, "looking at the sky from the bottom of a well," (*zuo jing guan tian*) one only gets a narrow and limited view. I benefited from the knowledge of different theories and approaches so that I could compare them and then take an eclectic attitude or have one theory as the basis and absorb good and useful points from other theories. My mind was often in confusion, but I began to think for myself in doing research. I felt as if I had placed myself amid a sea of multicolored and multifaceted world outlooks and viewpoints, and my mind became expanded and enriched and my individual self became stronger.

One interesting and original course that I took in the women's studies program was "Women in Contemporary Society." Its central theme was that women were not passive objects to be studied, analyzed, and categorized, but active subjects in recognizing our own value and bringing about our own progress while striving to analyze and understand ourselves during our research. Here women were taking the initiative to transform themselves and their situation. This course emphasized women taking the initiative. The most striking feature of the course was the study and analysis of one's self. This analysis started from the understanding of one's own physical body, including all the reproductive organs and the biological cycle of a female body, as well as one's mental and psychological state, one's feelings, emotions, moods, fluctuations, and spiritual being, drawing upon one's past and present experience and future visions. The purpose was an attempt to know one's strengths and weaknesses in every aspect, one's potential and value, and the power and rights one deserves through one's reflection and that of fellow students and teachers so as to cultivate an autonomous self. It was quite a unique course, which helped me a great deal by giving me (a person who grew up in a society where the moral codes stipulated that it was improper, indecent, and even obscene ever to mention the private parts of a human body, especially a female body) inspiration, courage, confidence, and method to self-dissection, -discovery, and strength to come to grips with myself.

After the Communist Party took over in China, the women's liberation movement was mostly launched from the top, and the broad masses of women were mobilized to take part in it. Women's issues were raised, and women benefited under the provisions set forth in the Constitution and the Marriage Law. Nevertheless, after the initial enthusiasm over women's issues, women were told that they were liberated and that they now enjoyed equal rights with men. Thus, Chinese women were on the whole in a passive state of mind, and there was little sign of initiative. I was co-teaching a course called "Asian Women" with some other graduate students and had shown intense interest in women's studies. I was invited to give presentations at some conferences and on other occasions that exposed me to a broader sphere in women's literature and women's studies off the school campus. Apart from learning about a wider range of topics concerning gender, race, and class in the different disciplines, I became aware of how freely people expressed their ideas and how they conducted networking and established relations between individual research and collective projects. This may be very common to people here in this country, but when I was in China, conferences and organizations were sponsored or organized only from the top by the Party and administrative leadership of different fields. The speeches or presentations were written and made according to designated guidelines and a set tone. Creativity was out of the question; if there was any, it was in the style of the writing or way of presenting, but never in the content.

Oddly, at first I still feared expressing my ideas openly and freely even in this country. At the first conference I attended, I was asked to speak about images of women in contemporary Chinese literature. Even though it was held in the United States, I still had the idea that at an open conference like this you never knew who would be present and what words would be passed around. My presentation was so structured that it was filled only with synopses of short stories or novellas and with little of my own analysis or views. Actually, in my original draft I started with some descriptions of the political background and social factors that inspired such characters and stories, but I discarded it even though it was very superficial and simple. I was afraid, but I didn't know clearly what I was afraid of. I was also ridiculously discreet when I talked to other participants at the conference. I think it was still this fear of becoming the target of criticism so deeply internalized that it became almost a conditioned reflex to suppress any personal views on public occasions. Keeping one's mouth shut was certainly the best way to save one's skin. One important reason for all this was perhaps my knowledge that I was going back to China after my studies. I would not have been able to stay in this country even if I had wanted to at that time.[25]

The longer I lived here and the more effect the freer scholarly atmosphere had on me, the more I began to loosen up. However, it was not until the incident of June 4, 1989 when I was given an opportunity to stay on in this country, that the lingering fear gradually faded. Even though it was still a somewhat vague feeling, at least I realized I had not been a free person for such a long time, both physically and mentally. This first phase was for me the beginning of a process of learning, observing, comparing, taking in new knowledge, trying to understand new experiences. It was a period of enlightenment and revelation, an initial awakening to an urge to free myself from old shackles, to rebuild an independent woman self. But how? I was still groping in the dark for a way.

WRITING MYSELF

The whole duration of writing my dissertation, three years from start to finish, constituted a second phase. I was working full-time plus teaching a course at another university, and wrote the dissertation mostly on weekends. Writing was an ordeal, yet it forced me to sort out my thoughts, to pin down those vague, unclear, and disorderly ideas, feelings, and emotions. My topic was a comparison between two American women writers living and writing at the turn of the century and two contemporary Chinese women writers. While exploring and analyzing the self and the woman self of the different authors, their various protagonists in their works, and their gradual awakening to gender consciousness, the process of my writing also became a process of discovering my own self, trying to understand and dissect it, as I could not help identifying and comparing my self and my own experience to those of the authors and their characters. It was a seemingly never-ending cycle of thinking, questioning and writing, and writing, questioning, and thinking. Instead of suppressing questions or doubts, or conforming one's thinking for survival, as when I was in China, in writing my dissertation, creating a work of my own, I had to think, and think mostly on my own, as hard and in-depth as I could.

There was no ready mold, no pattern to fit in, or anything to copy from. Then George Lukacs' words about Socrates struck me, "Socrates always lived in the ultimate questions; every other living reality was as little alive for him as his questions are alive for ordinary people."[26] Edna, the protagonist in Kate Chopin's *The Awakening*, says, "One of these days, I'm going to pull myself together for a while and think— try to determine what character of a woman I am; for, candidly, I don't know. By all the codes which I am acquainted with, I am a devilish wicked specimen of the sex. But some way I can't convince myself that I am. I must think about it."[27] The heroine "she" in Zhang Xinxin's *On the Same Horizon*, expresses similar sentiments when she asks herself, "What about me? Where have I got to? . . . Sometimes I really wanted to run off, find a quiet place, and work out exactly what I thought, hoped for and wanted for myself."[28] I found that I was in a similar state of mind.[29] I began to obtain a new understanding of darkness and light. In the past few decades in China, my life and work seemed to be carried on in a crystal clear pattern; however, my mental world grew darker and darker until the situation of the country changed. When I first came to the United States, the mental darkness and unknown future scared me. With increasing thinking, questioning, and writing in my life as a graduate student, light gradually permeated in my mind, and with it the boundaries of space vanished. Of course there will always be the unknown and the uncertain. Yet the little light has brought inspiration, strength, encouragement, and joy, the ability to observe and scrutinize as well as confusion, pain and sometimes even bitterness.

My life as a graduate student in the United States, especially during the writing of my dissertation, was so different from the life I had lived in China both as a student and as a teacher. I came alone, and it was the first time I had ever lived alone, by myself without any family. I knew few people in this country, and practically no one in the city where I studied at first. People were so kind to invite me to different activities, as they were afraid that I must have been terribly lonely. I did not really know and never gave a thought to whether I was lonely at the time since the studies overwhelmed me and occupied virtually all my time; besides, I was so used to casting thoughts aside. When I finished my course work and started to write the dissertation, except for the hours of teaching, I found all of a sudden that I had all the time in the world to myself to arrange what to do and where to go. I was not very used to it at the beginning. Now I did not have to report anything to anybody about myself, yet at the same time I had to think of and decide everything for myself. Is this the so-called personal freedom and privacy? I asked myself. Was this what I had been vaguely longing for before? I was not sure of the answer. In any case, my new life fascinated me, and I enjoyed it, cherishing the fact that I could be by myself with little disturbance. A sense of freedom overwhelmed me, followed by a feeling of relief, relief from the crowd and the clutter I had to cope with, the perfunctory role I had to play, and the facade I had to put on. I don't think I have ever felt lonely since I left China. Instead I have so much to do and think about that I am always pressed for time and trying ways to generate more energy.

In my writing, following closely the development of and analyzing and dissecting the women characters, their experiences and their inner world, I gradually became aware of the difference between loneliness and aloneness. I found it to be an important turning point, especially for a woman seeking genuine independence. When people asked me if I was lonely living by myself, I answered that I wasn't lonely at all because all my time was occupied by my dissertation and teaching. I was, however, offering only a superficial response. I had not understood the real implications of loneliness or aloneness. One can be very busy with almost every moment occupied and satisfied with one's outward or superficial satisfaction or immediate accomplishments, yet one can still be very lonely. It is a mental loneliness or emptiness that very often one does not realize as one's self is lost in the hustle and bustle of the routine life.

In the old days while I was trying hard to suppress the self that did not conform with the Party-inscribed mold, little by little deliberate hiding took the place of sincere suppression or discarding of my real thoughts. I further realized that self-dissolution was but a delusion. What Hegel identified as the distinguishing trait of Western Man, his capacity for being aware of himself,[30] always exists. The question is what kind of awareness one achieves and how one interprets and handles this awareness. I now recall that I sensed the distance and detachment between people even though we worked side-by-side and lived in close quarters in China. The heart-to-heart talk advocated by the Party was actually a formal conversation of criticism and self-criticism. During the Cultural Revolution this distance between people extended to family members in a number of cases and led to antagonism, hostility, and alienation from each other. This mental isolation or loneliness is no less painful than the physical, if not more, when one realizes it. The key of awareness of self is whether one can gradually build up a positive control of one's self—one's physical behavior and psychological being. In this endeavor, I gradually have found "being alone," both literally and figuratively, extremely important and indispensable to me.

ALONENESS AND CONNECTEDNESS

I was happy when I completed my dissertation, completed only in the sense that I finally put together into one piece what I had written in the last few years. Yet somehow I felt it was not finished. In the process of my writing I found I had embarked on a journey of continuous thinking, working, and writing,—thinking of and working on the self and the interaction between the inner domain and outside world, a journey of writing my life dissertation to an unknown destination. Thus, commenced the third phase of my diaspora life.

I had already started working full-time when writing my dissertation and continuing to attend scholarly conferences. The work I have been doing since is mostly teaching and translation. In my spare time I engage myself in the discussion, research, and activities on Chinese women and their issues and women's studies in China. In working together with my students and with friends on projects concerning women's studies and from the contact with different kinds of people from both countries, I have gained some new perspectives on the relationship between aloneness and connectedness, solitude and community, detachment and attachment. In China it was all the latter, and after I came here, as a reaction to my past experience, the emphasis of my search and exploration was mostly on the former. Now I began to see that aloneness and community can be mutually supportive, though it can still be mutually in tension. I was impressed and inspired deeply by my American, Chinese, and Chinese American students—through their enthusiastic discussion of the past and present of China and Chinese culture in and out of class, through their interesting papers that inevitably compared the East with the West, and through their cultures and peoples. My women students especially were not only eager to learn and raise questions about women's lives in Chinese society and the women's movement in China, but they also expressed sympathy and concern for their fate. I felt a sense of alliance, and their views and questions urged me to explore and pursue a more in-depth knowledge and understanding of Chinese women.

I am also a member of the Chinese Society of Women's Studies in the United States.[31] Although members of the Society live and work in different places in the United States, Europe, and China, we regularly exchange ideas and work on projects together. Our newsletter facilitates communication and provides information about our activities and the latest developments in Chinese women's studies and other related fields. This kind of group may seem very common to people here, but I had never been in any group like this before. The work and projects of the group arises from the members' voluntary initiative. We argue in friendly ways when different views emerge. Sometimes when we have contradictions or conflicts between us or complaints about each other, the solution is to talk things out face to face. I feel there is some kind of invisible bond between members, and trust and care for one another prevail. When I was in China, everyone belonged to an organization or a unit, but this was not a matter of choice. The Party's instructions guided the work and activities of the organization or the unit. People could maneuver only within the limited bounds. Therefore, I was excited that this was a group I really wanted to and could voluntarily join and participate in. This experience helped me to understand the dialectical relationship between the value of the individual self and other selves.

Situated in a diaspora positionality, often I am asked and I ask myself, "What do you really know about present-day Chinese women having been away from them most of your time?" "Is the research or activism you are engaged in now simply to satisfy yourself or serve as some kind of self-comfort for being divorced from their life and their predicament?" "What can you offer to genuinely contribute, or can you contribute at all?" These are questions I have to address at least to myself, frequently perhaps, as the tension of the physical distance will always exist and the supposed alienation assumed. I take these questions as constant challenges to my undertakings that will help and strengthen my efforts.

For a Chinese woman in diaspora, the question of "here and there" physically and mentally poses at once an antithesis of separation and connection. I was born and bought up and experienced most of my life in China. I have a deep understanding of and feeling for Chinese women of my generation living and working under similar circumstances. I keep in touch with the various changes occuring in China, through study and research and projects with our counterparts in China, which provide me with knowledge and food for thought. Family members, relatives, and friends fill me in on current happenings and incidents in their lives and express their ideas and reflections as well as those of others against the panoramic background. For me and in me the countless inherent, cultural, and emotional ties between "here" and "there" are indelible and forever continuous. Based on this deep-rooted connection, the separation may offer and is actually offering an advantageous and fresh perspective. Being "here" and "there" and exploring the "inside" and "outside" present possibilities for temporal and spatial studies in comparison from diverse angles. In the process of all the exploration, rumination, and activities, I try to comprehend and grasp the essence of the positioning of the self and the other (subject/object) or the self both in unison with and isolation from the other, thus gaining more courage and confidence in my endeavors and acquiring a better understanding of self/other. With the two countries and cultures in so many different respects and the constant tension of the inner and outer world in the individual, the struggle will always reflect complexities, conflicts and resistance. With this recognition of my situatedness and the tensions I hope to achieve some new insights and attain some new ground.

As for the question of "contributing," I view it as a question of "give-and-take." There is rarely a case where one side only contributes and the other only receives. The whole process of research is in itself a process of learning and being learned (the research result); so is exchange between people and cultures, which involves "give-and-take." The job of translation may be used as an example. I find rendering one language into another is in fact transmitting one culture into another. Translation is an act of creation in itself. A certain concept may exist in one language or culture, but not in another (for example, as the concept of "privacy" did not exist in China until recently); or a seemingly same idea may be interpreted with different meanings (such as the concept of "gender"). The translator has first to learn, comprehend, and acquire knowledge of the piece being translated, and then the translator puts it into another language for other people to learn, comprehend, and acquire knowledge, thus completing the whole course of "give-and-take" or "taking in" and "contributing."

In the midst of all this, I try to sort out bit by bit when I am reading, thinking, writing or translating by myself. It is in this state of conscious aloneness that I can look soberly into the past, present and perhaps future. It is in this conscious aloneness that I gradually feel the shaping of an independent woman self in me, a self with individuality and autonomy. It is in this conscious aloneness that I try to gain and regain the balance of a whole being, to lift the self beyond the mundane and transcend worldliness and cynicism, to work on reinstating my true self piece by piece, in an endless process, on a lifelong journey.

NOTES

1. The opening poem in Frost's "Mountain Interval" (1916), from William Harmon, ed., *The Top 500 Poems* (New York: Columbia University Press, 1992), p.900.

2. Xu Zhimu, "Leaving Behind," in *Selected Poems of Xu Zhimu* (People's Literature Press, 1994). This is my translation.

3. From Frost's "The Road Not Taken."

4. By using the word "darkness" here, I mean the unknown and uncertain future that lay in front of me. I would frequently have to grope in the dark on the path "less traveled by."

5. Mao Zedong Thought (*Mao Zedong si xiang*) became a theoretical concept parallel to Marxism-Leninism. It indicated Mao's theoretical creation, as it was claimed, summed up from applying Marxism-Leninism to the experience and practice of the actual situation in China.

6. I borrowed this term from Benjamin I. Schwartz, *The World of Thought in Ancient China* (Cambridge: Harvard University Press, 1985).

7. "Serve the People" (*wei renmin fuwu*), an article Mao wrote in the 1940s in commemoration of the death of a cook who worked hard all his life. The purpose of the article was to call on the people to learn from an ordinary person such as this cook his spirit of serving the people wholeheartedly. This article and two others, namely "In Memory of Dr. Bethune" and "How Yu Gong Moved the Mountains," formed what was called the "Three Old Articles" to be studied again and again during the Cultural Revolution.

8. "Criticism and self-criticism" (*piping yu ziwo piping*) was an idea advocated by Mao Zedong and used to resolve "contradictions among the people."

9. "To be on duty" (*zhiri*): In those days students took turns cleaning their classrooms (each class was assigned a classroom where students had their classes, held meetings, and did self-study) and corridors. The purpose of this

was to cultivate a "labor viewpoint," that is, to view labor, especially manual labor, with respect and love, to form a correct attitude toward labor, and, to be able to do manual labor.

10. In Mao's doctrine, "individualism" (*geren zhuyi*) is a concept that implies the consideration and putting first personal interest and desire involved in one's work, career, personal likings, and one's relationship with one's family, the collective or people one works with, and the Communist Party or its different levels of leadership.

11. A "backward element" (*lohou fengzi*) is a person who is unable to meet the requirements of the Party and disobeys the instructions or orders of the Party, thus assumed to be in a very low status politically, socially, and ideologically, which will definitely affect the person's present and future life.

12. The "revolutionary rank" (*geming zhenying*) was a term used in those days to mean the collective of people making revolution together or working for a common goal, as in a big family.

13. "Deepest of one's soul" (*linghun shenchu*) means deep down in one's heart and mind.

14. I am using some jargon, words, and expressions that were used so much in those days that they formed an inseparable part of the daily discourse and language until China opened up to the outside world in the late 1970s. Some of the words and expressions are literal translations from the Chinese terms. The meaning and implication of this jargon is limited to its meaning in the social and political context of that given historical period.

15. The aim and target of the Anti-Rightist Movement (*fanyou yundong*) was to repudiate and counterattack those "rightists" (*youpai fengzi*) who had supposedly slandered and attacked the Communist Party and socialist China.

16. "Rightists" who were considered to be involved in more serious cases were sent away to do forced manual labor in the countryside or on the farms or in factories. A number of them stayed there as long as twenty years.

17. Liu Shaoqi was the vice-chairman of the Chinese Communist Party and chairman of the People's Republic of China at the time. During the Cultural Revolution he was one of the earliest targets of attack of Mao Zedong. Liu was overthrown from his post and repudiated. He died during the Cultural Revolution. His book *On the Cultivation of a Communist* (*Lun gongcan dangyuan de xiuyang*) was taken as a classic to be studied not only by communists but also by people of the whole country.

18. By "original self" (*yuanlai de ziwo*) or perhaps I could use the term "primal self" (*yuansheng de ziwo*), I mean the self I used to be, the way I think, speak and act before being inscribed by the Party.

19. The "other self" (*ling yige ziwo*) is the one remolded, the one that put on a facade. In those days people talked about the fact that almost everybody had two faces or two selves, if not more than two.

20. Dough figure making (*nie mianren*) is a handicraft originated in the northern part of the country. The craftsmen usually make dough figures of famous characters in traditional novels or dramas or historical celebrities, and dough animals too.

21. Mao used the phrase from the ancient mythology in which the goddess Nuwa, who was the ancestress of mankind, was supposed to hold up the sky by overcoming natural disasters and beasts and enable people to live a peaceful life.

22. "Revisionist" (*xiuzheng zhuyi fengzi*) in the context of those days meant trying to revise or reform Marxism or the orthodox theory with deviationist ideas, concepts, or theories of the bourgeois class or the like.

23. "Struggle meetings" (*douzheng hui*) were meetings held during political movements against targeted "enemies," such as meetings in which landlords were struggled against during the land reform movement, "rightists" during the Anti-Rightist Movement, and all kinds of "bad elements" during the Cultural Revolution.

24 "Putting politics in command" was one the most important guiding principles the Chinese Communist Party advocated in adopting policies, making plans, and taking actions in all spheres and even in conducting personal life.

25. I was holding a visa that required me to go back and stay in my own country for two years before I could leave again. In fact, I really had not made up my mind if I wanted to stay in the U.S. at that time.

26. Georg Lukacs, *Soul and Form*, trans. by Anna Bostock (MIT Press, 1974).

27. Kate Chopin, *The Awakening*, (Norton, 1976), p.82.

28. Zhang Xinxin, *On the Same Horizon*, first published in the Chinese journal *Harvest* 6 (1981). Translation from the author.

29. *The Awakening* by Kate Chopin and *On the Same Horizon* by Zhang Xinxin are books I wrote about in my dissertation.

30. Discussed in Rey Chow, *Primitive Passions* (New York: Columbia University Press, 1995), p.180.

31. The Chinese Society for Women's Studies started as a women's studies group founded by seven Chinese graduate students of different discipline in the United States in 1989. It has developed into an organization consisting of about seventy members, including students, professors, scholars, and activists from different countries interested in Chinese women's issues and

women's studies. While most of our members live and work in the United States, we have members in Canada, Europe, Mainland China, Hong Kong, and Taiwan. Members of the Society work together with their counterparts in China on projects, organizing meetings, exchanging writings, and compiling books concerning women's studies in China and in the West promoting the contact and exchange of ideas among women from different professions and localities.

Deep into Småland[*]

Zhang Zhen

On a trip
I close my mind's eye.
The weather bounces around
and messes up my timetable.
Then in the middle of this lake,
a stretch of water about to be eaten by mud,
and the real colors start to appear.

Under my feet
the reeking graves of the past generation
torture me.
Not Tiananmen
not the Golden Gate Bridge
but coming back here is to arrive at a conclusion.
It's baffling as the perpetual rain.
No one else can know this.

I won't swim here;
the Asian-blood-happy mosquitoes would chew me up.
And through the clusters of lotus blossoms
water snakes thread,
their skin as beautiful as black jade.
Our eyes meet across the silence.

This sight
slowly sinks in me.

Now the darkness of this cypress and pine province

covers me with layers of silk,
fresh moss still spreading sweetness of the bygone,
wet and heavy.

The nature of this place
is a bad fit with my past,
yet sometimes I glimpse
my life's other half.

Sometimes I can think back that far:
the aged thorn trees and stone steps
force me to consider:
should I be buried in this foreign land
or drift back like white rain
and drop into the lake of my hometown?

—as if that place would ever let me return.

NOTE

*Småland is a province of Sweden known for its dense and dark pine forests. In the late nineteenth century, a huge number of the population immigrated to the United States from this poor region of the country.

Multiple Readings and Personal Reconfigurations Against the "Nationalist Grain"*

Zhong Xueping

A few years ago at an academic conference in North America, a group of (PRC) Chinese women scholars from the People's Republic of China presented papers at a panel discussing a contemporary Chinese woman writer. In different ways, the panelists focused on the writer's role as a woman and her ambivalence toward women's issues in contemporary China. After their presentations, the first question raised from the audience was for the panelists to "each tell us what your own position is in reading this Chinese woman writer [the way you did]?" Another question was put to them by someone who wondered aloud why the panelists were critical of this Chinese woman writer "who is very important to us" and suggested that their approach failed to do justice to her. In response, some of the panelists explained that there was a lack of gender awareness in this Chinese woman writer and this lack had to be understood within the context of her privileged social position in Chinese society. As is generally the case, there is never enough time for

*Part of the analysis on *Beijing Natives in New York* in this essay was presented at the 1995 annual meeting of the Association for Asian Studies held in Washington, D.C. I would like to thank Professor Malcolm Griffith and Susan Greenberg for reading and commenting on the essay, and for making stylistic suggestions. I would also like to thank Sharon Hom, the editor, for inviting me to contribute, for offering constructive suggestions and comments, and above all, for her enthusiasm in the whole project.

substantive exploration of ideas at a conference; the panel ended with a
little tension, leaving the question of positionality and many related
issues still hanging.

Looming in the background of this kind of tension is the
postcolonial discourse-influenced identity politics, a politics, as I will
argue later in this paper, that in many ways undermines the power of
those that the discourse proclaims to empower. As one of the panelists,
I have continued over the years to feel a similar tension whenever
issues concerning Chinese women, Chinese intellectuals, and China as
a "Third World" country were being raised and discussed. Every time,
the positionality of those of us—Chinese women scholars who are
currently teaching or studying in the West, especially in North
America, or "Chinese women intellectuals in diaspora" in Rey Chow's
terms—would continue to loom in the background as a problem in
those discussions. Being part of the tension, meanwhile, I have also
learned to enjoy its presence, especially after I realized that it is not
going to go away as long as many dichotomies (such as China and the
West, East and West, Third World and First World, Western and non-
Western) continue to exist as principal paradigms of debate and
discussion, and as long as there are those of us whose existence does
not fit neatly on either side. The way to "enjoy" the tension is to realize
that even though we tend to end up with more questions than answers—
hence the tension—questions are always part of life.

NOTES FROM/ON A *BIANYUANREN* (PERSON ON THE MARGINS)

I went back to Shanghai for the first time eight years after I came to the
United States in the mid-1980s. One month later, I left again. Another
two months later, I received a copy of a published essay written by my
sister, who is a journalist, on her impression of my visit.[1] Although for
me the eight years went by as if it had been only yesterday (because I
had not had the time to fully reflect), for her and my family, it was still
a mystery how I had survived that period. In the article, my sister
describes her impression about me through my positive and negative
reactions to the changes in Shanghai, my somewhat absent-minded
presence among family and relatives, the food I engulfed, the way I
acted in various surroundings—annoyed, surprised, pleased, or moved,
and above all, my somewhat inarticulate ways of trying to express my
thoughts in Shanghai dialect. Her journalistic observations made me

realize not only that I do have a journalist for a sister but also that I was both sister and an outsider to her as well. What struck me the most was the last paragraph in which she calls me a *bianyuanren* (person on the margins) and expresses appreciation (and understanding) for such a position. I could tell that she sensed my distance from "home" during my visit, but I could also tell that she interpreted it in her own way. It is true that my entanglement with "home" takes the form of a critical distance. But the critical distance is itself entangled with personal experiences that have been lived in small and big ways in conjunction with history. It can originate from unlikely places and moments.

I was just a child when the Cultural Revolution broke out. During a time when one could not learn much in school and when my childhood dream of becoming a pianist was broken, I took fancy in reading maps, encyclopedias, novels (whenever my older brothers could get their hands on one),[2] and learning English. Sometime in the early 1970s, Shanghai radio stations started broadcasting English lessons on a regular basis, and this is when I began my English lessons. Because I was listening to the Shanghai radio station only, I never got myself in any kind of political trouble by learning English openly. I was doing all of this during a time when no one (including myself) could see any purpose for doing so; I was just curious. I continued with my study of English and read whatever books I could lay my hands on years later when I was sent to work on a state farm on the outskirts of Shanghai. There I found myself being summoned to *tan hua* (have serious talks) by my superiors, who tried to stop me from continuing to study English. "What's the use? You can't do anything with it," they told me, apparently annoyed by my nonconformative behavior. Indeed, most of the youngsters around me paid little attention to books (and, as a result, me). (Many, however, were playing an even more potentially subversive and dangerous game—having sex.) I did what most Chinese would do at the time—*yangfeng yinwei* (to feign compliance) and continued the study (but more discreetly). If at the beginning my "studying game" was an innocent act of not wanting to conform, gradually, however, I began to feel at odds with the hypocritical practices of those in power in the name of "revolution." Since I was not inspired to be a hero either, learning or studying became my way of being, despite the fact that it often got me in trouble (but also benefited me under some strange circumstances). I could not comprehend the negativity attached to learning until much later, when I realized that in my case it was not what I was studying that was the issue but the fact that I insisted on doing so. Studying was, as we say now, a form of resistance for me.

It was only later when the nationwide college entrance examinations were resumed after the Cultural Revolution did my learning of English become "useful" and attached to things Western (during the Cultural Revolution, lessons in English were nothing but political slogans such as "long live the proletariat dictatorship!" or revolutionary stories as "*banye jijiao*" [midnight cockcrow]). Still, however, learning itself was more interesting to me than the fact that I was learning a Western (and First World) language. In fact, when I became an English major, I began to shift my interest and attention to other subjects including psychology.

It is being the daughter of two parents who indulged my desire to want to know more and instilled in me a belief that learning in and of itself was infinitely good and noble (because of their own rather naively but deeply entrenched belief in learning) that (perhaps ironically) produced in me a borderless sense of what I wanted to learn. And it is this very borderlessness that eventually led me to be more willing to see gray than black and white, to find any theory that compels one to ask questions rather than to answer them, to resist any form of easy labeling, and above all, to maintain a critical distance to, among other things, "home."

During my visit, I had many long and interesting talks with my sister. In one of them, our conversation wandered into *liuxuesheng wenxue* (literature by students studying abroad).[3] By then China had seen books, stories, and television shows written by many PRC Chinese who are currently residing in such places as Japan, Australia, Europe, and North America. Most of the writings (written in Chinese and published in China) pertain to their personal experiences of struggling to survive or succeed in those places. People in China seem to have an insatiable interest in their fellow countrymen's lives after their exodus. Such interest was manifested particularly strongly in the popularity of a television show entitled "*Beijingren Zai Niuyue*" (Beijing Natives in New York) when it was shown three years ago. The show is based on a novella written by a Beijing native who immigrated to the United States in the 1980s.[4] Both the story and the television series were written and produced for the Chinese in China. Meanwhile, like many people in China, my sister was also curious about how the PRC students in America responded to the show (and, for that matter, to other writings of this kind as well). She wanted to know if the story was "realistic."

My problem with the television show, I told her, is not simply whether or not it is "realistic."

READING FROM A CRITICAL DISTANCE

Both the story and the television series are written and produced for the Chinese in China. As a PRC Chinese (sometimes referred to as "Chinese Chinese") relatively new to the diasporic mass in general and to the ongoing struggles and negotiations of the various ethnic groups in North America (both in relation to the dominant culture and within and among ethnic groups themselves) in particular, my reading of this PRC production spins off from my daily personal and professional negotiation with the American dominant culture, Asian-American subcultures, and mainstream Chinese culture in China. I spell out my positionality here not for the purpose of waving a license for discussion but with the intention to make visible a connection between the subject matter of my discussion and my own position as a *bianyuanren*. It is a "double reading" in response to the ongoing debate in North American academia on "the politics of locality" (an improved version of identity politics?) inspired by the postcolonial discourse, and to the emerging discussions on Chinese diaspora,[5] and, implicitly, to my sister's questions.

If, as Lisa Lowe points out in her article "Heterogeneity, Hybridity, Multiplicity: Marking Asian American Differences," that "what is referred to as 'Asian America' is clearly a heterogeneous entity" and if the heterogeneity includes "the historical contexts of particular waves of immigration,"[6] in its own way, the television series *Beijing Natives in New York* adds yet another dimension of the Chinese diasporic experience: It is about the latest wave of immigration of the (mostly well-educated) PRC Chinese to North America. The difference here, however, is that the story is produced both by and for the Chinese in China.[7] More importantly, therefore, this difference begs the questions. In what ways is it different? How should we understand the difference? Why is understanding the difference necessary and important?

Beijing Natives in New York was first shown in China in 1993.[8] Based on a novella of the same title, it is a drama of twenty-one episodes about a PRC couple from Beijing trying to make it in New York. It was an ambitious first attempt on the part of the Chinese to make a "Chinese" representation of the (PRC) Chinese in America.

The story is about a couple, Wang Qiming and Guo Yan, from Beijing seeking to find their dreams in New York City. As they struggle to make a living in the United States, their marriage falls apart, with Guo Yan, the wife, leaving Wang to marry David McCarthy, a white man who owns a sweater shop.[9] Wang, in turn, finds another woman, Ah Chun, who used to be his boss at a Chinese restaurant. With her help, he starts his own sweater shop. Wang Qiming and David McCarthy become rivals, each trying to put the other out of business. Having lost his wife to McCarthy, Wang is determined to beat him in business and does manage to do so. Meanwhile, he becomes a rich man, gets his daughter out of China, and proposes to Ah Chun. The rosy picture, however, does not last long. Toward the end of the story, he is bankrupt (as the result of his bad judgment) and continues to face the cold reality of the business world in New York. Together with other subplots, the stories of Wang Qiming, Guo Yan, Ah Chun, and David McCarthy made this television series an instant hit and the most highly rated television show in China in 1993.

Meanwhile, popular as it was, the series has also become controversial since it was first shown.[10] Reportedly, most of the controversy comes from those Chinese who live abroad, especially in North America, those represented by the characters' experiences in the story. Many of them do not like the show because they find it highly unrealistic. The controversy, however, has also prompted a response from Jiang Wen, the actor who played the leading male character, Wang Qiming. In an interview, when he was asked about his view of the controversy, he replied, "*yuan kan jiu kan, bu kan jiu hui jia!*" (if you want, watch it; if not, go home!). In spite of the pompous tone of this *mingxing dawanr* (a term used referring to the celebrities in today's Chinese entertainment business), I am intrigued by his further claim that he was "only concerned with the opinions of the new immigrants from Beijing" (*wo zhi guanxin Beijing xinyiming de kanfa*). New immigrants from Beijing only? By "*xinyiming*," we know he was referring to the Chinese who left China in the 1980s. But the exodus from China in the 1980s is a nationwide phenomenon, why only Beijing? Is it because the main character is from Beijing and the series is called "Beijing Natives in New York?" Perhaps, but there is certainly much more than this. Given the complexity of other related issues, one can take issue with this claim in a number of ways. I take issue with it here on one point: a curious discrepancy between this Beijing-centered claim and the iconic existence of the image of Ah Chun, a character from the series who is not from Beijing, nor even from the PRC.[11] What, then, is the relationship between her "non-Beijingness" and the specific "Beijing" nature of the series identified by Jiang Wen? Why is it Ah Chun, rather than anyone else in the series, whose image has since effected an iconic existence in China?[12]

Let me proceed first by way of something seemingly small and insignificant—the name of this character: Ah Chun. In both the novel and the television series, unlike other major characters, such as Wang Qiming, Guo Yan, Bai Xiumei, and David McCarthy, Ah Chun is never given a full name; she is always "Ah Chun" to everybody and at every moment. Is this just a narrative accident that this particular character is named as such? Whether we check with the traditional Chinese notion of "name" or with the argument on "naming" put forward by contemporary critic Slavoj Zizek,[13] most of us would agree that name-giving is never completely an accidental or innocent act, and it always already involves an agency whose act of naming gives meaning to the named object. Without reading too much into the name of Ah Chun, I would nevertheless suggest that her name signifies something specific about this character. In fact, I suggest that in many modern and contemporary Chinese literary and cultural texts, if a woman has a name like "Ah Chun" or "*Ah+something,*" it can often conjure up culturally specific or stereotypical implications about her. Narratively, she often occupies a relatively marginal position in relation to other characters; culturally, she is usually a southerner (because the word "Ah" is commonly used in some southern dialects for addressing people informally), and economically and socially, she could be a vendor or a *laobanniang* of some sort (owner of a small food stall), or a woman from a humble background with a menial job (a worker, a maid, etc.), or sometimes a woman with "loose" character, or even a prostitute. In a similar vein, in this northerner-made television series about some Beijing natives in New York City, the name Ah Chun marks the character's difference from most of the other characters: She is a non-PRC Chinese, from the south (although exactly where she is from remains rather ambiguous, most would assume Taiwan simply because the character speaks with a Taiwanese accent), and already a successful businesswoman in the United States.

Visually, Ah Chun is brought into the scene (in the very first episode) in this way: She drives a red car to a Chinese restaurant, comes out of the car clad in a bright red cloak and high heels, walks with overflowing self-confidence to the front door, and throws the car key to a man standing there. In the next cut, we see her inside the restaurant walking between tables, smiling and looking after customers (and we realize then that she is the boss there). Immediately we see another cut, in which her smile is completely gone while telling Peter, an employee (with whom she may have had an intimate relationship before), not to come the next day because he is fired. With these scenes, the series sets her up as a confident, sharp, tough, but efficient businesswoman who also happens to be very attractive. Such an image is further enhanced visually in the following scenes when Wang Qiming shows up with a strong ambivalence for having to look for a job in a Chinese restaurant. There, she is given a number of close-up shots in which she delivers her lines of sharp words at him.

Both visually and narratively, the encounter between Wang Qiming and Ah Chun sets up the dynamic between a "new immigrant from Beijing" with little experience and knowledge about this "land of opportunities" and an ethnic Chinese woman who seems to have it all—looks, education, experience, and economic status—and she is an insider of the world to which Wang Qiming is inspired to immigrate. Once again, however, such a dynamic is not set up to show how different they are from each other. As the story line develops, the dynamics between the two also begin to change, but no matter how they change, one thing is already narratively determined: Ah Chun's life is hereafter going to revolve around that of Wang Qiming when from now on she is given an almost ubiquitous presence in his life in New York.

Narratively, the series also has its own logic for how both of their lives are going to change. She changes from being his boss to being his confidante, unofficial business consultant, financial supporter, friend, lover, and fiancée. Meanwhile, drastic changes also occur in Wang's life, from living in a basement apartment with his wife Guo Yan and washing dishes in Ah Chun's restaurant, to owning his own business, driving an expensive car, and living in a house on Long Island. The trajectories of the changes in their lives intersect with Wang Qiming occupying center stage; it is a story of how this Beijing man makes it in Manhattan. In relation to this underpinning narrative logic, changes in Ah Chun's life can only take place revolving around this central character. The interesting issue here is not just the question of whether this transition on her part is logical, but what makes the representation of this character work in spite of the fact that the portrayal in many ways cannot stand much scrutiny. This issue relates back to the question of "the naming agency," from which, in this particular case, stems both the name Ah Chun and image of Ah Chun, and how, through the camera, her image gets projected onto the television screen and manifests a fantasy about the *xiandai nuxing* or the modern female.

If we look into the media in today's China, similar images of women like Ah Chun can easily be found in a number of television shows and films (not to mention magazine covers), such as the film *Yanghang li de zhongguo xiaojie* (Miss Chinese in a foreign company) and the television series *Bieshu li de nurenmen* (Women in a resort community), and many others. What I am suggesting here is that the creation of Ah Chun is yet another manifestation of a fascination to perceive Chinese women within in a modernized setting, such as a *yanghang* (a foreign company) or a *bieshu* (a villa). Ah Chun, in this sense, is simply moved a little farther away geographically. She is, in other words, a Beijing-based creation projected back onto the screen for domestic consumption. Placed in an exotic setting (from the perspectives of the Chinese in China) like Manhattan, she is created with all the reference points back in China: recent Chinese history has gone through its love affairs with women workers, peasants, soldiers, cadres, educated youth, university students, and is currently deeply in love with the *xiandai nuxing* (the modern female) which is represented by the images of businesswomen, "miss office," "miss public relations," and so on. It is this new love affair with these newly emerged public roles for women that renders Ah Chun a positive character, and the appearance of such a new and modern female functions as an indication of China's modernization process. It is all of this that paves the way for Ah Chun, rather than any other woman character in the series, to become a possible candidate for a cultural icon.

At the same time, however, the Westernized/modern packaging is not the factor that sustains her image as a positive cultural icon. There is a deeper level of construction that makes the packaging of a seemingly non-Beijing and non-PRC Chinese woman a possible candidate. Instead of arguing that the television series objectively represents the value system symbolized by Ah Chun, I would suggest that the success of Ah Chun in China is the result of a repackaging based on a domestic fascination with notions of "the modern" and a desire to reevaluate the existing cultural system within. Ah Chun's real significance, therefore, exceeds her Westernized appearance and ways of doing things. Underneath such an appearance is a "Chinese heart" that has taken the steps to reject the West, a rejection symbolized by such things as: (1) her quitting the job at a big company, (2) her estranged relationship with Carter, a white man with whom she had a son and to whom she lost the custody of the child (although the story never makes it clear whether he is her ex-husband or ex-lover), (3) her knowledge that her survival in the United States is to fight "American battles" with Americans on their terms, and (4) most importantly, her relationship with Wang Qiming. The order of these steps demonstrates a trajectory of a Westernized Chinese woman moving eastward.

In the series, the positive implication of this direction taken by Ah Chun is further set off by the opposite direction taken by Guo Yan, the wife, and later, ex-wife, of Wang Qiming. The latter is depicted as a lost woman when she moves away from Wang Qiming by divorcing him and marrying David McCarthy, although her side of the story is told without much logic and in many ways does not hold up. Drifting away from Wang Qiming, Guo Yan's life deteriorates when she is eventually rejected even by herself and becomes an alcoholic. Her final return to Beijing is only the result of the "wrong" direction she took and is the only way out for having moved away from her roots. By comparison, in spite of her original image of a Westernized Chinese and a sharp businesswoman, Ah Chun's "eastward moving" is realized by her becoming increasingly domesticated in her relationship with Wang Qiming, from, once again, being his boss to being his creditor, his business partner, his lover, and his fiancée.[14]

This finally brings my discussion back to the claim that Ah Chun is a character liked by both men and women and to Jiang Wen's claim that he only cares about the Beijing *xinyiming*' (new immigrants') opinion of the show. The "liking," I argue, speaks more of a shared position between the show and its intended audience rather than the character herself. The character, in other words, represents a desire for a version of femininity that is both modern and domesticated. It is in this vein that the non-Beijingness of Ah Chun gets dissolved and she becomes an insider, while the alienating one turns out to be Guo Yan, who is represented for the most part as a lost Chinese woman who wanders beyond her boundaries and gets punished as a result. It is the domestication of the character Ah Chun that functions as the precondition for her image to become domesticated and accepted in China.

In the past two years, I have shown episodes of the series to students of the Chinese language on a regular basis. What may appear true and possible for the audience in China rings untrue to a group of ethnic Chinese who are familiar with the dynamics of being an ethnic Chinese in the United States and who watch the show within that very context. While we understand that the context in which Ah Chun is represented and accepted differs from that in which my students view her, the point of authenticity associated with their disliking of the character is nevertheless a valid one. It is valid just as it is valid when we question the misrepresentations of the "Other" in a Eurocentric manner, or when the Chinese Americans debate how to understand the representations of the revised Chinese myths by such authors as Maxine Hong Kingston and Amy Tan. However, it is not valid in the sense that we need to argue for an authentic representation (although I would still insist on the need for a better knowledge of the "other," which is more desirable than ignorance), but valid in the sense that it inevitably begs the question of why it is represented the way it is. While my students simply dismiss Ah Chun as an inauthentic representation of an ethnic Chinese residing in the United States, their negative reception is yet another point of departure in discussing the questions raised by this particular representation.

Again one of the reasons why Ah Chun is positively received in China is that she has maintained a "Chinese identity" in spite of being a Westernized woman. In this sense, then, there is an irony: In theory, at least, this maintenance of a Chinese identity seems to be in agreement with the desire and struggle of ethnic Chinese to maintain their cultural identity in the United States, and Ah Chun is depicted as someone capable of negotiating the boundaries of the ethnic and dominant cultures while maintaining her Chinese identity. At the same time, however, her "virtues" in maintaining that identity appear to be lost, to such an extent that my students, many of whom are ethnic Chinese, do not identify with her. To better understand this irony, we need to go beyond the image of Ah Chun alone. The negative reception on the part of my students is not just a rejection of Ah Chun for being inauthentic, but more importantly, it indicates a refusal on their part to identify with the gaze behind the representation of the character, a gaze that projects a certain perception that is rather alien to them. It is a perception that is rooted in a Chinese masculinist-nationalist discourse: representing "the other Chinese" for the purpose of creating a Chinese hero whose existence in New York subverts the American dominant culture "by defeating it on its own terms and with its own game." The discrepancy, in other words, suggests that what is at issue is the question of history and the historical contexts associated with both the representation of the character of Ah Chun and its receptions by different groups of (Chinese) viewers. My students' lack of identity with that "gaze" is overdetermined by the historical context within which they exist as ethnic Chinese (i.e. Chinese Americans, Hong Kong Chinese, Taiwanese Chinese, Vietnamese Chinese) in the United States.

This, incidentally, reminds me of the context in which Chinese American women writers such as Maxine Hong Kingston and Amy Tan negotiate their "Chinese" identities. Their (mis)use of Chinese myths and history (which is often a point of contention especially among different groups of Chinese) is conditioned by their own historical reference points: Theirs is one that orients around American dominant culture in negotiation for an ethnic identity. In this sense, one can argue that these Chinese American women writers focus more on the synchronic relationships between ethnic groups and the dominant culture, between one ethnic group and another, and among people within the same ethnic group. The synchronicity is conditioned, once again, by the ethnic politics in the United States, and it is part of the history of this country. Throughout American history, different diasporic communities have struggled to coexist and to be recognized. The notion of Chineseness is therefore often essentialized, in different ways, by both Chinese Americans (as part of their struggle) and the dominant culture (largely due to ignorance). The spatial importance of the ethnic Chinese is also overdetermined by this entanglement. In this sense, the depth and the intricate layers of Chinese history are also necessarily flattened into a spatial existence conditioned by the relationships between the American dominant culture and various Chinese diasporic groups.

READING AS A CHINESE WOMAN INTELLECTUAL

As a Chinese woman intellectual in diaspora as well as one of those (PRC) Chinese whose experience the television show attempts, at least partially, to represent, I find it difficult to celebrate what for some critics can be hailed as a Third World challenge of the First World power in a show in which a Chinese man is given center stage in a transnational context to voice his desire and to perform his struggles for success. I question the imprint of a PRC imaginary in the image of Ah Chun and argue that it is an imaginary that ultimately remains foreign to other groups of ethnic Chinese not only because of its Beijing-centered representation of the latest wave of Chinese immigration from the PRC but also because it stereotypes the experiences of other ethnic Chinese.

With my critical approach to the television show, if it were up to Mr. Jiang Wen, I should also be told to "go home." The irony, however, is that I may not have a "home" as such to go back to, depending, of course, on what he means by home. Judging from the tone of voice in his statement, one can say that Mr. Jiang could be telling those who do not like the show or who are critical of it to go away or disappear.

Symbolically, the complexity of "home" does not reveal itself only at the moment of one's return (or not return). Nevertheless, the act of returning does tend to register more meanings. At the end of *Beijing Natives in New York*, the viewer is told, via the captions on the screen, that Guo Yan, Wang Qiming's ex-wife, eventually returns to Beijing, where her "home" is. Her homecoming, however, is shown more as a sign of failure than anything else that may have resulted, in her case, from all the missteps she took. Indeed, most Chinese would feel no problem seeing her as a failure, for they like to believe she is the one who transgressed when lured away by white America.[15] Viewed from a perspective that presents her in an ambiguous light but which refuses to identify with her ambiguity, Guo Yan has only one way out—to the margins and to disappear by literally being made to "go home." The captions about her on the screen at the end read like inscriptions on a tombstone signifying a closure to her diasporic life.

At the same time, the stories of Wang Qiming and Ah Chun are left open even when toward the end they have lost their business. Early in the series Wang Qiming and Guo Yan decide to return to Beijing shortly after they arrive in the United States. When Wang goes to say good-bye to Ah Chun, he only encounters her strong contempt. She tells him that America is a battleground and that she feels sorry for those who mistake it for heaven and retreat when realizing that it is not. Ah Chun despises cowards, and so she will not retreat to "home." Her refusal to go home, however, is shown in a favorable light attached with a specific value: For her, "home" is to be lived as an entity that is different from the battleground in which she currently resides. As a result, even though she refuses the idea of physically returning "home", her relationship with "home" is highlighted positively against the background of Guo Yan's blurred and zigzagging movements between China and America, both of which are represented as problematic. When the series ends, therefore, Guo Yan's physical return does not identify her with "home" as positively as those who live away from it. In an amusingly frightening way, we find all of this reflected in the reactions given to the two actresses who played Ah Chun and Guo Yan. After the big success of the show, the former became one of the most sought-after actresses, but the latter had to go through a time being marginalized.

When I came to North America in mid-1980s to do graduate study first in English and then in comparative literature, my exodus intersected, intellectually, with Western critical (including feminist) theories and with the rise of postcolonial discourse. In some strange ways, while critical theories unleashed a sense of freedom in me and began to help me articulate how distant I felt about "home," the rising postcolonial discourse was carving out borders for me in relation to "home." Within the context of American academia, my own identification with "home" has thus been constantly contested by this intersection. Implicated by the postcoloniality, my physical journey or movement from the East to the West is also problematized. The "correct" (counter)moves seem to be for those who are identified as Third World intellectuals in diaspora to acknowledge that the vantage point from which they speak and write about their "home" derives much of its power from them being in the First World. Such an identification, however, often leaves my own sense of distance from "home" as well as from the First World hanging in a state of uncertainty, because not only are the borders often superimposed, but they are also in many ways limiting.

In her article "Against the Lures of Diaspora," Rey Chow points out,

> The space of the Third World intellectuals in diaspora is a space that is removed from the ground of earlier struggles that were still tied to the native land. . . . The unself-reflexive sponsorship of the Third World culture, including Third World women's culture, becomes a mask that conceals the hegemony of these intellectuals over those who are stuck at home.[16]

In naming "Chinese women intellectuals in diaspora," therefore, Rey Chow cautions that her naming is "to avoid repeating the well-worn discursive paradigm of Orientalism" and is "a way of *not giving in* to the charms of an alterity in which so many of the West's others are now called upon to speak." She addresses Chinese women intellectuals in diaspora directly, asking them to keep in mind the question "Why are we talking about modern Chinese literature and Chinese women in North American academia in the 1990s?" and to realize that "as such activities of speaking and writing are tied less to the oppressed women in Chinese communities in China than to our own intellectual careers in the West, we need to unmask ourselves through a scrupulous declaration of self-interest."[17] From these remarks, we can see that Rey Chow ties, with good reason, the speaking and writing practiced by Chinese women intellectuals in diaspora with where they are geographically located and the power that location commands.

To identify those of us who speak and write in the West as Chinese women intellectuals in diaspora is empowering, for it opens up a third paradigm in between the First and Third World intellectuals and makes it possible for us to address issues that are foreclosed by that dichotomy. Rey Chow's warning, at the same time, keeps one aware of the need to continue to problematize one's own privilege. Another way to think about the problem of privilege is to bring to the foreground in the debate the question of historical reference points, the problems of who (we are talking about), what (we mean by privilege), and why (it is necessary to question) when it comes to the question of privilege, and the multiple accountability in relation to those reference points. On the one hand, I could argue that as a Chinese woman scholar in North America, "speaking" or "writing" for me has never been just an exercise of power or display of privilege; it is also a means of survival, a self-interest both as mundane as having a job and as sublime as being reflected in the ongoing debate within American academia over the question of "who can speak." On the other hand, I am fully aware that the mundane and sublime dichotomy does not cancel out the relevance of accountability of such practices. Nor, more importantly, should it be reduced to just a trivial personal matter by turning it into a static and polarized paradigm—one is either privileged or not.

In winter 1995, at the invitation of the Shanghai Women's Cadre School (*Shanghai Funu Ganbu Xuexiao*), I went back to China to speak on media and images of women. The experience was very interesting, but what happened afterward was much more revealing. One (perhaps not so) amusing comment came from a woman who is very active in Shanghai media as a highly articulate woman expert on creating "femininity discourse." After being at my lecture, she was reportedly saying that those Chinese like me should not be taken seriously because we "have failed to enter the mainstream culture in the U.S." Another comment came from a man who is the head of a self-styled research group that helps design women's images (*Shanghai funu xingxiang yanjiu hui*). He complained to my sister one day when running into her on the street that rumor had it that I had questioned his role as a man in designing women's images. He said, with enough contempt but without any trace of irony, "What's wrong with a man designing women's images? Your sister lives in America. Doesn't she know that the most famous international designers are men?" Miscommunication and misunderstanding notwithstanding, I was sufficiently amused by these two accounts. What is ironic about all of this, however, is that in the eye of these privileged Chinese, I have little power to speak because I do not belong to the American mainstream culture and therefore I am not their equal. My intervention was not successful so far as these people were concerned, as it was not because of my privilege as a disaporic Chinese that made them resent me but rather because of my lack thereof.

If we push the analysis of the problems facing Chinese women intellectuals in diaspora further beyond its reference point—the hegemony of the West or the First World—we can argue that the West, or the First World is not (and should not be) the only reference point that we are concerned with as Chinese women intellectuals in diaspora in our investigation of issues concerning China and Chinese women. By "reference points," I have in mind Arif Dirlik's insistence on the importance of recognizing "local histories" in his critique of postcolonial discourse, histories that not only must be taken into consideration but also need to be examined as well. By "reference points," I also have in mind the existence of those positions that are less statically positioned, or more fluid (to use a fashionable word) in nature, in relation to those local histories, and which, as a result, have multiple accountability.

Here, I find Arif Dirlik's critique of the "self-referentiality" of the postcolonial rather illuminating. In his article "The Postcolonial Aura: Third World Criticism in the Age of Global Capitalism," Arif Dirlik challenges the postcolonial discourse.[18] For Dirlik, to use the term "postcolonial" (rather than "global capitalism") is historically misleading because, among other things, the themes of postcolonial criticism have been prominent in the cultural discourses of Third World societies that were never, strictly speaking, colonies, or that conducted successful revolutions against Euro-American domination, or like China, both. Nor are there clear temporal boundaries to the use of terms because the themes they encompass are as old as the history of colonialism. On the other hand, the term *postcolonial*, understood in terms of its discursive thematics, excludes from its scope most of those who inhabit or hail from post*colonial* societies.[19]

The historicism in postcolonial discourse, according to Dirlik's mapping, appears to be "without a sense of structure." Focusing on the location of the postcolonial critics—in the First World—and on the positionality of the critics themselves, Dirlik questions the postcolonial discourse as a "critique that starts off with a repudiation of the universalistic pretensions of Marxist language" that "ends up not with its dispersion into local vernaculars but with a return to another First World language with universalistic epistemological pretensions."[20] He argues that "postcolonialism's repudiation of structure and totality in the name of history ironically ends up not in an affirmation of historicity but in a self-referential, universalizing historicism that reintroduces through the back door an unexamined totality; it projects globally what are but local experiences."[21] Finally, he points out that there is an absence of "a consideration of the relationship between postcolonialism and global capitalism."[22] I quote Dirlik's unsympathetic critique of postcolonialism extensively here mainly to draw attention to the problematics I have tried to address here as a Third World intellectual in diaspora confronting the boundaries set up by the implications of postcoloniality. In conjunction with my discussion here, I want to echo Dirlik's point that, it is when "what are but local experiences" are projected onto those who are collectively labeled as "Third World intellectuals in diaspora" in the name of postcoloniality that problems arise. As Third World intellectuals in diaspora, or Chinese women intellectuals in diaspora, part of our reference point will always exist, among others, in what I would call "Third World capitalism," or the transnational capitalism in Third World countries, and the struggle there is not a mere transplantation of the First World and Third World power hierarchy with the latter being the one that we must always defend (in the name of the postcolonial).

On a recent trip to a Southeast Asian country, I was appalled at the huge gap between the poor and the rich. The rich are walled in behind concrete walls in big houses or compounds miles away from the ordinary people. To reach any of those areas, one can go only by car and by passing through checkpoints. While the rich have chauffer-driven cars and servants in their homes, and while they frequent trendy bars where they constantly bump into each other, slums, beggars, and homeless people are everywhere to be seen. The ruthlessness of the way the rich display their wealth and way of living are as appalling as the terrible conditions in which the poor live. And yet, in postcolonial discourse, one hears little about the class difference within a Third World country and its relationship with global capitalism. The self-referentiality of the postcolonial discourse developed in the First World is in fact, as Dirlik points out, the totality that tends to negate the importance of recognizing those other historical and local reference points.

In discussing the problematics concerning her positioning, Leslie Bow points out that "as an Asian American critic, I occupy a position that provokes ambivalence in others—I am either held in suspicion for 'making an issue' of my race, assigned honorary whiteness for being the 'good' kind of minority, or subject to racial erasure for being 'overrepresented.' My critical, intellectual, and personal authority are very much tied to this representation so that regardless of how I position myself critically, a certain amount of that positioning is done for me."[23]

The "positioning" done by the others in this sense is precisely a similar paradox of the postcolonial space in which Chinese women intellectuals in diaspora have found their authority to speak constantly contested. While the contestation of one's positionality keeps critics like me on constant alert, the question is why minority critics or Third World intellectuals have to sit on their hands trying to behave themselves as "good" minority critics. No matter how vigilant we try to be, we are often held on a seemingly higher moral ground for the totality of challenging Western feminisms and theories. At the same time, it is also a ground that actually commands little authority and power, because, as qualified members of a minority, our positionality is already overdetermined by what Rey Chow refers to as the "center and minor relationship"—that is, at the receiving end of the power relation set by the center. It is a position where those on the margins constantly find their own positioning being undermined, especially when they try to pull away from this center-minor dichotomy. In this sense, unless we localize the postcoloniality itself, our own local histories and historical reference points cannot be taken into serious consideration, and our positioning will always already be done for us with our voices marginalized and, like Guo Yan, with the complexity of our experience and its significance made to disappear.

Toward the last part of her article about my visit, my sister writes, "but after all she is a passing guest (*guoke*). After a month of listening, watching, eating, and talking, she was about to return (*huiqu*) again." In Chinese, when we use *huiqu*, we normally imply that the point to which one returns is where one's home is. Ironically, however, *huiqu* (or *huiguo*, return to one's own country) is also the word I (and most PRC Chinese) use when we go back to China to visit. Also ironically, I have always had trouble referring to wherever I live in the United States as home and usually refer to it as "*wo zhu de di fang*" (place where I live). While "home" for me could still be somewhere in China, like it is to Ah Chun (one more irony?), "home" is nevertheless not where I return to live. "Home" in this sense is simultaneously somewhere and elsewhere without definite borders and boundaries. It is perhaps because of that that I have become a "passing guest" even to my family. This paradoxical relationship between me and "home" also conditions my relationship to the place where I currently live (speak and write). It involves constant negotiations of boundaries and borders, as well as efforts trying to find a common ground where even when perceived as an "outsider" my voice can still be heard. To both places, in this sense, I cannot but be a *bianyuanren*, or a person on the margins. As my sister imagines it, however, this may be a more interesting position in which to be. Although it appears that she has also done a positioning for me, she does not do it from either a "center" or a "minor" position; she does it from a point where she sees me both as a sister and as a passing guest.

Although the term "in-between" has become rather overly used and has been criticized for romanticizing the cosmopolitan and its cultures, I still want to borrow it to describe the positionality of Chinese women intellectuals in diaspora. Unlike Ah Chun, whose image is eventually turned into a fixed model acceptable to one ideology, however, I see ours as continuing to remain both unsettled and unsettling, one that cannot be assimilated by one single identity, be it the center or the margin.

Here, I would like to come back, one last time, to the point concerning the character Ah Chun and her counterpart Guo Yan. As I have pointed out, Ah Chun is liked by many Chinese in China because she is represented as a Westernized woman who does not forget her own roots and is able to demonstrate her virtue by orienting herself toward a Beijing Chinese. This combination of both West and East is the ideal balance that makes a Westernized Chinese woman acceptable to the PRC Chinese. As her contrast, Guo Yan is represented, as I have also pointed out, as someone who loses her "center" by moving away from Wang Qiming and thus fails in everything else that follows and eventually has to return to China. The game of balancing is key to the success of the character Ah Chun. Symbolically, it is also a seductive part of the "lures of diaspora."

To move against such "lures," therefore, is to move beyond playing "balancing" games at the margins, to perceive the margins as entry for intervention or as positions for raising new questions, to learn to resist becoming Ah Chun—to resist being repackaged either by nationalistic claims or by any totalizing category, and to ask such question as "what about Guo Yan?"—so as to be able to question what has been erased and why it has been erased.

NOTES

1. Zhong Xueyan, "Jie cong meiguo lai" (Sister coming back from America), *Haishang Wentan* (World of letters in Shanghai) 3 (1995): 72—73.

2. Many people may not know that during the Cultural Revolution many youngsters (at least in Shanghai) could still find books they were not supposed to be reading at the time. Once they got hold of one such book, many would take the opportunity to read it. This is how I started reading, even though I was actually too young to read novels (just imagine the equivalent situation in this country where children of a certain age would not be allowed to watch certain types of movies). The irony is that, like many at the time, I did.

3. Stories written in Chinese by newly immigrated Chinese and published for domestic consumption constitute a particular school of literature in China called *liuxuesheng wenxue* (literature by students studying abroad). The literature itself, however, exceeds the boundaries of the experience of students to include all of those who joined the wave of exodus from the PRC since the 1980s. The richness of that body of literature is little known in the West because everything is written in Chinese and little has been translated except a few from an earlier wave (of Taiwanese students) in the 1960s. See Hsin-sheng C. Kao, ed., *Nativism Overseas* (Albany: SUNY Press, 1993). My discussion here, however, is not a study of this literature but an attempt to make visible

some of the issues raised in a Chinese representation of a kind of Chinese diasporic experience.

4. Cao Guilin, "Beijingren zai niuyue" (Beijing natives in New York), *Shiyue* (October 4 1994).

5. Chinese diaspora is becoming an increasingly hot topic in some academic circles, even though there are scholars who started writing about the issue years ago.

6. Lisa Lowe, "Heterogeneity, Hybridity, Multiplicity: Marking Asian American Differences," *Diaspora* (Spring 1991): 27.

7. I use PRC and China interchangeably in this article to refer to the entity called People's Republic of China to preempt questions such as, "Which China are you refering to?"

8. *Beijingren zai niuyue* (Beijing natives in New York), television series, directed by Feng Xiaogang and produced by Center for TV Production in Beijing, 1993.

9. A friend of mine pointed out that McCarthy is an Irish last name, and within American culture Irish identity (one made out by the mainstream culture) registers more than just being "white." She was wondering whether the Chinese producers of the show would have any knowledge of this cultural implication. Even though I don't have the hard evidence on this point, I would not hesitate to speculate that they don't and to them McCarthy is just an American white man.

10. See, for example, an article entitled "Dianshiju 'Beijingren zai niuyue' duanxiang" (Some thoughts on a Beijing man in New York), *Huaxia Wenzhai* 162 (1994): 12—14; Dong Mingyue, "'Liulang wenxue' de renwu yu zhuti" (The characters and themes of the liulang [wanders'] literature), *Wenxue Pinglun Jia* (Literary critics) 6 (1992): 23—27; Jiang Wen, "Yuankan jiukan, bukan jiu huijia!" (If you want to watch it, please do; if you don't, go home!), *Dangdai yuekan* (Modern age monthly) 37 (1994).

11. Since the huge success of the television series in China, Ah Chun, one of its major women characters, has also become a cultural icon. In an article titled "'A Chun, Xiang Dang Ge 'Hen Bang de' Nuren" (Ah Chun wants to be an "ideal" woman), the writer reports on the life of the actress who played Ah Chun. Instead of referring to her as Wang Ji (which is her real name), however, she identifies Wang as "Ah Chun" and writes that "while there are different views on the TV series of 'Beijingren Zai Niuyue,' everybody shares a positive view of the character Ah Chun; so much so that there are people who wonder why, when Chinese men like Ah Chun, Chinese women also like her as well. " Ji Jie "'A chun' xiang dang 'hen bang de' nuren" (Ah Chun wants to be a perfect woman), *Shehui Jiating* (Society and family) 2 (1994). In short, Ah

Chun is a favorite character of both men and women in China. Although the writer of the article does not show any data to support her assumption that both men and women like Ah Chun, I believe she makes the claim based on a general impression manifested in the iconic existence of the image of Ah Chun in today's Chinese popular culture.

12. The success of "Ah Chun" is such that the actress who played the character is trying to cash in on it by establishing a fashion company named after Ah Chun.

13. See, for example, Slavoj Zizek, *The Sublime Object of Ideology* (London and New York: Verso, 1989). See especially the chapter entitled "Che Vuoi?"

14. At this point, interestingly enough, I am reminded of another once-very-popular television series, *Earning* (*Kewang*), a fifty-episode television series first aired in China in 1990, which on the surface is almost irrelevant to *Beijing Natives*. *Earning* is about Liu Huifang, the embodiment of female virtues who is willing to sacrifice everything for the benefit of others around her. On the surface, Ah Chun stands as a sharp contrast to everything Liu Huifang stands for. The question, however, is this: Why did the same audience that had been strongly moved by Liu Huifang only a few years back find Ah Chun acceptable? What happened to the audience between this later show and the earlier one? One may attribute the change to the rapid economic development resulting in a shift from appreciating a virtuous woman like Liu Huifang to appreciating a modern female like Ah Chun. Still, however, I would argue that Ah Chun is not really the opposite of Liu Huifang. In fact, she represents an ideal combination that combines some virtues from Liu Huifang and the virtues of a modern woman. What makes her perfect and appealing is the fact that she is contained—domesticated—within the context in which her behavior and action make sense to an audience that shares a similar imagination as the producers of the show. She represents a kind of femininity acceptable to the mainstream culture—a woman whose heart is always in the "right" place. Although she is very Westernized (and her English "is even better than Americans'"), she is willing to take all kinds of risks for a "real" Chinese man and eventually becomes the loyal partner of this man's business venture, and more. In today's China, the fact that many men have both a wife who may resemble some of Liu Huifang and a mistress who may appear more like Ah Chun (or vice versa) signifies a desire for the ideal combination represented by Ah Chun.

15. Some are even reportedly accusing her for wanting it both ways: marrying an American and helping her ex-husband to lessen her guilt.

16. Rey Chow, "Against the Lures of Diaspora," in *Gender and Sexuality in Twentieth-Century Chinese Literature and Society,* edited by Tonglin Lu (Albany: SUNY Press, 1993), 41.

17. *Ibid.*, pp.40–41.

18. Arif Dirlik, "The Postcolonial Aura: Third World Criticism in the Age of Global Capitalism," *Critical Inquiry* 20 (Winter 1994): 328–356.

19. *Ibid.*, pp. 336–337.

20. *Ibid.*, p. 342.

21. *Ibid.*, p. 345.

22. *Ibid.*, p. 352.

23. Leslie Bow, "'For Every Gesture of Loyalty, There Doesn't Have to Be a Betrayal': Asian American Criticism and the Politics of Locality," in *Who Can Speak*, edited by Judith Roof and Robyn Wiegman (Urbana and Chicago: University of Illinois Press, 1995), 44.

[Per]forming Law: Deformations and Transformations

Sharon K. Hom

BEGINNING FORMATIONS

A frequent typo I make involves "from" and "form," typing one when intending the other. And indeed, the place(s) I come "from," the origins beyond territorial location, certainly shapes, "forms" how I am becoming who I am, and how I come to view the world. I was born in Hong Kong, a "borrowed place" that is on "borrowed time," in Rey Chow's words, a city that is "a particular kind of passage way, which was created by the accident of history but which nonetheless persists . . . with a uniqueness and resilience that is otherwise unknown in world history."[1] Carrying my colonial and immigrant past, in the identity alphabet of Chinese/Chinese-Americans, I am not ABC (an American-born Chinese), nor MIT (made in Taiwan), nor MIC (made in China). Technically, I might be a stubborn *jook-kok* (in Cantonese, literally the hard knot of the bamboo, used to refer to overseas-born), but growing up in the United States, I may have become somewhat empty like the hollow parts of the bamboo, a *jook-sing*. To write from and through these transitory diasporic locations requires excavations of sedimented layers of memory, history, and lived experience along the multiple axes of ethnicity, gender, culture, and class.

I was born during the monsoon season and in the midst of a great storm. My subsequent comfort as an adult inhabiting ambiguous spaces of transit—airports, hotels, train stations—may be connected to this birthing into a world in endless motion. I have also always loved rainy days. Unlike the Barbra Streisand song, on a clear day, I never felt I could "see forever," but rather only the sunny outlines of a deceptively stable reality against a blue sky. My childhood memories live on—

oranges bobbing by, pieces of furniture, eggs, floating by in the river of what was once our street—embedded deep evidence of the possibility of the destruction of apparent order(s) of "the ways things are." So I have always preferred the possibilities luminously inhabiting misty gray days.

Our one room Hong Kong flat in Daihang was located on a dead-end street that ended against a mountainside. My memories are mostly carried in my body—the sounds of water of a small stream or pond with goldfish flashing in the light, carrying a hot bowl of black medicinal tea for my mother carefully down the street, the cool incense-filled darkness of my grandmother's house, the smooth bamboo mat I slept on, and the public latrine I fell into and lost my wooden sandal. On a return trip as an adult I tried to find my way back to that pond, guided by my memory of the sound of water, but found only a dried up hole filled with garbage and dented soda cans near a boarded up temple. The old public latrine was still there with a sign "slippery when wet."

My best childhood friend in Hong Kong, Ping, and I used to explore and climb up the mountain paths, and one day, coming upon an opening, we saw (or thought we saw) an old woman, sitting behind a large steaming pot. She looked up at us, with a direct seeing into and past us, and I knew she was a witch. Terrified, I grabbed Ping and ran. We never told the adults, which is how I know it happened. Almost forty years later in New York, I ran into Ping, at an acupuncturist's office in Chinatown. She was lying on her stomach, her sweater neck was down and I could see the needles sticking into her back. She told me about her children, her work as a teacher's aide, and asked about me. I said, I teach law, I try to write, and even though Chinese parents are not supposed to say these things for fear of tempting the jealous gods, I said I have a wonderful teenage son. But my hands are bothering me, and I have shooting pains in my thumbs, perhaps from too long hours on the computer. Despite the distance of a lifetime apart, I just had to ask her about the witch in the mountains. I wanted to know if she remembered. She thought about it, and answered no. I pushed her, insisted on her searching memory, but she was blank. Lying there on her stomach under that cold fluorescent light, she was so certain of her memories that I almost envied her. Later, walking out of the acupuncturist's office, my hands somewhat tingling, the pain subsiding, I wondered whether I had seen the witch, or whether Ping, not being the obstinate journal and dream keeper I had grown up to be, had forgotten what we had seen.

An old photograph of my mother eight months pregnant with me at the Hong Kong airport—she is standing next to my very young, sad looking father, holding a raincoat draped over his arm, carrying his "paper son" immigrant status in his pocket. They are surrounded by my aunts, my uncle, and grandparents, all seeing my father off to America. My mother's mouth is tight, a thin line of anger, the wife left behind carrying an eleven-month-old baby in her arms and another on the way—me—heavy inside her. It was five years before my father could save up enough money to send for the three of us, my mother, my brother, and me. I remember the letter, or I remember my mother's reaction and preparation for the journey. She decided I needed to look "American" and gave me a perm, so that I would look pretty, and that meant of course, with curly hair. As it turned out, she overdid it, and my passport photo shows a chubby smiling, front teeth missing, little Chinese girl with an Afro.

On the eve of our departure from Hong Kong, my mother woke and was startled to see an elderly Chinese man with a mole on his cheek, bending over my sleeping brother and me. The story of my paternal grandfather's spirit visit was lost in the initial years of the exhaustion and alienness of our arrival. When my mother recounted this memory years later to my father, we learned that my paternal grandfather (who had passed away years ago in China, before our departure from Hong Kong) had a mole on his face. Perhaps he had come to see his grandchildren off, one of us already looking "foreign," as we left forever to another land.[2]

As a child in Hong Kong, I had imagined America where the father I had yet to meet disappeared to, was the *gamsan* (gold mountain), where I would have beautiful dolls and toys, where the houses would be grand, not like the small single room we lived in. But the route t/here and the arrival were not my imagined realities. Traveling alone with two small children, exhausted with air-sickness, my mother missed our connecting flight in Hawaii. My father slept overnight in JFK Airport in New York, holding onto his wilted, dying flowers and waiting for us anxiously. After the bumpy ride into Brooklyn, we arrived in the brownstone basement my father had rented. Surrounded by the bare concrete walls, the water heater facing us in the corner, I wondered how this could be *Meigok* (America, the "beautiful country"). In fading black-and-white photos of that first night, I look very exhausted, mouth slightly open, as if lost for words.

After a brief time in the Brooklyn basement, then a Chinatown walk-up apartment, we moved to the back of a laundry on the main street of a small Long Island town. When the bakery, the bank, and the other stores closed, we were alone—my mother, my brothers and I. Except for school hours and occasional outings, we lived isolated from the foreign world of the children who lived in large old houses in the tree-lined residential part of town, and who ate weird foods like cream of mushroom soup. My mother always took great pride and care that my brother and I were always well dressed and carried ourselves properly outside. While my mother cooked rice and chicken on Sunday nights, we watched Adam, Hoss, and little Joe on *Bonanza*, and the comings and goings of the male enclave of the Ponderosa Ranch. We did not connect the pigtailed Chinese cook with anyone in *our* family.

For many years, my father worked as a waiter, and for several years, in a restaurant far away. He rode the dark van that drove the silent men to and from the dormitory where they lived six days of the week. My father, who was an absent presence for the first five years of my life, became the disembodied voice at night talking, arguing with my mother. Our childhood was marked from the beginning by these absences, and yet the pervasive presence of unquestionable patriarchal authority ruled over our isolated family. Once a week, on his day off, my father would often take us to the dock to go crabbing. While my brother and I played our flashlight's circle of light across the water's surface trying to attract the crabs close enough to scoop up with our nets, my parents sat talking in indecipherable Chinese or silently stared at the lights of the bridge spanning across the darkness. When we went to the Carvel ice cream store, we could choose only vanilla, as no choices were allowed at risk of our father cursing us out for trying to be "different." Sometimes we went to a drive-in theater, where my brother and I were allowed to ride the carousel in our pajamas during the intermissions. The beginnings and the past flicker across memory screens permanently framed by the front windshield of a still car, as I watch from a back seat.

A yellowed framed newspaper photo of my brother pouring water over my head on the front page of the Brooklyn Daily News hangs in our living room. You could have seen the 5 cent price and the date had my mother not cut it off to make the picture fit into the frame she wanted to surprise me with. We always had different interpretations of what was significant enough to keep in the frame. The caption reads: "Cool cool kids: Paul Tom, 5, pours water on his sister Sharon, 3, as they swelter on the beach in Coney Island. The children are from Hong Kong, China, and this is their first visit to Brooklyn's haven from the heat. Thousands from all walks of life scurry to the beach as the thermometer hit 93. It was the hottest day so far this year." The reporter had gotten our ages wrong, and of course had used the new English names that the kind lady who was teaching my father English gave us. Without knowing that my Chinese given names were Kang (to be competitive) and Sheung (after the Moon goddess Sheung Wor), she named me Sharon, invoking the Chinese resonances of fertility and feminine energy. Embedded in our last name, Tom, are the multiple possible spellings of the same Chinese surname, the English transliterations of the dialects of Cantonese (Tom) and Toisan (Hom). Ironically though, in 1956, the *Brooklyn Daily News* was already referring to Hong Kong beyond its colonialist past, ignorant of its future recolonization by the "motherland." The temperature might have been 93°. But the rest of the story is always so hard to write, the complex lives embedded in a simple image, escaping the enclosures of the media spin of the headlines.

Yet, even as I attempt to read and transform my memory fragments into lived narratives, as I search fading family photographs for details of the past, my (re)imagined beginnings are already dissolving. Hong Kong, performing its colonial past and present with capitalistic confidence, is moving toward its historic political appointment in 1997. Lessons from taxicab drivers . . . like the taxi drivers in Beijing, the Hong Kong cabbies have a sophisticated no-nonsense view about everything. Thinking I was from Singapore, a cabby once explained to me the fundamental difference between the American political system and the Chinese system. He explained that Americans hold a deep respect for human rights as the foundation and basis of their system and the Chinese political dilemma was a misguided effort to separate economic reforms from political reforms. Like most Hong Kong Chinese, he believed there was no place in the world like Hong Kong. But those who have the money and connections will buy their permanent resident cards and relocate their families abroad as insurance against an uncertain future. The cosmopolitan and the affluent will leave if they need to, or become *taihongyan* (Hong Kong "astronauts" commuting between countries). Who will be left in Hong Kong? Those who have no roads out and those who have options but who choose to stay for economic, political, or other reasons and commitments of the heart. Imagine the future of a place shaped by them.

On my numerous transits through Hong Kong en route to and from China, I have always felt a strange sense of comfort, at-homeness, laced with imminent loss. Perhaps part of the comfort comes from the freedom to shift between English and Cantonese in midsentence and choreographing my own rituals of transit. I would often ride the last ferry back and forth from Hong Kong Island over to the Kowloon side and back, settle into the emptiness of the ferry, watch the tanned, sinewy old boat man throwing the ropes to shore, and follow the lights along the dark mountains rising against the night sky. It is as if I were holding a photo that is dissolving even as I trace the outlines within and beyond its frame. I wonder what my parents saw as they stared across the darkness during those Babylon nights down at the docks.

June 4, 1989

Paying respects to my maternal grandparents at the Taoist shrine where their spirits rest. We bring red and gold paper clothing, cars, money, and watches, all carefully folded to burn. An 86 -year -old caretaker presides over the incense-filled room, instructing us on how and where to burn the incense, where to stick the fresh flowers. My maternal grandparents look out of two small photos amid the top central row in the wall of pictures. The toothless caretaker points proudly to her own picture occupying the spot she has already purchased for her spirit's final resting pace. A good luck red strip of paper covers her face while she is still living. In the corner, two large stacks of violet, white, and red paper wait to be folded for the Taoist ceremony opening next month, all to be burned as a vigil to help ease the passing of the thousands who died in the Tiananmen massacre. In the midst of the complex fears and uncertainty of a whole people facing and trying to shape their political destiny and identity as a people, these rituals of tradition, death, memory, and hope for peace.

On the day I leave Hong Kong, hurricane Gordon approaches. Through the airplane windows, I watch the rain that starts to fall, the wind beginning to increase in force. My American passport securely in my carry-on bag, we take off. My last glimpse of Hong Kong—the storm and gray mists moving in and beginning to surround the mountaintops. The yellow rose given to me by my Hong Kong friends is tucked in the seat pocket, giving off a faint fragrance of petals beginning to open.

GETTING TO LAW AND OTHER EXCAVATIONS

Excavation. I like this word. It reminds me of memories of my childhood, when I inhabited books as escapes from my surroundings. Reading late into the night under the covers with a flashlight. I remember books about archaeology—the descriptions of bones, artifacts, and standing knee-high in brackish cold waters, the waters of an ancient past exposed to light. Something just outside my range of vision, lurks, its quick movement in the desert heat, a mirage reflecting the dangers of mysterious curses invoked by the breaking and entry into tombs, the resting places of dead cities, of kings. In those early junior high years, undaunted, I wanted to be an archaeologist.

In seventh grade, after the horse books, the dog books, Nancy Drew mysteries, the Red, Blue, Green, Yellow Books of fairy tales (how I LOVED the fairy tales!), I read books about flying. In between there somewhere, I read *Exodus, A Nation of Sheep*, and *The Ugly American*. I wanted to be a test pilot. I got books out on entrance requirements and the training programs. Then I read one day you had to have 20-20 vision, and I had already started to wear glasses. Strangely, I never wanted to be a lawyer. I recall an incident when I was a teenager, when immigration officials raided our family Chinese take-out restaurant. As the uniformed men terrorized and humiliated my brother, my parents, and me in a crowded store of customers, as they demanded to see our "papers," as they demanded to know if we spoke English, I grew very furious and shouted at them, "you can't treat us this way, we're people." As they told my father to tell me to shut up, as they walked away in the parking lot ignoring my screaming at their backs, "I want your badge numbers," I think the revelation of the law as an instrument of power (and disempowerment) began to emerge in inchoate ways. No, I did not dream of becoming a lawyer. Growing up, loving to read books, I wanted to be a writer because I was convinced this was the way one could change the world, create visions of a better world, better yet, create those worlds on the written page.

Despite violent opposition from my father ("education was wasted on a girl") and my own intense guilt at not staying home where I "belonged," I decided to go to college. After several academic and personal detours, I completed my undergraduate degree at Sarah Lawrence College. I concentrated in the performing arts, literature, and creative writing. Some of my happiest times were my intensive writing workshops and seminars with Grace Paley, Ed Doctorow, and the stream of poets that came through, and my dance classes, especially my ballet classes in sunny studios that opened out onto the grassy lawns. The realities of a close anorexic slide into oblivion of those days are muted, lost among memories of stretching and sweating on cool hard wooden floors, and the excitement and anxiety of performance. I also loved screening films for myself from the extensive college collection. Taking his dog for its nightly walk, my film professor would investigate the flickering shadows in the screening room. "Oh, it's only you," he'd say and then ask, "What are you watching?" I remember screening James Whale's *Frankenstein* over and over again, rewinding and stopping the film at frames of the monster's coming alive, mesmerized by the grotesquesness, innocence, and beauty of life created from death.

I lived in beautiful old campus houses with fireplaces, had many friends and wonderful encouraging teachers, and was active in student government. I went to my individual conferences with professors, where I was expected to talk about what I had read, or was reading. It was all so foreign to the childhood messages to conform, stay quiet, go safely unnoticed—to choose only vanilla. As a scholarship student, I also worked as a waitress at parties at the president's house and once baby-sat for his teenage daughter in their huge elegant stone mansion across from the college. At spring break, limousines or chauffeured cars would pull up on lawns to pick up students. One of my classmates went down the Nile on Christmas break, while I made my way on the Long Island Railroad to help out at my parents Chinese take-out restaurant.

Despite the pressures of my Sarah Lawrence classmates, many of whom were applying to medical or law schools, I decided to dance after graduation. I danced and performed for several years before ending up in law. Ironically, I think I loved dance because I didn't have to find words, and ultimately, I left dance in part because I also needed another way to speak again, enunciations that would connect me to the world, that would "be of service" and make a difference. Part of the impulse to apply to law school,[3] was this discomfort (guilt?) that simply performing began to feel terribly self-indulgent. Creating worlds on paper—poems, my little short stories—also seemed so intensely private, an intellectual indulgence and a moral luxury. What was the purpose of performing, of my personal explorations and disclosures? I did not realize until many years later, amidst a life in law, that law too demanded its own set of disciplining performances and enunciations, and ironically, that personal stories in law are strategic and contested interventions with subversive potential to undermine the legitimation and control moves of dominant legal discourses and institutional formations.

One of my jobs after college was in a youth program for Chinese teenagers, "gang" members. I spent my days counseling them back into school, tutoring English, visiting them at Rikers Island prison, and accompanying distraught, bewildered Chinese parents to criminal court, trying to translate an incomprehensible system that their children got caught up in. I also helplessly watched the revolving doors of "justice," as guilty pleas and sentencing deals were made. Working in underfunded and undertrained youth programs, after several teenagers I worked with were shot and killed, I began to see my role for what it was—futilely hauling children out of a river, into which they kept falling or in which they drowned. I recall accompanying a teenage brother and sister to their little brother's grave a month after the funeral. We brought the roast pork, the wine, the fruit, the meal to be shared among the living and the spirits, and spread it out upon the gravesite. I remember the silence and the coolness of the breeze. Before leaving, we placed some food and poured some wine over the grave. When I got home, I burned and then stepped over some newspaper at the door before entering my apartment, a Cantonese ritual to ensure no wandering spirits followed. I realized I could not accept the daily tolls of pulling drowning people again and again out of the river—nor to continue to bury children.

During my limited exposure to the legal system at that time, I was not inspired by any particular heroic models of law practice, but instead witnessed the pervasiveness and daily impact of law in people's lives. The cattlelike treatment of people caught in a foreign system resonated with my childhood memories and engendered a countervision. Unsupported by empirical or experiential evidence, my initial move toward law was motivated by a vision that law could be a tool for social transformation, for structural change, that law could contribute to making the world a more just and fair place. Perhaps it was naive faith that one could make a radical difference in the lives of people—poor people, outsiders, aliens, . . . children—that law was and could be about social justice. Perhaps it was an intuitive sense of the instrumentalist role of law coupled with the transformative potential embedded in the inherent contingency of any perceived order. Yet, my law school experience and past eighteen years in law was and continues to be a sobering struggle to resist the deforming pressures of law practice and to hold onto some vision of law as justice.

DEFORMATIONS AND OTHER OCCUPATIONAL HAZARDS

One day as I was attending a reception following a memorial service for a colleague at another law school, an elderly white man abruptly interrupted a conversation I was engaged in and demanded: "Do you speak English?"[4] Although this is not an unusual question put to me, I was stunned by his rudeness and responded, "Yes, I do." He then proceeded, "And you speak it fluently?" "I should hope so," I responded. At that point, another colleague intervened and introduced me as a law professor. "What do you teach?" continued the interrogator. "I teach contracts," I answered and before I could add, and international human rights and feminist jurisprudence, he peered at me, squinting back into the past to invoke his contracts professor and how all the great textbooks were written by members of that law faculty. At that point, of course, I should have offered to send him the new contracts text I just finished coediting,[5] but a new text that integrated race, class, gender, and sexuality perspectives in contract law did not seem to be a text he could "read" despite his apparent fluency in English. The "Do you speak English?" question or the amazed comment "You speak English so well!" is a common example of the kind of micro-aggression that thinly masks the challenge to my competency, my "foreignness," and my capacity to ever truly "belong" in the halls of power.[6] Yet, not all deforming effects of negative professional interactions are related to these kinds of disempowering micro-aggressions, these "citizenship" and competency challenges to "newcomers" (women and minorities).

A recent *National Law Journal* article discusses a *U.S. News and World Reports* ranking of the top twenty-five U.S. law schools and opens with the lead-in line "let the whining begin." Although there was disagreement among law school deans regarding the significance of the ranking,[7] I was particularly interested in the basis for the rankings, such as the per capita expenditure per student. Teaching quality and "intangible indicia of the strengths of a school were apparently deemed too difficult to "measure" to be included. However, the average salary upon graduation was an important factor in determining rankings. The choices of students to seek and accept public interest jobs, clearly not as well paid as corporate law positions, then had the effect of lowering their alma mater in this hierarchy of profit-oriented criteria. What kind of institutional message is this when law schools' explicit and implicit curriculum are complicitious with a hierarchical corporate model of law as a business? And not the business of justice, but the business of billable hours.

Somehow, in the course of being "processed" through the "hidden curriculum" of law schools,[8] the public interest concerns and public service aspirations of many law students are often undermined and distorted. Once in a family law class, in the midst of a lecture about divorce negotiation strategies and advice to demand custody even if your client doesn't want custody, I timidly raised my hand and questioned the use of a child as a bargaining chip and our role in exacerbating the human costs. The response from the professor was a sarcastic dismissive, "That's a good point, Miss Hom. Why don't you write a law review article about it?" In that power configuration, sitting at the back of a huge lecture classroom, instead of outrage at the implication of naiveté and irrelevance of my ethical concerns, I was silenced and humiliated.

I recall another incident during my second year of law school when all the students were busy jockeying for interviews at prestigious law firms. Knowing myself well enough to not waste other people's time or mine, I did not sign up for any interviews. I was in the ladies room one day, and a student came in breathless telling her friend she had received an offer at a very large prestigious corporate firm. After much screaming and excitement, her friend asked her whether she was going to accept it? The student stopped short. No, she didn't think so. She wasn't sure what she wanted.

By encoding the messages of a competitive culture of "success" alienated from one's interests, commitment, and responsibilities to multiple communities, law schools are implicated in a structural and ideological complicity in the privileging and maintenance of the hierarchy and elitism of the legal profession. In light of the dismal statistics for law graduates choosing public interest law careers,[9] and the studies on the professional and personal alienation and frustration many lawyers experience,[10] it is important to critically interrogate these dominant narratives that betray the demands of justice and that impoverish our lives in law.

Choosing law as a life just one generation ago, I had to attempt, though never really got the hang of it, a gendered, raced auto-ventriloquism of the languages of white masculinist power. That I am able to speak at all, and without an "accent," is a source of amazement and interrogation for some law students, professors, and others. Yet, the masked speaking of the law is often left uninterrogated. Law pretends to speak in an unmediated objective language of rationality and universal truths. Its logic, "thinking like a lawyer," demands the cognitive and emotional ordering of the messiness of the world into its limited and limiting categories. A complex human reality must be reduced to a tort, or contract, a crime, or some other substantive label. Even with multiple theories of legal recovery, the claims must be structured within these categories. There are rules of course. But who makes them? Who enforces them? Who interprets them? Who assigns the meanings to these rules? These questions call for the exposure of the meta-narratives that enclose, legitimate, and domesticate text-making, world-making, and interpretation.[11]

Unlike feminist projects in which personal narrative is part of a recovery and legitimation of excluded voices and experiences, narrative in law is suspect, or more accurately, certain narratives, recounted by certain people are suspect. This is so even though we all know that law is about storytelling, and a masked story of power. Anyone who watched the O.J. Simpson trial, also knows that law is also about contested stories. But for law to admit its own narrative partiality and agenda is to expose the Great Wizard of power, the Great Oz, as just the tiny man behind the curtain manipulating the smoke and thunder. In referring to law in its hegemonic formation, I am not suggesting that law is a faceless force unmediated by human agency, only that it presents itself via *masked* human agents as faceless, neutral (justice as a blindfolded woman balancing scales), and unmediated. Yet, law is raced, gendered, and classed even as it races, genders, and classes.

Recently, I was asked to review some of the essays by a group of Asian American law professors for a colloquium issue on affirmative action, diversity, and critical race theory.[12] I was struck by the apparent ease with which almost every contributor used the "I" voice, told stories, wrote in a play format, referenced novels, and explicitly engaged the power and political dimensions of legal discursive debates. I thought of the intellectual and political debts we owe to each scholar, teacher, and activist who transgressed discursive boundaries so that each of us who followed could survive deforming formations and inhabit an enlarged potentiality. I thought of my former CUNY colleague Pat Williams who struggled years ago to write her brilliant, fiercely moral visions and give us her poetic gifts of "intelligent rage." She reminds us: "Nothing is simple. each day is a new labor." [13]

TRANSFORMING PERFORMANCE(S)

I would often arrive in Hong Kong, check for messages and find short cryptic notes: "performance tonight, ticket held for you at the box office." Or "come to studio, we are rehearsing new piece." So it is that my Hong Kong transits have usually been deeply marked by and filtered over the years by the evolving performances and political work of ZUNI ICOSAHEDRON, the controversial, experimental, and activist Hong Kong theater group. ZUNI appropriates the language of "film transposed into theater," and deconstructs the "deep structures" of Hong Kong and Chinese society. Well into an apparent "beginning" with performers running around, an announcer's voice reminds the audience that pictures, recording, smoking, drinking, and eating are not allowed and that all beeping devices should be turned off. Like the television schedule announcement played at the end of ZUNI's *Romance of the Stone* (1987), the perceived sources of guidance for order and meaning and the perceived sources of apparent authority and rules may often be meaningless background noise or irrelevant. The audience is often left with only a context that keeps shifting and the choice of passive or engaged spectatorship, or committed performance.

Danny Yung, the artistic director of ZUNI, once said, "The stage is a place to be honest; it is not a place to exercise power or oppress people." Anyone can perform; anyone can be a powerful presence in the lives of others; and anyone can claim this power to choose the stage for any performance he or she chooses and to create the language of our performance(s). The source of this power does not lie in the role assigned us or the role we choose, but in the totality of commitment we make to each particular moment. In ZUNI movement, each gesture, word, image, or sound is discovered and reinvented each time it is "performed," the "essential gestures of a social being" in Roland Barthes phrase. I have always read ZUNI's texts as political invitation and inspiration for imagining a post-1997 Hong Kong, and as gestures pointing toward the kinds of subterranean fissures that might enable social performance of our complex, multiple, and fluid identities.

As a law professor, to focus on one identity marker, I am clearly a privileged member of a professional class. In the intersectionality analysis plotted along the axes of race, class, sexual orientation, culture, and ethnicity, called for by critical race and feminist theorists, our effort as academics to address class issues immediately invokes the tensions inherent in our privileged class positions. How can we can begin to talk seriously about class when the talking is already in the registers of privileged discourse? How do we avoid a Maoist romanticization of the working class that lurks beneath some radical intellectual posturing? Yet, as a Chinese/American female law professor, I often also experience what I call an "Alice in Wonderland" effect of sudden size shifts of significance, of authoritativeness, as I "land" in different "rooms," mediated by the ideological operation of gender and race, performing my multiple roles for shifting audiences. As a visiting professor standing in front of an American law class of predominantly white students, as a Chinese/American Fulbright scholar teaching in China, as a professor in my home institution, a diverse and public interest community, I grow and shrink in perceived size, power, and authority, sometimes within seconds.

Yet, growing up in the back of that main street laundry, I carry with me the imprints of social marginality. Then and now, despite outward social fluency, I often still find myself feeling awkward, uncomfortable, an outsider to the histories, connections, and privilege of the foreign worlds of social privilege. The points of alienation are subtle: references to private boarding schools of children, names dropped of connected friends and relatives, exclusive vacations, and law school classmates now in high positions of power. To disclose this class-engendered social discomfort is not to invoke epistemological privilege or to assert authenticity of a working-class-origins subject position. I am wary of the politics of authentication, especially for ethnic "minorities" inhabiting a diasporan space. In his eloquent passionate reflections on the doubling effects and challenges of inhabiting postcolonial locations, R. Radhakrishnan asks, "If a minority group were left in peace with itself and not dominated or forced into a relationship with the dominant world or national order, would the group still find the term 'authentic' meaningful? The group would continue being what it is without having to authenticate itself. My point is simply this: When we say 'authenticate,' we also have to ask, 'Authenticate to whom and for what purpose?' Who and by what authority is checking our credentials? Is 'authenticity' a home we build for ourselves or a ghetto to satisfy the dominant world?"[14]

When I wonder if I have "passed"[15] or whether I am still just intellectually cross-dressing, I find a shift from authenticity debates to multiple performance possibilities to be a trans-form-ing strategic move. In her provocative and insightful article arguing that we are all transsexuals, except that "the referent of the *trans* becomes less and less clear (and more and more queer)," Judith Haberstam writes "we are all cross-dressers but where are we crossing from and to what?" This destabilizing of the *trans* and the empowering suggestion of multiple possible points of crossings underscore our interconnectedness, accountability, and complicity for mutually empowering or disempowering, transformative or deformative performances of power[16]—that is, from intellectual cross-dressing, from a politics of authenticity toward a politics of accountability and multiple commitments.

To write not only in law, but beyond the logocentrism of law, from and to situated human realities, requires critical readings of ourselves and examination of the professional performative acts demanded of us. My law writing has focused on Chinese law reform, international and domestic human/women's rights law, and gender in the context of the intersectionality of race, class, and culture. I have also drawn upon my international human/women's rights advocacy and training work to inform my research and writing, to pay explicit attention to the policy and strategic implications of any legal or theoretical analysis. Perhaps due to these applied theory interventions, I have never felt comfortable with a paradigm that locates the activist in opposition to the scholar. I have always viewed the disciplining reality-checks of activism and the discursive power of theory as mutually necessary and implicated. Within the disciplining scripts demanded by law as rational discourse, I try to negotiate the demands and expectations of the authoritarian, authoritative footnote and the required "objective" voice of the text. The struggle to reclaim my narrative voice was and continues to be simultaneously undermined and empowered by ongoing legal discursive and political debates in the field.

Yet, while writing this personal essay, I realized that I have been surreptitiously trying to write it without being aware of this, for a very long time. Through the years, despite the pressures of tenure and the disciplinary valences that privilege "hard" law (writing about "substantive" areas of law rather than the "soft" areas such as feminist theory or legal education), I was encoding bits and pieces of intellectual biography, of memoir, in the margins and footnotes of my law review articles. I was safely italicizing my stories, signaling to the law reader an interdisciplinary poly-vocal intervention. I was reading literature outside of law, trying to ground myself, conducting interdisciplinary raids into foreign territories. I read and wrote about the texts of films, my dreams, and inserted numerous "Jamie" stories about my son until he announced recently that I might be violating his "copyrights."

However, on my last birthday card, my son writes inside: "Thanks for being supportive, pitiful, lenient, funny and etc. You've made my childhood fun and distinctive. Happy Birthday!" "Pitiful"? His childhood over at age fifteen? I thought of the time he stood in my bedroom doorway a couple of years ago, feeling sad and nostalgic for our Beijing home. He wants to know if I remember, if I am sad and miss it too. I am struck by how my son, a young Chinese-American male, is able to express his feelings and his appreciation for emotional support. I overhear him talking—secure, happy, funny—with his friends. When I question the "culture" aspect and the "Chineseness" of his Chinese culture club field trip to a New Jersey mall, he explains that it is part of the culture of Chinese teenagers in the United States—no denial of Chineseness, just an appropriation of the right to name his experience. Even as he eyes bikini-clad life-size posters of models in store windows, he criticizes the sexism and racism in television commercials or store interactions that we witness. Amid the reconstructed fragments of my own childhood, I think of the Chinese expression "Green comes from, but is deeper than blue," a phrase generally suggesting the pride and hope of teachers for students who surpass us. Negotiating his hormones, his out-of-control adolescent body, the enormous peer pressures, and yet, my son is perhaps writing a different script of manhood, of social being.[17]

Bob Chang urges: "Whatever path you choose, fill your life with passion for what you do. This passion will not come from the drumming of native blood within you. It will come from the compassion and commitment you feel for the communities you choose as your own."[18] With many possible birthing places, we all come from somewhere, usually somewhere else. Upon "arrival," many of us live in marginalized social spaces, in social "basements," the backs of laundries, the Chinatown walk-ups. We all hold within us distant memories that we try to sort out, multiple traditions, allegiances, and multiple languages, literal and symbolic. In biographies of me, in introductions to my guest lectures or academic presentations, I continue to include my immigrant genealogy. Embarrassed and impatient with my persistent insertion of the personal into my professional world, my younger brother used to argue, "Who cares where you were born." But these personal markings inscribe the past onto the present—traces of the dead-end mountain street in Daihang, the monsoon rains and the smells of incense burned by my grandmother praying at night, the existence of embedded power, of witches. These memories connect me to my communities of origins even as I negotiate my communities of choice. I try not to forget even as I try to resist romanticizing memory. I try to remember and write other languages.

In my attempts to choreograph the multiple, contradictory professional and personal performances of a politically accountable life, I try to make sense of my ancestors whispering, shouting, and laughing at me, or bending over my family in our dreams as we embark on yet another journey. In my own multiple crossings, I attempt to name the daily micro and macro aggressions, often embedded in casual social and professional interactions, that disempower so many of us. I try to read for the symbolic resources embedded in my memory and dream archives. In a recurring dream, I am climbing the rocky surface of a cliff in the dark. Behind me, a disembodied voice whispers, *"sometimes you have to approach from the sea to catch the shore by surprise."* Even though the languages of my waking life abhor the infinite borderlessness, the koans of my dream-time, I dutifully record my nightly travels, and retrieve my memories in tattered journals kept over the years. These dreams, voices, memories, and stories, these reminders of other agentiality whispering our capacity to write new languages, are rich spirit resources for (re)imagining the traversings possible, toward transforming performance(s) at the shifting horizon's edges.

I dream about finding some ancient Chinese dictionaries. I am in a dark wood bookstore and I crawl under a counter, a kind of crypt-like space with shelves lining the walls. I discover three sets of blue silk-bound volumes on folding panels of rice paper, nestled in oval bamboo baskets. I ask the man at the register how much, and he replies $89.90. I say, that's not too bad, and almost buy them with my credit card, but I think it's too expensive and plan to return another day. When I awoke and for a long time afterward, I regretted not purchasing them, because try as I may, I couldn't find my way back to that dream store again. It was only when I was working on my Chinese-English Lexicon project of women and the law[19] that the dream revealed a different significance. I didn't/couldn't buy the dictionaries not because they were too expensive, but because ultimately they were not purchasable. The price had all the lucky numbers of longevity and fortune, but like the murmur of numerous disembodied voices that comes to me at that the split second before waking, the vision and the tactile memory of holding them, gesture toward a discovery beyond a market exchange. I couldn't buy them. I had to help write them.[20]

> *The night fades along a line of red staining*
> *the edge of the horizon which keeps moving beyond us*
> *the edge of worlds which keeps dissolving*
> *In the dead of night surrounded by the intimate*
> *sleep of strangers filled with the hum of jet engines*
> *I am moving towards you, away from you.*
> *Simultaneously. We are breathing*
> *Inhaling and exhaling long even breaths*
> *ten thousand miles of dreamtime*
> *separating us, connecting us*
> *The sudden sharp daylight*
> *through the closed shades*
> *Exposing Time's contingency. Again and again.*
> *I am back. I am gone. At the Horizon's shifting edges.*

NOTES

1. Rey Chow, "Things, Common/Places, Passages of the Port City: On Hong Kong and Hong Kong Author Leung Ping-kwan," *Differences: a Journal of Feminist Cultural Studies* 5, no. 3 (1993): 179.

2. In a recent family discussion, I share the progress of this project and mention the story of grandfather's spirit visit. An immediate disagreement follows. My father insists that my grandfather's spirit visitation occurred upon the eve of *his* departure from Hong Kong, while I was still in my mother's womb. My mother wavers, not sure of which departure it was. I decide to leave my text as it is, and footnote its contested retrieval.

3. Actually just one, New York University School of Law, because of its public interest Root-Tilden fellowship program.

4. I name these identity markers to signal the context of this person's social location and the way it reflects embedded institutional markers of power.

5. Amy H. Kastely, Deborah Waire Post, and Sharon K. Hom, eds., *Contracting Law* (Durham: Carolina Academic Press, 1996).

6. The inscription of foreignness onto the professional lives of Asian Americans has been thoughtfully critiqued by many scholars. See, for example, Robert S. Chang, "Toward an Asian American Legal Scholarship: Critical Race Theory, Post-Structuralism, and Narrative Space," *California Law Review* 81, no. 5 (October 1993): 1241–1323; Margaret (H.R.) Chon, "On the Need for Asian American Narratives in Law: Ethnic Specimens, Native Informants, Storytelling and Silences," *UCLA Asian Pacific American Law Journal* 3, no. 1 (Fall 1995): 4–32.

7. Ken Myers, "Deans Disagree on the Usefulness of Magazine's Annual Ranking," *The National Law Journal* 18, no. 34 (April 8, 1996): A19. The debate continues and alternative assessments of law schools are being explored by various bar associations, the Society of American Law Teachers, and special professional task forces.

8. Howard Lesnick identifies a "hidden curriculum" of law schools as encompassing the attitudes and practices reflected in all areas of law school life such as "the admissions and placement processes, relations of faculty and students with the non professional staff, and bases on which we choose people to speak at school functions, receive awards, judge moot court, or have their pictures hung on the walls." See footnote 3, Howard Lesnick, "Infinity in a Grain of Sand: The World of Law and Lawyering as Portrayed in the Clinical Teaching Implicit in the Law School Curriculum," *UCLA Law Review* 37, no. 6 (1990): 1160.

9. Many law graduates saddled with staggering loans and debts often feel they have no other choice but to seek high-paying corporate positions. This economic bind underscores the interrelated institutional, economic, and structural factors that maintain the current system of valuing corporate values and that limit the career choices available to many law graduates, particularly students from working-class backgrounds. For a description of a study of debt, career choice, and race and gender, see Lewis A. Kornhauser and Richard L. Revesz, "Legal Education and Entry into the Legal Profession: The Role of Race, Gender, and Educational Debt," *New York University Law Review* 80 (October 1995): 829–964.

10. A 1990 follow-up to a 1984 lawyer survey concluded: "Never have so many who earn so much been so unhappy." Quoted in footnote 33, Susan Bryant, "Collaboration in Law Practice: A Satisfying and Productive Process for a Diverse Profession," *Vermont Law Review* 17 (Winter 1993): 466. Susan Bryant summarizes a variety of causes contributing to this rise in professional dissatisfaction: fatigue, the lack of a warm and personal atmosphere, waning

sense of disrespect from superiors, not enough personal time, the individualistic and competitive nature of practice in large legal organizations, and difficulties created by joint work organized in bureaucratic, hierarchical ways, and burnout for legal services and legal aid lawyers. *Ibid.* at p. 467.

11. Narrative in law has engendered an extensive literature, most visibly in a law and literature movement, in feminist legal theory and jurisprudence, and in critical race theory and "outsider" scholarship. For a good survey discussion of the critical literature, see, for example, Robert S. Chang, "Toward and Asian American Legal Scholarship: Critical Race Theory, Post-Structuralism, and Narrative Space," *California Law Review* 81, no. 5 (October 1993): 1241–1323. For a recent volume of collected essays, see Peter Brooks and Paul Gewirtz, eds., *Law's Stories: Narrative and Rhetoric in the Law* (New Haven and London: Yale University Press, 1996).

12. Keith Aoki, "Colloquy: The Scholarship of Reconstruction and the Politics of Backlash" (Participants: Keith Aoki, Margaret Chon, Garrett Epps, Neil Gotanda, Frederick Dennis Greene, Natsu Saito Jenga, Peter Kwan, Alfred Yen), *Iowa Law Review* 81 (summer 1996).

13. Patricia Williams, *The Alchemy of Race and Rights: Diary of a Law Professor* (Boston: Harvard University Press, 1991), p. 130.

14. R. Radhakrishnan, *Diasporic Mediations: Between Home and Location* (Minneapolis: University of Minnesota Press, 1996), p. 211.

15. I am borrowing from discursive debates on "passing" in the context of race and gender. As Elaine K. Ginsberg suggests, "passing" metaphorically may suggest the trespass of an individual who crosses a racial or gender line or boundary to assume a new identity, escaping the subordination and oppression of one to access the privileges and status of another identity. She contrasts class, ethnic origin, and sexual orientation as easier to enact or disguise. Yet, the "passing" is not a simple binary, but rather exposes the truth that identities are multiple and contingent. Elaine K. Ginsberg, "Introduction: The Politics of Passing," in *Passing and the Fictions of Identity*, edited by Elaine K. Ginsberg (Duke University Press, 1996), pp. 2–5.

16. Judith Haberstam, "F2M: The Making of Female Masculinity," in Laura Doan, ed., *The Lesbian Postmodern* (New York: Columbia University Press, 1994), p. 212.

17. Following our "copyright" discussion, I adopted the practice of reading to my son the stories I write about him before they are published.

18. Robert Chang, Keynote Address: "Passion and the Asian American Legal Scholar," Asian Law Journal Spring Banquet (April 19, 1996).

19. Sharon K. Hom and Xin Chunying, eds., *English-Chinese Lexicon of Women and Law (Yinghan funnu yu falu cehuishiyi)* (Beijing: China Translation and Publishing Corp. and UNESCO, 1995).

20. I recount this dream in Sharon Hom and Robin Paul Malloy, "China's Market Economy: A Semiosis of Cross Boundary Discourse Between Law and Economics and Feminist Jurisprudence," *Syracuse Law Review* 45, no. 2 (1994): 829–830.

Coming to Terms with History

Vivien Ng

PRE-HISTORY

The phone call came out of the blue. "Vivien, this is Rose. Rose Wang. From Maryknoll, remember? I'm calling from California." It took me more than a few moments to register what she was saying, but yes, I remembered who she was, an old school pal from my "prehistory" days in Hong Kong. I vaguely recalled that the last time I saw her was nineteen years earlier, in 1972, when I stopped over in Minneapolis on my way from Ohio to Honolulu to start my graduate work at the University of Hawaii, but I wasn't sure. It did not matter. A strange sensation coursed through my body at this reconnection; I was both pleased and dismayed at being "found" after all these years. She called to tell me about a class reunion to be held in Hawaii. "The entire gang will be there," she assured me (and presumably to entice me). I asked for more time to consider the prospect, and we spent the next few minutes chatting about other members of the gang. It seemed that they had all married and settled down to a comfortable upper middle-class life with their husbands and children. Most of them lived in southern California. I began to lose interest in the reunion. During the next few months, Rose, Beatrice, and others pursued me aggressively, refusing to let me off the hook, following me from New York City, where I was spending my sabbatical year, back to Norman, Oklahoma, where I had made my home. I went along and played the game of hard-to-get, because even though I had already made up my mind to skip the reunion, I was not ready to let go of that tenuous tie with my past now that the re-connection had been made. We were a close-knit group at Maryknoll Convent School; some of us had been friends since kindergarten. We did everything together and at one point even designed a ring especially for ourselves. When Rose called that day in 1991, happy memories of my Hong Kong past surfaced to my consciousness; for a brief moment, I was "home" again.

Hong Kong was my childhood home because my parents thought it was a better place to rear their children than New York City, where the rest of the Ng clan resided. Although they never admitted it, I think they believed that their children would have a better chance at growing up unfettered by racism in colonial Hong Kong than in the United States. It mattered also that my mother's family had deep roots in Hong Kong; one of her great-grandfathers was a *compradore* (Chinese merchant acting as a middleman for British traders) during the early colonial days in the nineteenth century. Ironically, because my parents were very protective of me and would not let me explore Hong Kong without them, and there were so many places that were off-limits to me with or without them, I did not partake of the rich diversity of Chinese cultural life that Hong Kong had to offer. To be fair to my parents, I was content with my life at home and at school and did not show any interest in exploring the world unrelated to these two spheres.

Maryknoll meant the world to me during my formative years. Its single-sex environment sheltered me from sexist notions about women's and girls' ability to do math and science, and since we were expected to excel in academic subjects, being brainy was not a stigma to be avoided. It was there that I was taught by the nuns the meaning of service to community. It helped also that the six-acre campus, with its brick buildings, cobblestone paths, manicured lawns with gorgeous displays of spring flowers (mostly azaleas), outdoor swimming pool, along with the convent sitting solidly on top of the knoll, exuded an air of prosperity and stability. Small wonder, then, that long lines of mothers (and some fathers) would form every year around the time when application forms were made available to the public, every one of them harboring the hope that their daughters would be among the chosen few to be accepted. More than anything else, however, Maryknoll meant to me the circle of close friends forged out of common interests and similar backgrounds. We competed against each other academically, but we sustained each other emotionally as well. It was this circle of friends that I cut loose from after I moved to Honolulu to pursue a new academic direction.

It was almost preordained that I would be a scientist or at least a medical doctor. When I was in the fifth grade, I asked for and got a chemistry kit for my birthday, and I spent many weekends playing with and mixing the different chemicals in the kit. The following year, my parents gave me a microscope and the first samples I examined were cells scraped from my father's cheek! A subscription to *Scientific American* soon followed. When I was skilled enough to dissect insects and small vertebrates, my father bought me a set of German-made dissecting instruments, and my mother would go to the fish market in search of dogfish for me to cut and examine at home. There was never any suggestion from my parents that as a girl I should set my sights lower; rather, they impressed upon me at an early age that they would be greatly disappointed if I squandered my potentials and settled for only a bachelor's degree, especially in the humanities. I learned from them that science was a worthier intellectual endeavor than the humanities, but my own inclinations and passions were in chemistry and biology anyway. Thus, at school, when it came time for us to choose either the science stream or arts stream (in Hong Kong secondary school students had to make this choice by Form 4), I naturally opted for the former. So, too, did all my friends. Membership in the Science Club gave us access to the biology and chemistry labs on weekends and during the summer vacation, and our projects ranged from making soap out of coconut oil to using chloroform to extract caffeine from coffee and tea. One summer, my friend Miriam and I tried unsuccessfully to obtain permission from a narcotics control agency to test the effect of marijuana inhalation on mice, but we continued with the experiment using airplane glue instead!

In the end, I did not follow the straight and narrow path to a scientific career. Several developments converged to deflect me from my preordained objective. I entered college in the fall of 1969, when President Richard Nixon was escalating U.S. war efforts in Vietnam, but for much of that first year I was oblivious to the growing antiwar sentiment on campus, because I was too busy with schoolwork. But in the spring quarter of 1970, I enrolled in a botany class that changed my attitude toward scientific research forever. I regret very much that I have forgotten the professor's name, but I think about him often, especially his signature conclusion to every lecture, which was a reminder to his students to be always mindful of the ethical implications of the experiments that he had just taught us about. None of my other science teachers, in high school or college, had ever challenged me in this way before, and invariably I would leave his classroom in a reflective mood. It was also during that term that Nixon made the fateful decision to invade Cambodia, and not long after his televised speech to the nation, on May 4, 1970, the Kent State massacre happened. Almost immediately, protests against the invasion and the incident at Kent State erupted on the Ohio University campus, the National Guard moved into town and the university shut down for the rest of the academic year. When the resident advisor woke us up in the middle of the night to tell us that we had less than twenty-four hours to vacate the dorms, it was a different wake-up call for me. Overnight, I shed my political apathy for good.

When I returned to Ohio University the following fall quarter, I continued my chemistry studies, but without the passion that I felt previously for the subject. Protests against Dow Chemical, manufacturer of napalm, were daily reminders of the lesson my botany professor taught me, and I began to worry about whether it was possible to do scientific research without making a bargain with the devil. I combed the library shelves for enlightenment and soon found myself reading all the books that I could find on Robert Oppenheimer, the "father" of the atomic bomb. I interpreted the choices he made as a cautionary tale for me. The new friends I made that year were philosophy and english majors, some of whom were active in the campus antiwar movement. At their urging, I took John Cady's "History of Southeast Asia"—the first history course I took in college besides the requisite U.S. history survey. The turning point came in April or May 1971, when John King Fairbank of Harvard University came to give a lecture in honor of Cady's retirement. The lecture was ostensibly about Chinese history but it was in fact a subtle anti-war speech (at least that was how I heard it). In his quiet, low-key way, Fairbank put forth his argument that throughout much of its history, China seldom pursued a policy of territorial expansion through military means. By implication, he suggested to the audience that U.S. foreign policy makers had completely misread Chinese history and that their flawed domino theory had led the nation needlessly into a misguided war in Southeast Asia. I sat in rapt attention in the audience, appreciating his message but at the same time doubting his knowledge of Chinese history. I told my friend this, and he turned around, put his hands on my shoulders, and said, "Why don't you take a Chinese history course next quarter, to find out what actually happened? There is no point in just relying on your gut feeling, is there?"

It is true that there was no factual basis for my skepticism. Although Chinese history was a required course at Maryknoll, it was taught in a most perfunctory way. In any case, I found Chinese history boring and irrelevant and therefore paid very little attention to it. In fact, when I was growing up, I was unreflective about my ethnicity and about Chinese culture in general. To be sure, I enjoyed all the traditional festivals and the feasts and other goodies that were associated with Chinese culture, but I considered these observances to be part of family life and not part of cultural life. More than anything else, the main reason I did not concern myself with my ethnicity and politics in general was that there was no occasion for me to do so. I lived in a comfortable cocoon, shielded from realities outside my realm by the privileges that my parents and my school provided; as long as I had my books and science experiments and friends who shared similar interests, I was happy. So, when my friend at Ohio University suggested that I try out a Chinese history course, my immediate reaction was, "you must be kidding," but I did not dismiss it entirely. After a summer's reflection, I decided not only to take Chinese history courses but to aim for a graduate degree in East Asian history as well. The Vietnam War, my doubts about the ethics of unreflective scientific research, and John King Fairbank's lecture converged at the right moment to allow me to come to terms with Chinese history. It was a good thing that I permitted myself to listen to my inner voice and took the necessary steps to reorder my life. One year after Fairbank's lecture, I graduated from Ohio University and headed out to Honolulu. I picked the University of Hawaii for graduate school not only because of its excellent Asian studies curriculum but because its geographical location afforded me physical distancing from my previous life. I don't think that I consciously made the decision to cut loose from my old Maryknoll friends, but my brief stopover in Minneapolis on my way to Honolulu in 1972 was the last contact I had with any of them until Rose rang me up that day in 1991.

REINCARNATION

I do believe in destiny. When I arrived in Honolulu, I fully expected that I would have to flip hamburgers to support myself, because turning to my parents for financial help was out of the question. After my first year in college—after Kent State, to be more precise—I stopped sharing my political views with my parents (my father was very hawkish in his views), and my correspondence with them became empty rituals. They did not know that I was contemplating a career in history until I had been accepted by the University of Hawaii, nor did I seek their approval. (Estrangement may be too strong a word to describe my relationship with my parents at this time, but I was feeling increasingly disconnected from them as well as friends from my prepolitical past.) As it turned out, just days before the new academic year began, one of the teaching assistants failed his master's examination and as a result lost his assistantship. His loss became my gain, and I was assigned to work for B. J. Miller, who taught one of the huge World Civilizations sections. It was a fine stroke of luck that Miller was my first mentor in graduate school.

I remember my first meeting with Miller very well. Right away he told me that I needed to know two things about him—that he was gay and that he did not believe in objectivity, especially as it related to the writing and teaching of history. He warned me that he had strong political convictions and that these would be reflected in his lectures. He asked if I would have any problems working with (not for) him. His disclosure threw me off completely, because his take on history was totally alien to me and I had not met an openly gay person before; moreover, I felt intimidated by the passion of his convictions. However, because I needed the teaching assistantship, I took a big gulp and assured him that it would be just fine working with him. Thus began my long apprenticeship as an intellectual with a social conscience.

In 1972 it was rare to find an "out" gay academic, thus Miller's openness about his sexual orientation made him a controversial figure in the history department. Not too long into the fall semester, some of his colleagues began a vicious campaign to destroy him professionally, although none of them had the courage to state the real reason for wanting to dismiss him. I was squeamish about his homosexuality myself, but when one of my Chinese history professors—a powerful member on my master's committee—tried to snare me into the anti-Miller camp, I balked. As the hate campaign unfolded, it became clear to me that his detractors had wild notions about the way his classes were conducted. They imagined him prancing across the platform, flirting openly and shamelessly with male students. They seized upon his lectures on Roman decadence and cultural constructions of sexuality as evidence of his depravity, and because Miller was also openly opposed to the Vietnam War, his choice of *Antigone* and Franz Fanon's *Wretched of the Earth* for class assignments also came under attack as examples of the way he managed to politicize the classroom. During the spring semester, a departmental hearing was held to determine if Miller's contract should be renewed, and a number of witnesses (I was one of them) were invited to answer questions concerning his professionalism, especially his ability to be an objective historian. It was a farce, and at the conclusion of the hearing, the committee of his peers delivered what had already been predetermined, that Miller's contract would not be renewed and that he had one year to look for a job elsewhere. Harassment continued during his final year at the University of Hawaii in the form of anonymous letters sent to his prospective employers warning them about his homosexuality and professional "misconduct." The last time I saw him was in the summer of 1975, when he returned to Honolulu for a short visit and stopped at my office to talk about the bad old days. I have since lost touch with him.

The lessons I learned during my first year as a history graduate student were not at all what I had imagined or hoped for when I decided to study Chinese history instead of chemistry. Chinese history was to be a safe haven where I would learn about my cultural heritage and at the same time escape the kind of ethical choices that I would have to make as a research chemist. I would specialize in the modern period and write a thesis on the student activists of the May Fourth Movement as a way for me to connect with China's past (I was struck by the coincidence of the two dates: May 4, 1919, in China and May 4, 1970, at Kent State). When I enrolled at the University of Hawaii my original plan was to stop at the master's level, transfer to a library school, and pursue a quiet career as an East Asian bibliographer. Instead, my association with Miller and his oppositional stance opened my eyes to the prospect of a meaningful (and ethical) life as a historian with conscience—as an oppositional intellectual. In time, I would understand that coming to terms with history was a moral choice and not one of safe escapism and that it was this distinction that separated an historian from an antiquarian. My "awakening" was tweaked further by a required course that I took during the first semester—historiography—taught by A. Kuzminski, who, besides Miller, was the most misunderstood member of the history department (he eventually resigned on his own accord to become an innkeeper in New England). That first semester, under his tutelage, our class read (with great resistance) Foucault, Freud, Marx, Wittgenstein, Vico, Norman O. Brown, and Chomsky, protesting the irrelevance these theorists seemed to have had to our business of studying history, especially Asian history! (It was not until years later, when I was teaching at the University of Oklahoma and had begun the arduous task of revising my dissertation for publication, that I came fully to appreciate the influence the course had had on my maturation as a historian. Without being aware of it, my understanding about language, structures, time, historicism, and historicity had been shaped by those readings. I realized that even my choice of dissertation topic and the research strategies that I had adopted to bring the dissertation to fruition had been influenced by that course.) The net result of my first year, which shaped my orientation in the future, was that learning about Chinese history became less important to me than the broader question of what it meant to be an intellectual. My alienation from the field of Chinese history would deepen after I came out as a lesbian and had to confront the resistance of the profession to the work that I had committed myself to do.

The way I met my first lesbian lover was pure destiny. I did not have to sign up for the "History of Tokugawa Japan" seminar in the fall semester of 1975, but because I opted for it at the last minute, my life would never be the same. I noticed her on the first day, sitting across from me at the seminar table, and felt a connection even before I found out her name. I knew that she was new to the university because I had never seen her before, and I decided immediately that I wanted to get to know her better. It was not love at first sight, however, at least not love as I understood it at the time. There was nothing in my background (or hers, as I found out later) that prepared me for the attraction that I felt for her. What ensued during the rest of the semester, for both of us, was a long process of deciphering the nature of our feeling for each other— in other words, of unburdening ourselves of heterosexist baggage.

Perhaps if we had met in 1995 or even 1985, we might have recognized immediately the sexual nature of our attraction for each other; but in 1975, we did not have a clue (at first). In 1975, Miller was the only gay person that I thought I knew, and although I was a history graduate student and read newspapers and news magazines regularly, I did not know about the Stonewall rebellion of 1969, nor the nascent gay and lesbian liberation movement that emerged in its aftermath. Except for Miller, none of my professors thought that the subject of sexuality was worthy of inclusion in their syllabi. In other words, in 1975 I lacked the context to understand what I was experiencing at the time. The homosocial aspect of my upbringing at Maryknoll, where I developed intense friendships with my classmates, might well have camouflaged the sexual attraction that I felt for another woman.

We met practically every day and would leave notes for each other at our carrels in the library, and very soon we started talking about renting an apartment together, but we did not have a clue. I would visit her at her studio apartment for dinner (mostly unsavory salads with tropical dressing), and after dinner we would go up to the roof to look at the Honolulu skyline and make up stories (mostly mysteries) to regale each other. We would hug and touch, and still we did not have a clue. She would sing "Black, black is the color of my true love's hair," yet I could not recognize what was happening between us. Perhaps she understood it first, because I have just recently discovered a note she wrote to me around Thanksgiving 1975 urging me to have the courage to take risks and not to be afraid of falling flat on my face; the note was too cryptic for me, though, and I filed it in an obscure book and did not see it again until 1996. Happily, when I finally woke up to the new reality, on New Year's Day 1976, I welcomed it. My reincarnation into a new person was thus complete.

OKLAHOMA!

When I landed the job to teach Chinese history at the University of Oklahoma in 1982, my friends at the University of Hawaii rejoiced with me because 1982 was an especially difficult year for job placements in history. By the time I arrived in Norman, Oklahoma, I was grateful to have a job and determined not to do anything to undermine my security there, and so I decided to keep quiet about being a lesbian, at least during the first year. I must not have done a good job hiding my true identity because toward the end of the first semester, one of my students came up to me and asked quietly if I had read Rita Mae Brown's *Rubyfruit Jungle*. I recognized immediately that she was sounding me out, testing her "lesbian radar," so to speak, but I had no choice but to answer in the affirmative. She gave me a broad grin and proceeded to tell me about a bookstore in Oklahoma City that she thought I might be interested in, and offered to drive me there the following weekend. It was thus that I was introduced to Herland Sister Resources, a lesbian feminist collective in Oklahoma. Later in the spring semester, developments on campus forced me to edge further out of the closet. In March 1983, I noticed a rash of homophobic chalkings on sidewalks all over the campus and was told that every spring, some of the fraternity "boys" would designate one week in March as Gay Bashing Week and the chalkings that I saw were part of their hateful campaign. There were also letters published in the student paper quoting the Bible to denounce homosexuality and bestiality. I knew that

I could not remain silent under these adverse circumstances, but I was not yet ready to come out to the entire university community. After much soul searching, I hit upon a strategy that I thought would allow me to confront the issue of homophobia without disclosing my own sexual orientation—I brought my copy of John Boswell's *Christianity, Social Tolerance, and Homosexuality* to my Chinese history class and read sections of the book to my students, to educate them about a reality different from what they had learned from their preachers. I might as well have declared that I was a lesbian because very soon rumors began to circulate that I was a "manhater" and that a man would have to be a fool to take my courses. When I heard these rumors about me I decided that it was time for me to come out on my own terms. My first move was to put a lambda sign (symbol of lesbian/gay liberation) on my office door.

My first year at the University of Oklahoma was a difficult one because I felt alone in a wasteland of homophobic sameness. My colleagues in the history department were in fact very hospitable and my weekends, especially during the first semester, were usually spent having dinner at their homes. However, because of my reluctance to talk about my private life due to fear of retribution (Miller's mistreatment at the University of Hawaii was never far from my mind), I was not able to connect with my colleagues at more than a polite but superficial level. During this time, my long-term (and long-distance) lesbian relationship was breaking up, but there was no one in Oklahoma I could talk to about it. Although in my later years at the University of Oklahoma I became closely identified with the women's studies program, I was unable to break through their parochialism during the first years. I had a lunch meeting with members of the women's studies program at the beginning of my first semester there, but nothing concrete came out of it. Because my field was Chinese history, a subject they knew very little about, and my dissertation was on criminal insanity in Qing China (1644–1911) and not about women in China, the women's studies faculty did not immediately see me as a potential colleague, nor did they recognize the relevance of my work to women's studies scholarship. In any case, I was not invited to join the program for at least another two years, not until I had already established a reputation in Oklahoma as an outspoken feminist activist and they were able to overlook the fact that I still had not written about women per se. What sustained me were my students in my Chinese history classes. Their enthusiasm for the subject matter motivated me to come up with innovative ways to introduce them to Chinese history and culture, and I taught with obvious passion. Most of my students were from Oklahoma and their cosmopolitan outlook forced me to abandon my early perceptions of Oklahoma as a land of tumbleweed and grapes of wrath. My students made it possible for me to come to terms with my decision to teach Chinese history at the University of Oklahoma, but it was not enough; by the end of my first year, I realized that my survival strategy needed a complete overhaul.

The lambda sign that I put on my office door began to attract a steady trickle of students (not enrolled in my classes) to my office; often, they were too shy to do more than just say how nice it was to see the sign on my door. Understanding the meaning of the sign required a level of "literacy" that I did not expect to find among the students at the University of Oklahoma; in fact, almost immediately after I put it up, my doubt about the usefulness of the sign was reinforced by a colleague who noticed it and remarked, "How nice of you to put 'enter' in Chinese on your door!" (The Greek alphabet lambda does look a bit like the Chinese character signifying "to enter"!) I found out later that a handful of students did recognize the sign, and they soon spread the word around that there was a Chinese American lesbian history professor on campus who gay and lesbian students could turn to for help. It was thus that my new survival strategy was devised—that the best way for me to maintain a full life at the university was as an "out" professor fully committed to mentoring students who might need a sympathetic ear during their coming out process, and who would speak out against homophobia. I remembered why I decided to become a history professor in the first place. I reminded myself of my ambition to become a fully engaged intellectual with a social conscience, and told myself that job security that required making political compromises was not worth it. It was the most liberating decision that I had ever made in my life. Soon afterward, I plunged headlong into Oklahoma politics, especially in the pro-choice and lesbian and gay rights movements. Not surprisingly, many of my colleagues found my political activism to be incompatible with their definition of a scholar's life, and when it came time for my tenure review, they voted against me. It was the first time that the history department sent up a tenure recommendation that contained a high number of negative votes. Having made my peace with myself, I was unfazed by my colleagues' action; in fact, on the day of the tenure vote, I was giving a paper at the Second Annual Lesbian and Gay Studies Conference at Yale

University! It was one of the high points in my life at the University of Oklahoma.

My lesbian activism infected my work in Chinese studies as well. When I wrote my essay on rape laws in Qing China, for example, I decided to include a section on the felonization of consensual homosexual relations and characterized the change in law as a form of state homophobia. I accepted an invitation to submit the essay to the *Journal of Asian Studies* for consideration, and the long process of anonymous review turned into a nightmare for me. One of the anonymous readers was especially hostile to my thesis, and after my second attempt to revise the manuscript to meet her or his objections, this reader came back with the startling statement that "the author should come out of the closet and state outright what her politics are." The field of Qing legal history was very tiny at the time, thus it was not surprising that the reader knew my identity; after all, I had presented it as a paper at the Association for Asian Studies annual meeting. I refused to revise my manuscript any further and fortunately for my career, the editor agreed with me and finally published my article in the February 1987 issue. In 1989, I published two articles on male homosexuality in Chinese history and soon consolidated a notorious reputation in Chinese studies for forcing Western sexual constructs on Chinese culture. I would find myself excluded from a number of conferences that addressed the topic of Chinese sexuality, even though my articles and papers would be brought up and discussed by the participants. In time, I became increasingly alienated from the field of Chinese studies and began to identify myself primarily as a scholar in lesbian and gay studies.

POSTSCRIPT

After living and working in Oklahoma for thirteen years I moved to Albany, New York in 1995 to become the new chair of the department of women's studies at SUNY-Albany. The first course I taught at my new academic home was "Introduction to Lesbian and Gay Studies," which drew more than eighty students. I am finally at a place where I do not have to teach Chinese history anymore and can devote myself entirely to teaching and writing about lesbian, gay and queer issues. I have never felt more Chinese or more at peace with being a historian than at this moment in my adult life. I do not know how this came about, but when the first budget crisis hit us, I turned to the *Tao-te ching* (a Taoist classic) for inspiration and solace. When the second and even more serious crisis developed, I told my colleagues with a "straight" face that I would consult the ancient text *The Art of War*. In the classroom and at my office, I find myself telling women's studies students they need to know the history of the subject that they are researching, that they must know the historical contexts. I am now pushing to add more history courses to the women's studies curriculum. I don't know what all this means; perhaps I am finally coming to terms with being a Chinese historian.

Too Many Things Forgotten . . .

Zhang Zhen

Too many things already forgotten
But we still want to do this and that, go here and there
To seek limelight or play the coquette
We forget things we did, right or wrong
We forget people we knew, loved or hated
We forget too our experience in the womb before birth
Forget the fear that came with first menstruation
We are too anxious to become strangers to ourselves
As though the farther we fare from the starting point, the better
We forget too many things
Forget friends' names and the meaning of many words
Forget that some are in jail for our sake
Forget pretty clothes we wore in childhood
Forget the taste of others spitting in one's face
Just as though we live only to forget
Just as though we only belong to things forgotten
Everything that has been denied
Our future will also be erased
Our diaries and letters will be sent to ragman's place
Perhaps, in the fire, we will remember ourselves
Remember some extraordinary sunrises and sunsets
Certain indications are at last connected to others
Remember how our soul was caressed and then devastated
Finally, realizing the significance of all these
The bits and drops that were forgotten
Should tell us how not to waste a life
—If possible

—Tokyo, January 1989

Moving into Stillness

Eleanor S. Yung

BEGINNING JOURNEYS

When I was about four or five years old, a great typhoon swept through Hong Kong. My family lived in the New Territories, above the factory that my father managed. Across from us was a field of lotus, and beyond that were hills. Sometimes we would see people in boats picking lotus seeds among the blooming flowers. Other times we would see people trekking up the hills. As children, we would wonder excitedly whether they were smugglers. Most of the time, there weren't too many people in sight. On the other side of the road across from where we lived was a little store that carried knickknacks and candies. It was really only a wooden shack with an open front. The family who owned the store had several children, ranging from very young to teenagers, and they all lived in the back.

I don't remember much about what happened during the typhoon. It was the calmness after the storm that I remember. There was a great deal of flooding, and the lotus field was submerged under muddy water. The water covered the road, so you could no longer see where the road ended and where the lotus pond began. Some vegetation that was used to feed pigs floated on the surface, slowly drifting away. The flood was so high that the little store was half under murky water. There was only the music from the small radio playing in the store. One of the older children in water up to her waist was cleaning the store. She was using a broom to sweep the water surface. As she swept the floating vegetation, leaves, and paper junk out toward the street, other things continued to float into the store to take their place. However, she did not seem to think this activity futile nor did she seem to mind. She was in no hurry either, but continued this unusual chore. As a child, I remembered this scene in relation to the peacefulness after the storm. As I grew older, it came to mean many other things.

I was born in Shanghai the year after Japan surrendered in World War II. When my mother was pregnant with me, there was finally peace and she felt peaceful. She always tells me that is why I was a happy child. When I was little, I danced all the time, at home, in school, up and down the movie theater aisles while people were waiting for the movie to begin. My family gave me a lot of encouragement. I felt everyone loved to see me dance.

I took dance classes when I was growing up in Hong Kong. Mrs. Cook, a wonderful ballet teacher, taught in a bright, airy church with a high steeple and tall, narrow windows that opened to the trees and birds outside, and to the sky. I also took some Chinese folk dance classes, but they were repetitive, not very interesting, and I didn't study very long. When I was older, I studied Peking opera with Chi Tsai-fung, a contemporary of Mei Lang-fang. He taught me the composure and beauty of simply standing still. I learned a great deal of the aesthetics of this classical art form, which could not be learned from books or other visual materials. But Chi Tsai-fung passed away before I could study further. I graduated high school from Maryknoll Convent School in Hong Kong. For my high school certificate examination, I received a distinction for music because I had had the best piano teacher for eight years, Betty Drown, a remarkable woman whom we called Auntie Betty. She never sat down and played for her students, yet she trained many of the best musicians in Hong Kong. What she taught me in music theory and structure played an important part in my life and my career in dance.

In the late 1960s, I followed in the footsteps of my older brothers and went to the United States. I attended the University of California at Berkeley, where I studied sociology, and I found the study of society and its people fascinating. It especially touched a chord in my heart when a surge of Chinese people immigrating to the United States in the late 1960s posed a myriad of issues, in terms of assimilation, acculturation, or simply adaptation to a new life-style. I felt particularly for the children of these immigrants, most of them struggling to learn the unfamiliar language and to cope in school as well as at home.

In the early 1970s, I studied dance education at Teachers College in New York and, with Teddy Yoshikami and Sin Cha Hong, organized the Asian American Dance Theatre. Aside from choreographing dance pieces, I became involved in the complexity of arts funding and the laborious task of administrating a small dance company with the obscure goal to create "Asian American" dance. For the next fifteen years, I was very busy. Not only was I creating dances and putting on productions, but I was also giving dance classes, coordinating programs, writing proposals, balancing budgets, advocating for contemporary and traditional Asian dance, and complaining and protesting about the lack of support for ethnic and minority community arts.

During these fifteen years, against the backdrop of the changing landscape of Asian America and the nation, the Asian American Dance Theatre evolved constantly in response to its changing environment. When the dance company first began in the early 1970s, it was to demonstrate that Asian people in America could choreograph and dance contemporary works just like other artists. I would meet people who would first be surprised then commend me for my English-language ability. When they heard that I danced, they would assume that I danced only traditional Chinese dance. After a few years, in response to the limited of knowledge about Asian people and culture on the part of mainstream American society, the company began to include traditional dances in its repertoire. Even most Asian people had limited exposure to Asian dance: Chinese dance was often equated with the ribbon dance, and Japanese dancers were expected to look like dolls. I realized the purpose of the company should include educating the public about the diversity, intricacies, artistry, and beauty of Asian dance.

I was sometimes criticized though, because we were performing traditional Asian dance under the banner of the Asian American Dance Theatre. Some people in the audience at one of the performances even walked out in protest. They did not consider Asian dance to be Asian American, even if it was created in the United States, danced by United State citizens and residents, and part of community culture. In promoting Asian American culture, the dance company expanded to include a community school, touring activities, education programs, as well as the annual New York season at major concert halls. The organization further evolved to include visual arts and folk arts programs as well. Soon the Asian American Dance Theatre changed its name to the Asian American Arts Centre to reflect its diverse programs.

Although Asians have been in America for many generations, and continue to be a growing population, the history of Asians in America and their activities are not in the mainstream consciousness of this nation. This lack of appreciation of our presence drives us to seek affirmation, and as cultural workers, to create more arts programming.

It is as if there were an insatiable thirst for acknowledgment for our arts, and as many cultural programs as there were, could provide only a drop of cultural nourishment to those immigrants, whether they were first, second, or third generation. As community culture workers, we found ourselves reinventing the wheel again and again.

MAKING DANCE

In the old Chinese classics, it is said that, poetry is the voice of intention; songs, the tonal recitation of sounds; and dance, images through movement. In other words, poetry explains the contents of thought, songs (music) express the sound of thought, and dance is the outer appearance of thought. The three are closely connected, often referred to collectively in classical Chinese as *yue.* The character "*yue*" has many meanings. Pronounced "*yue,*" it refers to the genre of music. Pronounced "*le,*" it means "happiness," "enjoyment." Pronounced as "*yao,*" it means "to like," "to love," "to prefer." Dance is inferred in all these meanings.

In the Book of Odes, the oldest Chinese collection of poems and songs, it is said, "As the heart moves, it moves into words. When words are inadequate, arms and legs begin to dance." This we can see in body language. When I talk and gesture, and I find that my words are not enough to express myself, I then use my arms, hands, fingers. The birth of dance arises from the need to express thoughts and feelings. As human beings of mind and heart, everything we do responds to this dual mind/heart element. Without the mind/heart content, dance becomes empty, as if without a soul.

The duality of mind/heart creates intention. Whether we intend to have a big dinner, whether we choreograph a dance, write a book, or decide on a career, is based upon intention. We may be the only species on earth with awareness of our intention. If we are aware of our intention, we can make conscious choices. When we are focused and confident, and when we persevere, our intention can be powerful. When the Wright brothers built their airplane, their intention was to fly. Similarly, when people dance, their intention plays a big part. Their intention may be to dance to entertain and inspire others, to enjoy or challenge themselves, or to speak to the gods, or they may have multiple intentions. In Beijing for example, elderly women often gather in the park in the early morning to dance. Sometimes they put on colorful costumes, wear makeup, fix their hair, bring music, and do group folk dances. Other people practice t'ai chi chuan or some other form of martial arts, or take morning walks. Recently, one can see Western social dancing in the early evenings on a regular basis. To understand our own dances or the dances of other peoples, it is useful to think about intention.

Figure 1: *Passage* **floor pattern**

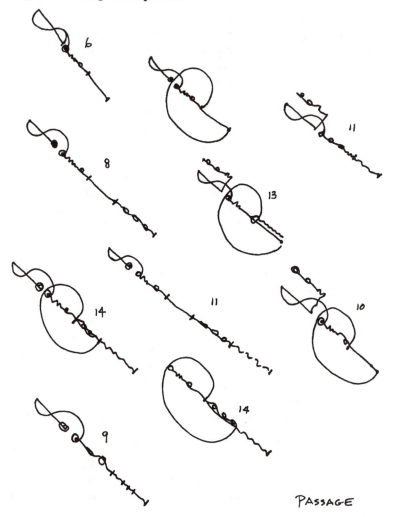

PASSAGE

In the late 1960's, I initiated an English tutorial program for children at the Chinatown Y in San Francisco. The plight of immigrants, their uprootedness, their hidden sense of uncertainty and great fear made a deep impression on me.

In the late 1970s, I choreographed *Passage*, one of my earlier major group dances, which explored this dilemma of immigration, leaving one's familiar home to live in an alien land, moving from one culture to another, and was about transformation. I used improvisational Korean shamanistic music, which was also about transformation. I have always been fascinated and moved by the process of initiation, the slow and forced passage of many dimensions transforming a people, a culture, into a somewhat different entity. This entity, as it evolves, must constantly renew to sustain itself. While doing so, it undergoes extreme stress and labor. The outcome, however, while open-ended and sometimes painful, is often very different and beautiful.

I wanted to use egg masks (white masks in egg shape with no openings for eyes or nose), but I couldn't because of the technical problem of dancing while wearing them. This was an extremely demanding piece for the dancers. The primary concern was their focus. Each had to develop a keen sense of focus towards the direction she was traveling onstage. Kwok Yee Tai, then CETA artist, designed the costumes. The dancers were in colorful, elaborate, traditional-like robes, made from sheer, shiny fabric, and patched to look like the paper dolls used for burning in rituals for the dead. As the piece developed, layers of this costume were shed until finally the dancers were in neutral solid colors of beige, pale blue and gray cotton shirts and pants. Another visual aspect of this piece was the long strips of black cloth tied to each dancer's crown. These strips hung behind down to the knees and would twirl as the dancers moved, a striking accent to the costumes.

In creating my pieces, I choreographed with the vocabulary that I knew, ballet and Chinese dance. Modern dance concepts became the structure by which I could speak my language. It worked for me because I did not prefer some of the choreographic treatment of movement combinations and arrangements of traditional ballet and Chinese dance. They are meant to convey only "beauty" and so they do not carry any purpose for me. We can also notice how this standard of beauty and appreciation changes, sometimes quite rapidly over time.

My piece, *Kampuchea*, was a response to the destruction of one culture by another, and its reemergence from within the aggressor. It was not a depiction of the atrocity in Cambodia at that time; it was an exploration of my responses to such horrific situations. The aggressor inevitably must redefine itself, while the culture that was seemingly destroyed almost always reemerges in different forms from within the aggressor. *Kampuchea* was in three sections. After I choreographed the first two, I had the hardest time creating the third. How does one resolve a situation like that in Cambodia? What can one gain from such horror and degradation? What generosity of insight, of revelation, is possible? *Kampuchea* remained two sections for a long time, and was danced to beautiful Cambodian music. The tradition of a people, their culture, and their existence would endlessly continue but for the interruption imposed on them by foreign objects. The problem of resolution brewed within me as I could not find anything to offer until suddenly the third section came to me as if from nowhere, with no shape nor form. Introduction of the new elements was powerful and exciting. It was Shiva, birth and destruction at once. It was vibrant, sensuous, powerful, and deadly. In the end, dancers signifying aggression identify themselves, show their faces, exist like the rest of the world, and, ultimately, reflect images of the totality.

Although *Kampuchea* was one of my favorites, it was a difficult one for me. It was difficult to convey the message through the dancers. It was hard for the dancers to express their intent, as they did not always understand or resonate with the intention of the piece. The structure of the piece was not like my previous pieces *Passage* and *Madhouse* in that it did not provide a focal point or the framework in which the dancers could present themselves with the intensity necessary for the piece to communicate effectively. Without such intensity, the piece was frail and could not convey the fullness it should have. However, this is still one of my favorite pieces.

In the early 1970s I choreographed three solos: *Water Portrait, Sheng Sheng Man*, and *Ribbon Dance*. All three dances were based on traditional Chinese dance, but they deviated from the classical form. Bell, my oldest brother, a musicologist, helped me with Water *Portrait* by suggesting a story line to the dance. It was the first dance I choreographed in a narrative form and I became aware of the use of time and timing. Although the movements were completely based on my training in Chinese classical dance, they reflected only the essence of fluidity, roundness, and the inter relatedness of the body, and none of the pure form of classical dance. The music was an ambient sound track of birds and flowing water. The fluidity and flexibility in movements of this piece are very much a trait of Chinese culture.

Sheng Sheng Man was a dance to a poem by a Sung Dynasty poet, Li Ching-tsao, recited by Shiao Fong-fong. The choreography was composed of three phrases. The first was strictly traditional Chinese dance performed in silence, which was then repeated to the recitation. The third phrase was a free interpretive development of the traditional phrase again danced to silence. Music was not used. After one performance, a friend commented to me that he thought he could hear music. I attribute this to the beautiful dancing of Junko Kikuchi, who had performed this piece.

Ribbon Dance was also in many ways a deviation from traditional form. Instead of the red ribbons commonly used for dances during the new year celebration, I used double ribbons, one black and one white. The emphasis of this piece was my stillness to emphasize my presence. The piece opened with me standing squarely facing and slowly approaching the audience, which was not proper in traditional Chinese dance. I always considered presence an essential part in dance. For my particular purpose, my presence emphasized the presence of the totality of me, history, culture, lineage, heritage, and my people. In a later version, Josephine Ting performed the dance using purple and yellow ribbons, colors of the royal emperor. Mrs. Ting thanked me after the performance because it gave her daughter an aura and a sense of dignity and elegance.

Asking what Asian American dance is is like asking about one's identity. Our identities are labels. What I am interested in, is not my identity but what I am after I rid myself of all my identities. If we want to identify something in relation to something else, the labeling is only a reaction to something else that needs identifying. Asian American dance was different from the Asian American dance that I see now. The new generation of choreographers is quite different, most being at least twenty years younger, with different education, upbringing, and exposure. Their languages and the ways that they identify themselves are also different. That's why when people ask me what Asian American dance is, I have to say I don't really know. It can be anything you want it to be. Then asking whether it exists is like asking whether you or I exist. The answer is that Asian American dance is as real and diverse as you and I. Yet, to me, we are all on a continuum of the past reaching into the future.

Figure 2: Ribbon Dance, Photographed by Tom Yahashi

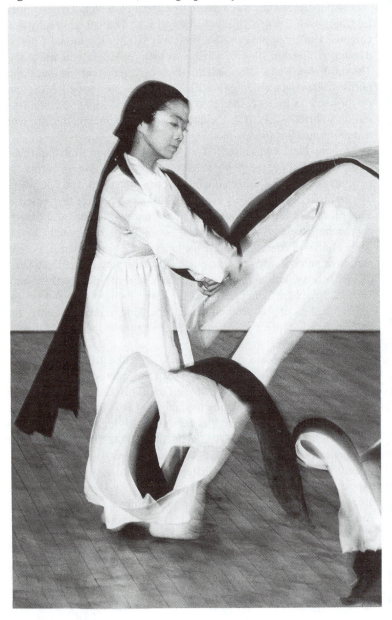

Figure 3: *Crystal Rainbow* **floor pattern**

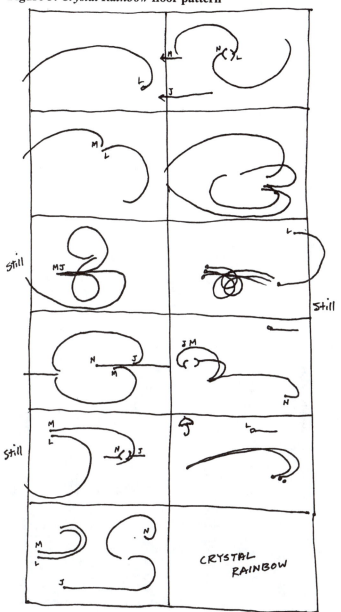

Figure 4: *Identification in Progress,* **Photographed by Tom Yahashi.**

My earliest group piece was a three part collaboration with my brother Danny, entitled *Identification in Progress* (see figure 4). Danny designed a structure for the entire piece, giving it a definite shape. He helped me realize space, both positive and negative, and the unlimited potentiality of its use. My two brothers played a significant part in the formulation of my choreographic style.

In *Crystal Rainbow*, I used many Chinese props: fans, a huge one with a design and two black ones; a farmer's hat; sparkling silk handkerchiefs; the dancers wore brightly colored coolie shirts and black pants. This was also a traveling piece. The dancers began the piece in dark shadows and moved across the stage in a boat vignette, crossing the stage repeatedly before opening into large sweeping patterns that circled the entire stage. I choreographed *Crystal Rainbow* when I was pregnant with Onie so I was restricted in my movements. I therefore created movements that were similarly restricted, yet creating a light and airy piece, full of dreams and hope, wonder, and enchantment. (See Figure 3.)

Origami emerged from images of origami cranes, blown in the wind, or flocks of pigeons flying freely and whirling patterns against the blue sky. I expanded on the crane images and used extensive circular floor patterns to create spirals and spirals amid spirals. It was a dance of grace, with dancers moving swiftly and lightly sweeping through space. It was a light and enjoyable piece. This dance could vary from a three-minute solo, to a six-minute duet, to a nine-minute trio, to a fifteen-minute dance for five dancers. The piece was choreographed in this way for practical reasons, such as the availability of dancers and time, and the requirement of programming.

Silk Road was choreographed on a fellowship, in collaboration with visual artist Zhang Hongtu. *Silk Road* commemorated the 200-year trade anniversary between the United States and China. This piece was performed to Kitaro's dreamlike and mystical music. It was also a travel piece, dancers traveling from point to point, like the merchants passing through the caves of Dunhuang bringing with them tea and spice over 200 years ago. It was a cross-cultural exchange between China and the countries west of the caves, including India, Afghanistan, and the other near Eastern countries. I based many of the movements on the stone carvings found in the caves, which originate from Buddhist motifs. Many of these motifs were of strength and power, while others were light and ethereal. I used long silk ribbons, not in the conventional manner, but to create flow and atmosphere. The piece was organized in sections, that ran from one into another without pause. This seven-dancer piece shimmered and glowed. The piece also featured my daughter Onie's two-minute debut when she was four years old. Her delicate and fine movements were light and pure and she won the hearts of the audience. She was a beautiful little dancer, with soft gesturing hands and expressive tilting of her head, and she had very good focus. *Silk Road*, like many of my other pieces, was intended to capture a moment in time and space. It was a glimpse into the past, the mystery, and the enchantment of a place and time long ago. *(My husband Bob writes: For me your earlier pieces opened doors, and with this dance you walked through those doors, this was a stage of great maturity, of triumph, of a full sail forward, historical only as a reference to your current moment, a spiritual discovery.)*

Since I often choreographed to convey a message, I was never interested in creating difficult movements for dancers per se. In fact, I often prefer the natural flow to intentionally challenging the physical ability of dancers. The challenge in dancing is to bring the work to life, and not simply the execution of movements. That is why my movements are often considered simple but difficult to perform well. In my work, I do not have main dancers or supporting dancers. To me, the dancers are all participants in a situation in which they are equal participants, each of whom must be aware of the others' presence. My works would not be complete without the dancers establishing silent communication among themselves, as it is of utmost importance for the dancers to build a rapport with each other.

Madhouse was based on a poem that explores the horror of uprootedness and dislocation. It touches upon the madness of oppressive power, signified by the great bird, and the immense sense of loss, signified by the repetitive act of weaving. It was a physically powerful piece, as the dancers at many points in the piece run forward, backward, and sideways (weaving) in loops, creating tunnels of whirlwind. This piece was selected for a choreographer's showcase and was performed in silence, with only the muffled sounds of running. Running in this manner, the dancers had to develop trust and an unspoken acknowledgment of their fellow dancers. But more importantly they had to develop confidence in themselves, in their ability to be in control of their movements, in their peripheral sight, and in their self-awareness of the powerful context of the piece.

I often put dancers in a state of uncertainty that requires confidence and consensus. They are to be challenged, not only technically, but in their existence. They must have a full sense of presence onstage. In *Passage*, the dancers were required to exit downstage and to reenter upstage almost immediately. This kind of demand created a sense of urgency, and resulted in a different form of performance. The dancers no longer had time to think about the present, but had to constantly be aware of the immediate future and the direction they were heading. They were to worry only about their being at the right place at the right time and focusing in the right direction. Every second of the performance counted, and in this way, the piece reflected the actual plight of immigrants.

The stage to me has always been a segment of space only seemingly limited by the frame. The stage could be extended beyond the proscenium and the walls. What happens onstage is only a captured moment of a much bigger picture. It is like watching television. While the camera lens can show only a certain area, the area beyond the lens continues to exist. What we can see whether onstage or through the lens does not encompass the entirety. In fact, space being limitless, provides room for all our imagination. While designing what is onstage, I think also of what could be offstage. Therefore, not only are entrances and exits of particular significance to me, the patterns on stage must also provide room for expansion beyond the stage.

MOVING TOWARDS STILLNESS

After fifteen years I was exhausted and have long since stopped dancing. The joy I had while dancing has disappeared. The battle of fighting for the arts, in my case Asian American dance, was an uphill one, and years of concrete work seemed to dissipate. In the past, my energy was at such an intensity that I worked seven days a week late into the night. It had its tolls. I was extremely unpleasant and, looking back, unhappy. These days, when I see young, aggressive, idealistic cultural workers pushing their way forward, I shudder because they remind me of myself of those early years.

Now, my expectations have become less, and are more flexible. I remind myself each time to begin from ground zero and to keep doing what needs to be done. As I reflect and slow down, I enjoy watching members and former members of the dance company get married, have children, receive their doctoral degrees, develop their own styles, get interviewed on public television, and continue in some form related to the art of dance and the art of living.

I improvise every day, enjoying the things that I do, and I do them at a comfortable pace. Sometimes, I challenge myself by executing a difficult "step," such as giving a talk in public or writing. I no longer do choreography, that is, the design of movements and the manipulation of the design through time and space. To choreograph, I must have something to say. In the future, when I have a better sense and control of my real self, I can venture again into choreographing with a message I feel comfortable with. But first I need to develop better control, which is really discipline. I am not referring to choreographing a dance to be performed onstage. I am really thinking of choreographing a pattern to live by, one that would have some benefit for everyone involved.

When I was in China in the summer of 1986, I began the practice of chigung exercises. In 1989 I met Master Koo in New York and have since studied t'ai chi chuan with him. Twenty or more years ago, my husband, Bob, had tried to teach me. He was really into it. But at that time, I found t'ai chi too slow and I had no patience. My idea of movement was that it had to be creative and expressive. T'ai chi was neither. At the time I began studying with Master Koo, I was burned out from my dance work. I was receptive and ready for change. Both my body and my mind were exhausted. I felt I was in this ocean with billows pushing from all directions. My actions in life were conditioned by internal and external forces that I could not fully control. While I liked to think I had self-determination and was in command, I was driven.

Since I began practicing t'ai chi, I feel the subtle alterations in directions of my life. I realize aspects of me that I never knew before, and likewise, aspects of people around me. These revelations are enlightening and continue to affect my thought process and actions. I have been discouraged many times in my practice, feeling like I was taking one step forward and two steps back, but I gained new insights each time into the intricacies of my physical makeup and its deep and strong relationship with my entire being.

I am also involved in the study and practice of Buddhism and sitting meditation. The combination of movements, stillness, and recitation has had a powerful effect on me. I realize that I have embarked on a new journey. I am fortunate to bring my memories and experiences with me on this journey. I have only begun to understand my existence and the potentiality of what can be. I can understand my limitations, and the invaluable lifetime that I am so very fortunate to have.

The chigung and t'ai chi revitalizes and provides me with energy to continue each day's work. The recitation and meditation clears my mind. Without the clarity of our minds, we can easily become unfocused. Our pursuit in life becomes hectic and hazardous, and our perspectives become distorted. It is only with clarity of mind that we can realize our existence and our purpose. Half an hour of stillness every day can make a whole life of difference. Sometimes, in the middle of the day when I find myself caught in a web of work and potential anxiety-producing situations, clearing my mind for merely a minute amazingly gives me not only a new perspective and outlook, but renewed energy and spirit. It is as if my mind has been given a break, and I can begin anew again.

In reaching for a state of stillness, I begin to look at the dimensions of time and space differently. As a dancer/movement person, space and time are the parameters of movements. We move through space, and we move through time. Using these two elements skillfully, movements can be manipulated to create a dance piece. Yet, there is really no stillness. When I am seemingly still, my body is moving tumultuously inside. My heart makes the loudest thunder and there are waves upon waves moving within. Everything is red hot, and then sometimes, everything becomes cool blue. I try to keep my mind still. That too is a difficult task. My mind is a galloping horse running wild, darting here and there, doing disappearing and reappearing acts. It laughs, and sneers, makes excuses, and falls asleep.

Trying to figure who I am,
>   When I laugh, I ask "Who
>   is laughing?"
>   In sitting, I ask "Who
>   is sitting?"
>   Without name,
>   body,,
>   characteristics,
>   personality,
>   What
>   am I?

To arrive beyond my identity, I practice being dead. In my mind I have died, and I eliminate everything I can which I know of is my life now. In this way, I reduce myself to almost nothing.

As I sit and contemplate,
wandering in time,
reliving fragments and pieces,
I see movements of my past -
>   blue hue in the sky dissolving,
>   meshing into streaks of red
>   while the sun slowly disappears
>   behind the dark mountains on the horizon.
Is it my eyes, or is it my mind?
As I listen
each musical note
fills the present time -
quickly disappears and becomes the past.
As it becomes the past, it no longer is.
>   Where has it gone?
>   Where did it come from ?
As I reflect,
my thought fills the present time—
quickly replaced by another.
>   Where did the last thought go?

It is the element of time which arrives and departs continuously bringing with it everything of that time. As I am the perceiver, everything evolves around me while I am seemingly still. The New York skyline I see from my window, as it appears now, immediately becomes the past. The space it occupies dissolves with the passing of time.

Traveling through time and space,
whether in a car, on a plane,
sitting motionless,
I think I am still
while the world moves
quietly and

                         tumultuously around me.

My stillness
It gives me tranquillity, peace and grounding.
So I would like to believe.
But I know while sitting still,
the world inside of me moves quietly and

                         equally tumultuously.

The tranquillity and peace that I experience is only in comparison to the tranquillity and peace that I experienced one fragment of a second ago. And the grounding? How could that be possible when the ground moves as much as I am moving internally. How is it conceivable when my concept of groundedness is changing as quietly and tumultuously as the groundless ground.

We are accustomed to viewing the universe from the standpoint of earth. If a black spot appears in the sun, the earth is affected. If there is a nuclear test in the Pacific Ocean, our food chain is affected. If a tree falls down in the Amazon, we have one less tree in our natural environment. However, I am also one of the changing variables in this huge design of things. In flowing with time and space in meditation, I ask, "Who is flowing with time and space?" As I reduce myself to nothing, my mind merges with and becomes connected to and a part of all things. When that happens, the mind disappears and stillness sets in.

I remind myself of this stillness amid my daily routine. Changing with the changes around me, I remain open and willing to become a different person. I become a reflection of what I see. Likewise, everything becomes a reflection of me. Although stillness, like chi, cannot be explained, I remind myself to stay always at zero.

A MEDITATION EXERCISE

If you put your hands on your lower abdomen, just beneath the belly button, this is the lower dan-tien. "Dan-tien" means literally the "field of elixir." It is where the essence of life collects and is maintained. It is like a caldron where heat accumulates and provides warmth for the body. Breathing with the lower *dan-tien* is like fueling it. Because working with breath is work, we need also to use our mind and be aware of what we are doing. To work with our minds when we work with our chi is different from how we normally work with our minds. We must work on discarding baggage. We do not think, or analyze, the work involved is actually the opposite; we work not to work. We try to keep our minds clear, with no thoughts.

I would like you all to think about what is on your mind, your plans for the future, your worries about your family, your responsibilities at work. You may feel anxiety, excitement, or frustration and anger toward something, or some people. Put all of these thoughts and feelings in a parcel, put the parcel in an imaginary closet, lock the door, and put the key in your pocket. You can get to these later. But let us clear our minds, and breathe with our abdomen. Apply a little pressure to your abdomen with your palm to feel and contain your breath. Every time, we exhale, we relax. Every time, we inhale, feel the pressure on the abdomen against your palm.

> Now, keep all your thoughts out.
> This is time for your-self.
> Try to not let your heart leave the room, visit friends, go
> traveling. . .
> to keep your heart in your-self.
> When we talk about heart, we don't mean the organ heart,
> we mean figuratively heart, as in love, and warm feelings.
> We keep all that within us.
> Be aware of your breathing with your lower dan-tien.
> Be very calm, relaxed.
> You have all the time in the world.
> There is no limit, no end, no hurry.
> Simply be here, be your essential you.
> I am going to be quiet for a while.

There will be silence.
Listen to the silence inside yourself.

ELEANOR S. YUNG: MAJOR CHOREOGRAPHIC WORKS

Reminiscence
Premiered at the Asian American Arts Centre, 1988

The Camp
Premiered at the Asian American Arts Centre, 1986

Dreams and Fantasies
Premiered at Pace University Schimmel Center, 1985

Silk Road
In collaboration with Hong-tu Zhang, visual artist
National Endowment for the Arts Choreographers Fellowship
Premiered at Riverside Dance Festival, 1984

Origami 3, Origami 5
Premiered at Riverside Dance Festival, 1983

Origami 1, Origami 2
Premiered at Marymount Manhattan Theater, 1982

Kampuchea
Premiered at The Open Eye, 1981

Crystal Rainbow
Premiered at Dance Theater Workshop, 1980

Passage
Premiered at Clark Center for the Performing Arts, 1979

Madhouse
Premiered at Clark Center for the Performing Arts,
Choreographers Showcase, 1978

ID 1, 2, 3
Identification in Progress: An Asian American Experience,
in collaboration with N.T. Yung
Premiered at Synod House, Cathedral of St John Divine, 1977

Sheng Sheng Man, recitation by Fong-fong Xiao, 1976

Water Portrait, 1976

Ribbon Dance, 1976

Beijing Two

Zhang Zhen

Shaking open your letter as if shaking open an old umbrella
A handful of fallen leaves from last autumn
The scenery you describe
Like slender cold currents
Piercing through between my teeth
That kind of gracefulness is unbearable to the eyes.

We are shining shoals of fish
Having swept through all sea waters
But still, the creatures caught by the net
Belief, no longer transferable
Already washed off among reefs and coral
A place where the autumn light cannot reach

The widespread comet tail
Sweeping over another busy season in Beijing
The Square is too remote to be remembered
By now the process is at last completed
But those permanent footsteps of first love
Bleakly, are reflected on the time's river

When everything seems to have been said
All must regain respite
Let's dive into winter into warm currents
In deep water again open our eyes
The sobering sky is watching you, with profound meaning
Embrace it, this flash of time

Therefore I have no strength to seal the envelope
I feel the sea water is swaying inside of me

My arms are as lithe as blue seaweed
But the hollow sky behind is sucking hard
I must immerse myself, I must get far away
My field of vision is full of the hints of fallen leaves

Growing Up Colonial and Crossing Borders: Tales from a Reporter's Notebook

Ying Chan

During the year when I was a Nieman fellow[1] at Harvard University, I was one of 25 journalists, 13 from the United States and 12 from all parts of the world, including Poland, Korea, Argentina, Brazil, Namibia, and South Africa. As a reporter from New York, I am a US fellow. But as I often told my pals in the program, I also feel very much international, depending on my mood of the day. Another way of putting it is that I never feel truly U.S. or truly international. I don't know if I think more in Chinese or in English. I suspect, however, that I am constantly switching back and forth between the two without my conscious self registering it. I don't know if I dream more in English or in Chinese either, except that my English seems to be much better when I talk in my dreams, which tend to be very verbal. In my waking hours, I used to think that I write better in Chinese, though now I don't know anymore.

The fact is that even though I've been a loyal New Yorker for twenty-two years, I'm connected by blood around the globe. While my mother, a sister, and two brothers still live in Hong Kong, everyone in my husband's family, except for his mother, who came to the United States to live with us ten years ago, is in Brazil: his two brothers, a sister, and their families. In the United States, we don't have relatives to go to for Thanksgiving or Christmas dinners or for Chinese New Year celebrations. My husband hails from São Paulo, though he is really Chinese. His family immigrated to Brazil from Hong Kong—after an earlier transplant from China—when he was ten years old. Six years later, he came to the United States to attend college and never returned.

To complicate matters further, my sister in Hong Kong, Vicki, is married to a native Frenchman. (Their only son, who was born in London, also claims British nationality.) My older brother, Alex, has a Filipino wife, while another brother, Nicky, has a child who was born in Mauritius. (He worked there briefly in the 1980s and has many in-laws, all Chinese, on the African island.) In Brazil, a sister-in-law was born in Taiwan, while a niece is married to a Brazilian-born Japanese. And who can keep up with the dating habits of my dozens of nieces and nephews? I stop tracking at the next generation.

In China, I have still more relatives, half-brothers and - sisters from my father's first wife, whom he left behind when he fled the communists for Hong Kong in the late 1940s. When I visited my seventh sister in Guangzhou and met her for the first time in 1985, the first thing she did was draw a family tree to help me figure out who's who. (It turned out to be quite an elaborate tree with many intricate branches.) Since then, at least one half-brother has immigrated to Canada, while a niece has settled in New Zealand for good. Together, the two sides of my family can form a mini-UN. We are the living proof of the Chinese diaspora.

I am typical of my generation from Hong Kong, baby boomers whose parents' experiences were shaped by the Second World War and the Chinese communist takeover. For us, it all started in China, and then Hong Kong. Until recently, Hong Kong was a British colony. In the parlance of the local media and government pronouncements, the place was known as "the territories." But up until July 1, 1997, when China took over, it was still a colony.

When growing up, we thought we had the best of both worlds, since we had holidays for Chinese New Year and the regular new year (also known as the Western New Year). There was no school on the Queen's (British) birthday, Confucius' birthday, and Sun Yat-sen's birthday (modern China's founding father who overthrew the imperial dynasty). We also had no school when we celebrated Easter and the Chinese festival of Ching Ming, when we visited our ancestors' graves and paid homage to the dead. Christmas was a major holiday too. So was the Mid-autumn Moon Festival, when we ran around with candle-lit paper lanterns, enjoying special pastries and another day off.

In those days, all the smart Hong Kong people in important places spoke English—they had to in order to get good jobs in a city where

99.8% of the population was Chinese, but English was the only official language. Not only was English used in commerce, it was also the lingua franca of the courts, government offices, and the best schools. To become somebody, you had to learn English and learn it early. After all, the only university at the time, Hong Kong University—founded as a training school for local civil servants in Her Majesty's service—held its very exclusive entrance exams in English. Except for a very small Chinese language department, it taught everything in English. And in those days, all professors were British, who, not surprisingly, didn't speak Chinese.

These days, there is a consensus in Hong Kong that the state of language—Chinese and English—among the students, college graduates included, is terrible. "They are bad in English and they are bad in Chinese. They can't write a decent letter in anything," an editor friend in Hong Kong has told me. To remedy the problem, my friend, who oversees a Chinese language news weekly, has been importing writers from Taiwan and Singapore to staff his entry-level reporting jobs.

Among educators, there is also a growing consensus that the reason for this sorry state of affairs is that children are totally immersed in English at too tender an age (say three or four, when they enter pre-pre-kindergarten), and that the English they learn is almost always badly taught. They don't learn Chinese in the right way either, since it is mostly taught as a second language in the schools, even though it is the mother tongue. Worst of all, children find it hard to learn mathematics, science, or history, since they have to study these subjects in English—a hurdle before they can get to the subject matter. So when a child has difficulty with a math problem, it is often because he or she doesn't understand the English instructions rather than for the lack of math skills.

In recent years, there has been a movement among enlightened professionals in Hong Kong to restore Chinese-based teaching in all subjects—even up to the high school level, complemented with a strong curriculum of English-language training. But many ambitious parents and schools that want to attract the best students, have little confidence in this language program. So it is not hard to imagine why I have always been a little mixed up in my language skills. It could be much worse.

I was lucky I was able to get away from learning English until I turned nine years old. When I started school in the 1950s, the English craze had yet to reach the toddler level. Somehow my parents chose to send me to a neighborhood school that didn't start teaching the alphabets—and English as a second language—until the third grade. Everything I know about Chinese, math, science, and everything that is important to me I learned during those six years of solid traditional schooling.

My luck soon ran out. By the sixth grade, every kid had to take an SAT-type exam that would decide which middle school (the equivalent of junior high and high schools in the United States) he or she would go to. As expected, all the best schools—the Hong Kong Stuyvesants, the Andover's—are English-based schools, run by the government or by missionaries like the Jesuits or the Maryknoll nuns. The handful of children whose scores were good enough for these schools have a good chance of getting into Hong Kong University, the very exclusive local university, and eventually make something of themselves.

I was a good student then. I did well in the test and was accepted into an all-girls school run by the Canossian Sisters from Italy.

I still remember the first day I started at the big school. Perched on a hill overlooking Hong Kong's beautiful harbor, the main school building consisted of two wings that spread like a mighty eagle, awashed in white and supported by hand-carved columns that rose four stories high. On both wings, the classrooms were lined by immaculate French verandas, from where one could watch the oceangoing ships shimmering in the sun. To a neighborhood twelve-year-old, the school and the people were indeed daunting. So I tried to be brave, until I heard my new teacher speaking English, and English only. Most of the kids, who had come up from the same school, seemed to understand her. I was totally lost, like I was in a foreign country.

Things quickly turned from bad to worse when she gave the first instruction for the new school year. "Give me your English name tomorrow, if you don't have one already," she said. That day, I ran home in a state of panic. My parents didn't know English and not many people I knew spoke English. What was I going to name myself? After many agonizing hours, I finally stole the name of a friend's older sister. By next day, all the girls had adopted a new identity, as Marys, Lucys, or Daisys—names that were popular in Hollywood movies then. Television still hadn't appeared on the scene. Since Chinese tend to share common last names even though they are not related, there must have been at least ten Mary Chans and ten Lucy Wongs in the thousand-pupil school.

My name was Winnie.

I was to live with the name that was imposed on me, one that I never quite got used to, for the other Hong Kong part of my life. It would go on my high school certificate, my college documents, and my Hong Kong passport and identity card. The name that my parents gave me receded into the background.

My chance of reclaiming that part of my identity came only thirteen years later in 1972, when I left for the United States for graduate studies. I dropped my English name, a symbol of my colonial past, from my official papers when the first occasion presented itself. I have not used it since. In school, I began to understand my teachers in class. I also learned a lot of English, though I hated it with all the rebelliousness I could muster in my young mind. Growing up, I never imagined that I would one day make my living writing English for a big-city daily newspaper.

"HOW DO YOU FEEL?"

Anita Hill was coming to town, and I was assigned to cover her for the day. Hill, a law school professor, had charged Supreme Court Justice nominee Clarence Thomas with sexual harassment. He denied it. The country had just watched on national television as Hill stood her ground in a face-off with some white-haired male senators in nationally televised congressional hearings. Love her or hate her, Anita Hill was hot. She was going to speak at Hunter College, her first appearance in New York City since her bombshell allegations rocked the nation.

I was living a double life at the *New York Daily News* then. Four days a week, I wrote about immigrants and the issues that affect them. On Saturday, I was one of a handful of reporters on the mayhem watch, marking events that even a city that averages three murders a day would find gruesome. I chased after ambulances, hunted for relatives of murder victims, and went to funerals.

Covering Anita Hill was a welcome change of pace.

Armed with a tape recorder, I arrived at Hunter's auditorium early. I asked a few women their thoughts on Hill, recorded some quotes, and surveyed the surroundings to collect some "color" for the story. Settling into a front seat, I watched the crowd, mostly women, swelling to the four walls and buzzing with anticipation. Wearing a purple knit dress, Hill was as cool and commanding as her appearance on television. She talked about women's tough fight in the legal jungle, the roadblocks to excelling, and her unflinching faith in her cause. The crowd responded with great sisterhood warmth, breaking into riotous applause often. Anita Hill was a homecoming queen, a heroine who had survived enemy fire in the trenches of the battle of the sexes. I was glad to be there and almost felt I was watching history unfold.

Then the beeper on my belt went off. It was my office calling. But if I were to leave the hall, I would not be able to get back in. Blasting off like crazy, the beeper wouldn't stop. What could be the problem? The editors must need me badly. But they should know that I'm with Anita Hill. I began to lose track of what Hill was saying. The crowd became a blur.

As soon as Hill finished thirty minutes later, I dashed off to the closest pay phone and called. Sure enough, something awful had happened.

"The police just arrested four teenage prostitutes. They are Asians and said to be Stuyvesant students," said the editor, referring to the most selective public high school in the city. "Can you go to their house in Flushing?"

"There's a lot of interest in the story," he added, meaning that the story might get a prominent place in the paper.

"What about Anita Hill?" I asked.

"Forget about Anita Hill," he said.

Jumping into my banged-up 1982 Toyota Tercel, I raced to Flushing, Queens. It didn't take me long to find the teens' house and get myself invited into the basement apartment, a filthy dump littered with books, clothing, and lingerie. There were no beds, only mattresses. The rooms were otherwise bare, except for a portable stereo and some CDs in the living room.

The women had just been released from police custody and were packing. I got one woman to talk to me briefly and hung out long enough to see her mother arriving in a Mercedes to take her troubled daughter home. Not surprisingly, the teenage runaways had gotten into the unseemly business on their own, without their parents' knowing. It would be a routine story of lost children in a big city except that the women were of Korean descent. One was indeed a Stuyvesant kid. And Asians are supposed to be model immigrants. Their kids are supposed to work hard, get good grades, and stay away from trouble.

It was an easy job. I got what I needed and felt good that it would be a scoop. Since I was the only reporter there when the mother and daughter sped away, I was sure that my competitors would have no way of finding them. I even got to ask the distraught mother the penultimate reporter's question: "How do you feel?"

The next day, I woke up to the horror of a *Daily News* front page photo: four thinly clad teens squatting in a police van, their hands in handcuffs and their smooth long hair flowing behind their back. On the inside page two of them had turned away from the camera, but one face was clearly visible. Above the giant picture, the headline screamed: "Pricy Teen Hooker Ring."

The Anita Hill story was relegated to page 26, a brief story from the wire service that conveyed none of the euphoria I had witnessed. There was no picture of her.

At the office, my phone rang off the hook. Friends, strangers, and agitated readers wanted to know why the *News* would subject these women and their families to such indignity. A few asked if it was legal to print the pictures of underage teens. I referred all queries to the editors. I also told the callers that I felt sorry for the teens but that I had a job to do.

The little incident made the "media watch" column of an Asian American magazine a month later. After blasting the *News* for its cruelty, the commentator was forgiving to the offending writer, noting that I had been known as a "good reporter." "Her editors must have made her do it," he declared.

So much for my life as a city reporter.

Don't take me wrong. I enjoy working for a paper of the masses, writing for the working stiff and on things that affect people's everyday lives. My colleagues write about the schools, the subways, and the zillions ways little people get shortchanged by the crooks and the powerful. They go after celebrities, the O.J. Simpsons, Sheik Abdul Rahmans, or Donald Trumps, always looking for the outrageous, the irreverent, and the grit. I write about the city's newcomers and the not-so-newcomers: the last Jewish tailor in Chinatown, an Ethiopian Jew trapped for years in a nightmare of federal jail and bureaucracy, or the sons and daughters of Korean greengrocers making it big.

As a writer for the working people, you learn to write simply and directly: no big words, bureaucratese, or convoluted sentences. You learn to see through phony and pompous writing, nine-tenths of which can be chopped with no meaning lost. You learn to tell the story straight: who kicked whom? Who did what to whom? You also learn to be funny, human, and a little smart-alecky.

I even took my Saturday runs in stride, sometimes racing to distant neighborhoods to be the first reporter on the scene. I need to talk to people while they are still "fresh" with the most spontaneous response to the tragedy that has befallen them. More often than not, it was heartbreaking work, like the time when I visited the same storefront funeral parlor in the South Bronx two Saturdays in a row. Each time, it was for a small child who had lost her life to some senseless violence. I would see the children up close in their tiny coffins, and dutifully record the color of the teddy bears they clutched on their way to heaven. I've seen other deaths: young and old, the only sons or only daughters, beloved husbands or wives. I've seen the remains of a blasted brain on a sidewalk outside a Chinese takeout, evidence of an overnight carnage. As some medic's plastic gloves lay in the gutter, the morning people would rush by without even a sigh. Yet I would never say that I have seen it all. The job has taught me to approach each death with respect. For however lowly, each lost life is unique. It is my job to uncover those sparks that have dotted his or her path.

COMING TO AMERICA

It has taken me a long time to get to the *Daily News*. By the time I graduated from Hong Kong University (HKU) in 1970, colonialism had lost much of its luster and the colony was slowly changing. Inspired by China's Cultural Revolution and the 1968 youth rebellions around the world, young people were growing restless and clamoring for change. At HKU, I spent most of my time on the student newspaper, including a year as the editor. The paper reported on real news instead of campus social events, and we wrote about labor unrest, and the school's archaic curriculum, and we shamed campus groups for their obsession with barn dances, formals, or "social gets." We also pushed for the government to make Chinese the second official language.

But I was floundering and had no clue what to do with myself. The options before me were limited. First the government turned me down for a job, since I was considered too much of a troublemaker and a radical. The mere thought of working for business seemed a betrayal. The prospect of grass-roots politics looked grim, since Hong Kong has long been a place whose future is decided in Beijing and London. My saving grace came only when the University of Michigan offered me a generous fellowship in its Ph.D. sociology program. Without second thoughts, I told my mother I was leaving for the United States to study to become a college professor. I didn't mention that I needed to break away because Hong Kong was too small, its political and social horizon too suffocating.

The self-exile would last for thirteen years, when in 1985 I returned to Hong Kong for the first time, on assignment from my employer, a Chinese newspaper.

At Ann Arbor, Michigan, my academic ambition soon fizzled, in spite of the nice professors and the good money I was paid. (I had enough money to send mom $100 a month.) I decided that I was not professorial material and fled again, this time for New York City. Preparing for the drive east with my new husband, a labor and community organizer, I couldn't fill a Ford Pinto with all our belongings.

That was 1974. New York has been my home ever since. I spent the first two years there as a social worker and the rest as a reporter and editor for Chinese-language newspapers, until I joined the *News* in 1990.

My career at the Chinese papers ended quite unexpectedly. One day, the boss told me that a Chinatown godfather was upset about my stories about the slumlords and the gangs. He had offered the paper $30,000 advertising if it would get rid of me. "I told him no; I can't do that," he said at the time. Two months later, I was let go. It turned out that the firing was one of the best things that could've happened to me. Unemployed, I began writing for publications in Hong Kong. With $2000 borrowed money, I also bought a used Macintosh computer and began writing in English. A few of my stories got published. The firing forced me to take risks, to reach out and learn new things.

Then Jim Dao, a friend who was then working for the *News*, called. His editor had asked him to go to China to investigate its growing people-smuggling trade to the United States. He could use some help. Would I be interested? So I started at the *News* as a temp. With neither a desk nor a phone, I would camp out at other people's desks when they took off for vacations. From the far end of the sprawling newsroom, Jim pointed out faces of people: star columnists, published authors, and top editors.

But the newsroom was a lonely place, where everyone seemed too busy to bother with a new face. Little did I know how the air was thick with mistrust and resentment, poisoned by ugly contract talks between the unions and the paper's then owner, the Chicago Tribune Company. When I arrived, both sides were waiting for the other shoe to drop.

Besides Jim, the only person who would talk to me was a business reporter, a mother of two. "If I were you, I would get out of this place as soon as I can. Make them send you to the bureaus; that's the best," she would say as we ran into each other in the ladies' room.

One day, I walked up to another reporter to introduce myself, telling him how I had admired his work and that I had followed his exposes of city malfeasance for years. Without looking up too much, he shook my hand across the desk, his lips tight, his body hardly moving.

The people-smuggling project went well. Jim and I went to Hong Kong, China, and Bangkok and produced the first extensive American report on the topic—three years before the *Golden Venture*, a tramp freighter with nearly three hundred smugglees on board, grounded off New York shore and propelled the modern slave trade into the national spotlight. At the end of the project, Matthew Storin, then managing editor at the *News*, hired me for good.

"Ying, you've made history, " a friend told me from the West Coast when he heard about my new job.

He was almost right, since I would become one of the few journalists from the ethnic press to cross over to the mainstream media. But I never expected what I had gotten myself into. A month later, Jim called again at night, "The union walked out. We are on strike and can't go in now," he said. "Just go to the union tomorrow."

The rest of the strike story, as people say, is history.

The next day, I would sign a union card and join a walkout that lasted five bitter months. Three or four days a week, I walked the picket lines and passed out flyers to urge people to boycott the stores who continued to advertise in the paper. One memorable moment was the day when a man, baseball bat in one hand and Mace in another, stormed out of a bedding store to attack me and a fellow reporter as we were passing out leaflets outside. We ran as fast as our feet could carry us and escaped unharmed.

In the end, the workers won a contract. But the victory soon turned hollow, as management declared bankruptcy and put the paper up for sale. Robert Maxwell, a tycoon from the United Kingdom with supposedly deep pockets, bought the paper and saved it from doom. Just when I thought my job was safe, I arrived at work one morning to learn from the wire service that the new boss had disappeared while yachting in the Atlantic Ocean. By late afternoon, his body had surfaced and his death was declared a suicide. Not long afterward, his two sons, who had pledged their commitment to the paper, were arrested and charged by British authorities for conspiring with their father to scam millions of dollars from worker pension pensions. (They were eventually acquitted .) Once again, the paper teetered toward the valley of death. Once again, a white knight came to the rescue, this time a real estate mogul named Mort Zuckerman. On the day Zuckerman took over, 180 workers lost their jobs in what has come to be known as the January 7 massacre of 1993, a day of infamy for *News* employees. In a brutal execution, all the staffs were told to go to a room downstairs to pick up some envelopes: a thin one for the fired and a thick one for the hired. Throughout the day, *News* veterans stood on line with rookie reporters for the fatal package. No questions allowed. No explanations offered.

Somehow, I survived. When it was all over, I still had a job. Through it all, I would also make a lot of friends, including Gene Mustain.

I first met Gene on the picket line outside the *Daily News* building a few days into the strike. Wearing a black beret and black leather jacket, he looked somber and distant as we exchanged greetings. With a sharp wind blustering from the East River, we were in no mood for small talk—especially not on the sidewalk of 42nd Street on a cold December night.

Hands stuffed deep inside our pockets, we stomped the pavement in mindless circles behind police barricades. Above, Christmas lights dazzled against Manhattan's night sky, as festival banners fluttered from high. Below, placards announcing the strike hung on our chests.

So there we were, Gene—who had just finished a book on John Gotti, the infamous Mafia godfather—and me—a new kid on the block still struggling for bearings. But a strike has a magical leveling effect: On the picket line, star writers or office clerks are all out-of-work equals.

By the time the strike ended, I returned to work and found that I not only had a desk and a phone, I even got Gene and the coauthor of his book, Jerry Capeci, as neighbors. A third-generation Italian American, Jerry wrote a weekly column called "Gangland," the only regular column on organized crime in the country. The fourth member of the quadrangular pod was Tom Robbins, a community activist turned investigative reporter, who is always in hot pursuit of slumlords, corrupt union officials, and misbehaving bureaucrats.

Gene, the writer of the odd pod, would never budge whenever I asked him to look at my writing. After reading it with meticulous care, he would tell me—with a gentle pat on the back—whether a word, a sentence, or a paragraph "works." Jerry would share with me his encyclopedic knowledge of the gangster underworld, plus all the fascinating tidbits that could not get into print. Tom, the ever sober political mind, would always remind me of my bearings, that instead of taking cheap shots at lowly officials or the small people, we should keep our eyes on the prize: the powerful and the mighty.

For my part, I brought to the pod who I am: my languages, my culture, and the many wonderful worlds I am connected with—the Chinatowns, Asian America, Hong Kong, China. I am also the immigration expert, having written about U.S. immigration and its fiascoes for more than a decade at Chinese papers.

Over the years, we would collaborate on stories—kick ass, as they like to say in New York City—and have fun doing it. We must have bonded on the picket line.

I also bonded with others, especially women reporters who have to cope with a newsroom culture dominated by the other sex. We would share our trials and tribulations as women, wives, and working mothers, or celebrate our small victories in the management of our double or triple roles. In my weaker moments, they would always be there to listen and to give a hug.

Jim, who also went on strike, soon left the *News* for the *New York Times*, leaving the paper with even fewer Asian American staffers. For almost two years after the strike, I did not speak to the few among them who had crossed the picket line. They didn't talk to me either. The discomfort was mutual.

"Race" and "ethnicity" are sensitive words in newsrooms. It's plain wrong that in a country where minorities make up 24 percent of the population, they make up only 11 percent of the newsroom staff. To survive, newspapers need to reflect the changing face of America. We need people from different ethnic backgrounds, men and women, to bring together different perspectives and write good stories. We need diversity. But then the next question becomes: representation for whom and to what end?

Race and ethnicity matters, but they are not all that counts. And often, basic justice and fairness count even more. I would prefer working with reporters of any race who are fair and unafraid of telling unpopular truths. I would rather have friends who walk on my side of the picket line.

A HARVARD SOJOURN

"I'm falling apart. no detergents. laundries piling up. have skipped the gym for two weeks. bills to do. the cafeteria is closed. i have no milk, no crackers, no food in my room," I sent a friend an e-mail from my temporary home, a one-bedroom suite with a working fireplace at Lowell House, a beautiful undergraduate Harvard dorm near the Charles River. For the year, the Lowell House had kindly taken me in as a visiting scholar.

"End of year college student disintegration. You're like a graduating senior," shot back the friend, a bored New York lawyer.

It was June and my Nieman year was coming to a crashing end. Horrifying reentry trauma gripped me. I still faced deadlines for two essay projects and was preparing a presentation on Asian gangsters. Besides, I was building a personal Web page, knee-deep in this strange computer language called HTML. I was trying to overcome my Chinese shyness and tell the world about myself, my friends, and put some of the favorite stories I have written into cyberspace. Until then, the stories had not been available electronically. The World Wide Web was mesmerizing, empowering, and liberating. Surfing the Internet for hours every day on Harvard's high-speed computer network, I could feel an outpouring of energy surging through the modest laptop into my wired suite, connected to millions and millions of people around the world. On the Net, writers have become self-publishers and Web editors, putting their work directly on the Net in a grand experiment to become their own bosses. For most of the independent Web wizards, it is a labor of love, an adventure in technology's brave new world where one can only guess what the future holds. In the mythical cyberspace, a glimmer of hope seems to have arisen for a new age of freed scribes. It could be a false promise. But for now, Karl Marx must be happy to learn that for the first time in history, intellectual proletariats have finally found the means of production within their reach.

I should have had better self-control and turned down some of the tasks at hand. Yet bad habits die hard. Without deadlines, I can't focus. I need the process of producing something to organize my being.

The Nieman year was my first real break for as long as I have been a reporter and a mother (my oldest son, Malcolm, turned nineteen that December). Before heading for Cambridge, I was growing myopic, unable to see beyond things New York. I could not read anything unless it was immediately relevant to my work. I would not travel unless I was on assignment. A sinking news junkie, I would be satisfied by nothing else. Harvard was my chance for air. With Malcolm in college and his brother, Freddie, who was fifteen, in high school as a sophomore, the Nieman gift couldn't have come at a better time. Both agreed that mom needed a break and could take a leave from the family.

So for ten months, I gobbled up the intellectual feast before me, going to classes and seminars seminars, and learning from renowned professors, fellow Niemans, and new friends. I read. I wrote journals, letters, short exercises, and a lot of e-mails—quick snaps or lengthy ramblings as I reconnected with friends in Hong Kong and around the world. For the first time since college, I also "have a life," going to concerts, hopping off to Maine and Cape Cod, strolling along the Charles. It was a year of comradeship and unfettered thoughts. Every day, I lived like there was no tomorrow.

I was especially struck by Tillie Olsen, who most passionately writes of her tortured writing life as a mother and wage earner, and of her exhilaration when she was awarded a writing fellowship at Stanford University.

"Now, like a woman made frigid, I had to learn response, to trust this possibility for fruition that had not been before," she writes.

And there's her description of the circumstances for the creative process, quoting Rainer Maria Rilke: "Without duties, almost without external communication, unconfined solitude which takes every day like a life, a spaciousness which puts no limit to vision and in the midst of which infinities abound."

> unconfined
> solitude
> spaciousness
> vision
> infinities

Such were the magical states I found during my Harvard year.

Fleeing a colony powerless over its future, I ventured to academia in a far off land. Bored with a university's sheltered life, I headed for the bright lights of the big city. Now having met the test of adulthood, I have returned to academia to claim my reward, ten months for myself with no strings attached.

At Passover, some Niemans put together a beautiful seder, my first. I was intrigued by the words "unrewarded worth," buried in the prayers. All good journalists must have too much of that.

The Cinderella year was almost over. So much to do, so little time. In between writings and deadlines, I rushed to final lunches, final dinners, yet more lunches and dinners with fellow Niemans—twenty-five strangers thrown together for a year of mutual professional and personal growth. Beer and wine flowed. Having survived the snowiest winter in history, we even pulled off two softball games, crowned with postgame haikus and lyrics. It was a maddening dash toward the finish line.

Reentry would be a breeze if only journalists these days can do the work they love without so much pain. Newspapers are in troubled times: shutdowns, cutbacks, union-busting, mega-mergers, corporate greed, self-doubt, drive-by journalism, O.J. overdose. Bosses are going cheap and racing for the bottom line. Hungry young men and women are begging to work for free just to get their foot in the door. The best journalists I know have said they would not want their kids to follow in their footsteps, at least not into the print world.

Even amid Harvard's golden steeples and ivy walls, disturbing news from the world of journalism kept arriving to bombard my refuge. There would be no peace of mind, as the Chinese would say: "The tree wants to stay still but the wind will not rest."

When the Nieman year began in September, reporters, drivers, and other workers at two Detroit newspapers were going into the third month of their strike, fighting back management demands to squeeze more profits from them. Ten months later, when I was getting ready to return to New York, the workers were still out on strike while the papers had hired scabs and continued publishing. More than half of the reporters and newsroom employees have returned to work. For those who chose to stay out, the prospect of winning a decent settlement is dimming by the day.

From the north, across the border, a Canadian tycoon has been swooping up newspapers. After taking over one paper, the new master summoned employees to a hotel, where they were sent to different rooms. In one room, some lucky people were told that they still had a job. The rest, who were sent to another room—which came to be known as the "death chamber"—were told that they had been dumped. "Drown those kittens," the tycoon reportedly told his minions. Some employees were sent to the "chamber" by mistake.

Then one bright spring day, an e-mail titled "disturbing news" arrived to say that Bill Wong, a columnist at the *Oakland Tribune* for seventeen years—one of the only two Asian American columnists in the country—had been fired, ostensibly for money-saving reasons. The veteran journalist was given fifteen minutes to leave the building. As shell-shocked colleagues burst into a chant of "we want Bill," Bill was escorted out by security guards,—with only enough time to collect his Rolodex and the family photo on his desk.

Bill's firing prompted a storm of protests from the local community as well as from Asian Americans across the country. As angry letters and subscription cancellations flooded the *Tribune*, journalists, politicians, and community leaders held a spirited rally outside the paper, demanding Bill's reinstatement. A few months after the self-inflicted public relations fiasco, the *Tribune* corporate honchos replaced the editor who fired Bill. But Bill still has to get his job back.

At my own paper, the *New York Daily News*, management finally unveiled a contract offer to its workers, who, in spite of the presence of a union, had been working without a contract since Mort Zuckerman took over. The proposal would cut the minimum wages for new hires by as much as 50 percent and give management sweeping control over every aspect of our work, including firings and transfers. Workers would have no recourse if they were wronged. To sweeten the bitter bill, Zuckerman offered each worker a $1000 bribe if the contract was accepted. Battered as they were by years of fruitless battles with one boss after another, the workers rejected the humiliating proposal by a vote of 188 to 8, another hollow victory since they were still without a contract.

I have a job to go back to—that's the good news. It's also the bad news—that there's work to go back to.

I did not go into journalism because of some noble call, even though the college paper gave me a sweet taste of it. Nor have I looked back since I started in my first newspaper job. Somehow, I have come to embrace the craft as a way of life, for good or for bad. Like many colleagues and some of the best in the trade, I have never imagined that I would do anything else for a living—except for some fleeting dark moments when the pain that comes with the job seems so unbearable.

A reporter's obsession is to write and make sense of the world. Distrustful, unabashed, and curious, we like to ask questions. We trust that if we ask the right questions, stay true to the facts, and challenge the powers-that-be, we'll be doing the right thing.

It would be nice if life could be that simple.

In her essay "Silences," Tillie Olsen writes of the many ways the creative process has been stifled, and of the silences inflicted by censorship, deprivation, and the duties of motherhood. There are also "silences where the lives never came to writing. . . those whose waking hours are all struggle for existence; the barely educated; the illiterate; women."

If Olsen were around today, she would add that reporters have also been silenced by corporate intimidation, firings, downsizing, job insecurity, fear, cowardice, newsroom politics, and the cult of trivia worship. She would also note that it's only fair for the survivors who have a voice to bear witness to what has been lost and silenced.

CROSSING BORDERS

Sometimes it bothers me that I don't feel offended when people ask the familiar question: "Where are you from?" "I am from New York. I'm also from Hong Kong," I would say. To an immigrant Chinese, I would say, "Oh, I am a Lao Huaqiao (old-timer overseas Chinese). I came from Hong Kong long time ago, too long." Nor do I mind people complimenting my English or asking: "Where did you learn English?" It's my chance to give a quick lesson in colonialism, and the way masters impose their language and culture on their subjects.

Reporters are used to questions, though they are usually more comfortable asking the questions. But the bottom line is that I am not a good representative of my tribe. That is the real reason I don't easily take offense at potential swipes at my ethnic origin or my "Chineseness." As a mother of two and a working journalist, I have never had the luxury of an identity crisis, real or imagined. I have enough worries meeting deadlines—stories, dinners, picking up a kid at school or at the baby-sitter's, tax returns, bills.

Hong Kong natives like me also tend to be more practical, for sentimentalism is a luxury we can't afford. To be born in colonial Hong Kong meant that you were destined to be a permanent exile, a Chinese without a China to call home. The Hong Kong-born are Chinese but are not as authentic as people born in mainland China. They are born British subjects but are not "real" British people either, since the Hong Kong-born can get only a second-class British passport, which does not permit the holder to permanently reside in the United Kingdom. Still, Hong Kong is my first home and my first love.

Since coming to the United States, I have become a Chinese American who speaks English with a Chinese and a Brooklyn accent! I am as Chinese as much as I am American, a permanent settler as much as a sojourner. I am a transplanted immigrant, but I am also more, considering the many years I have been here. On Memorial Day, I found myself choking up as I watched America's aging veterans, their faces plowed and stoic, marching down a deserted Harvard Square. My heart has also gone out to the children of the Tiananmen massacre, bleeding as I sat glued to the television set during those June days of 1989.

Hopefully, ethnic and geographical markers will fade away some day, as stereotypes and cultural expectations give way to a habit of taking people as they are, in all their shades and dimensions. Already, my children are outgrowing me. Maybe they will care about Hong Kong and China. Maybe they won't. I am sure only that their lives will be a littler richer and a little more complicated because of their parents and grandparents. I am also gratified that in the matters of names, my two sons are happy with their Chinese and their American names. Unlike their mother, they can't be bothered.

POSTSCRIPT: TWENTY-FIVE REASONS WHY I AM A JOURNALIST

These are tidbits that I've picked up along the way and therefore can't claim absolute originality.

1. You can write about anything you know absolutely nothing about.
2. You can always learn by talking to the best brains.
3. You can ask the dumbest questions and not be embarrassed.
4. You can call anybody and expect them to talk to you.
5. You can embarrass anyone who refuses to talk to you.
6. You can ask people any crazy question and expect them to answer you.
7. You learn something new every day.
8. You have deadlines to force you to produce and deliver.
9. You are not expected to deliver the perfect product, only the best you can with the time you have.
10. If you are not happy with what you have produced, you always have another chance with the next job. There's always another deadline.
11. You never think your work is good enough, so you'll always try to improve and indeed get better.

12. Nothing in your life will go to waste. You can write about your depression, your operation, or with a little bit of foresight, your own death.
13. You can take notes at your best friend's wedding or at your mom's dinner table.
14. You have editors who clean up your writing, without too many people knowing (but stay away from editors who overdo it).
15. People will forgive you for not sending them Christmas cards: They know you are busy.
16. You don't have to take sides in those nasty debates: welfare reform, immigration cutbacks, abortion, you name it.
17. You can get both sides to talk to you.
18. You have excuses for being an obnoxious driver (illegal U-turns, speeding, turning from the middle lane—you get the idea.)
19. You can beat parking tickets—sometimes.
20. You always have an excuse to skip a horrible event: I'll be on assignment.
21. You can pull a no-show even if you have promised to show up: Something unexpected happened at work.
22. If you show up inexcusably late, you know the excuse.
23. You can't be bothered by the bosses because you have a job to do.
24. If you get fired and decide to do something else with your life, congratulations, your life can only be better.
25. If you get fired and decide to stay in journalism, congratulations, your life can only be better.

Just beware, you can love your job so much that you are tempted to do it for free.

NOTE

1. The Nieman fellowship is the oldest midcareer fellowship for working journalists in the United States. Every year, the Nieman Foundation at Harvard University brings together up to twenty-five U.S. and international journalists at the university, where fellows attend classes, learn from each other, and pursue a study program of their own design. Too many people have crossed my path, in big ways and small, to make me who I am. Even this short essay owes its being to the generosity of others, too many to name. For this small accomplishment, I wish to thank the Nieman Foundation for giving me a gift of time, the

wonderful Nieman year; Bill Kovach, curator of the Nieman Foundation, veteran journalist and true professional who tells us to keep the faith; the Nieman class of 1996, especially members of my writing class, who most generously listened to my stories and told me theirs; Rose Moss, the wonderful teacher of the writing class, who insists that I can write; my friends at the *Daily News*, and those who have left, for showing me how to persevere and keep our dignity through bad times and not-so-bad ones; and finally, Sharon Hom, a friend and this collection's editor, for refusing to give up on me.

Roundtable on the Fourth World Conference on Women and the NGO Forum, 1995

Participants: Sharon K. Hom, Ma Yuanxi, Tan Dali, Wang Zheng, and Zhong Xueping

Edited and introduced by: Sharon K. Hom

In 1975, the United Nations launched the UN Decade for Women to focus on pervasive and persistent gender-based inequality and its interrelationship with global development and peace. Since 1975, several world conferences have been convened to address the progress in these areas. These include the World Conference on Women in Nairobi (1985), the Rio Earth Summit (1992), the World Population Conference on Human Rights in Vienna (1993), the Cairo International Conference on Population and Development (1994), and the 1995 World Summit on Social Development in Copenhagen. From September 4 to September 15 the official UN intergovernmental Fourth World Conference on Women (FWCW) was convened in Beijing and a parallel NGO (Nongovernmental) Forum was held August 30-September 8, in Huairou, 40 miles away. Over 38,000 people registered for the forum and at least 30,000 people attended the forum. Under the themes of the conference—equality, development , and peace—the governmental delegates examined a range of issues, including violence against women, women's access to political decision making, environmental protection, sustainable development, rights of the girl child, and the global feminization of poverty. At the forum, there were over 3,000 events organized by local, regional, and international NGOs focusing on issues of violence against women, international economic policies and structural adjustment programs, participation by women in decision making, health, and the rights of the girl child.

The FWCW adopted the Beijing Declaration and the Platform of Action that had been drafted and negotiated during the preparatory process leading up to the conference. The Declaration recognizes the advancements in the status of women and the inequalities and obstacles that remain. The Platform of Action addresses, analyzes, and invites action by Governments and the international community to carry forth a global agenda to take strategic action in the following critical areas of concern: poverty, education, health care, violence against women, economic structures and policies, decision making at all levels, human rights, media stereotypes and access, management of natural resources and safeguarding the environment, and the rights of the girl child (Earth Negotiations Bulletin, September 1995; Sullivan 1995; Bunch, Dutt, and Fried 1995). Following a proposal by the Australian delegates, supported by NGOs, the FWCW became a "Conference of Commitments" in which participating states were invited to announce implementing initiatives during their plenary speeches. Some of the governmental commitments announced included plans to open working women's centers, to allocate percentages of the GNP or specified amounts to women-specific and gender-oriented programs, to initiate poverty elimination, education , and social services programs, and to increase women in decision making by targeted percentages, and to create development funds.

The United States, for example, announced its commitment to a series of initiatives targeting domestic violence, health education, political participation program, legal rights education dissemination initiative, and efforts to enhance micro-enterprise development. At the same time, in its interpretative statement and reservation filed after the adoption of the Platform, the United States made clear its position that it did not view the Platform and its "commitment" as "legally binding." Over sixty delegates from other states and the Holy See noted their interpretations and reservations to the Platform. These included reservations to parts of the text that were viewed as not in conformity with Islamic law, for example provisions on abortion, reproductive health, sexuality, and family. The Holy See and a number of Catholic countries also noted their reservations to interpretations of terms such as "family" or "sexuality" to refer to anything other than a heterosexual family unit created by marriage. Thus, despite the adoption of the Platform as the agenda and the framework for commitments to advance women's status into the twenty-first century, its actual implementation will depend upon continued advocacy and monitoring by NGOs, international bodies, domestic decision makers, and global political and moral pressure.

In the aftermath of the Conference and Forum, women's rights activists and scholars, women's human rights organizations in the United States, and many other individuals and groups organized numerous debriefings to share experiences and to develop follow-up "bringing Beijing home" strategies. The roundtable discussion below brings together several U.S.-based Chinese women who have been active in exchanges with women's groups and Chinese women's studies scholars in China. The participants were asked to discuss their experiences at the conference and NGO Forum and reflect on the impact of these two international meetings for women in China.

INTERNATIONAL AND ASIAN FRAMES: MATERIAL AND DISCURSIVE STRUGGLES

Sharon Hom: I think it's important to begin our discussion by locating these international meetings within a global and historical context and against the backdrop of current Asian human rights debates. A mapping of the "shifting material cartographies" of our century underscores what is at stake in these international conferences. By "shifting material cartographies" I am of course building upon Chandra Mohanty's term "cartographies of struggle" and her call to Third World feminists to wage our feminist struggles at the ideological and material levels. By "shifting material cartographies" I am referring to both the "material, experiential, daily-life level which focuses on the micropolitics of work, family, sexuality" that Chandra Mohanty identifies,[1] and also to the macro levels of global, national, and regional institutional formations of power.

To foreground Asian discourses on human rights as the background of our discussion also helps to surface the discursive and political slippages that often occur across geopolitical terrain and the odd political alliances that are formed in defense of patriarchy. For example, in the negotiations on the Platform of Action prior to the Conference, the Holy See wanted all references to "gender" removed from the text. In the final document, it entered a "concerned statement " elaborating its opposition to the use of the word as well as its opposition to the use of the term "family" to mean human relationships other than a heterosexual marriage. The Holy See's position as an alliance with Muslim and Catholic countries might seem at first glance to present strange bedfellows, but then again, from a patriarchal stance, it is not surprising.

In addition to the discursive challenges to the racist and sexist norms embedded in the theoretical and practice genealogy of "universal" human rights, other key terms have been deconstructed and reformulated to empower human flourishing and support environmental sustainability. For example, the term "security" in human rights and development usage has expanded to encompass not only military strength, but economic and social security, the security that comes from not only absence of war, but the nurturing of the conditions for peace. Under the auspices of the United Nations Development Programme (UNDP), in the introduction of the Human Development Index (HDI), as an alternative measure to the quantitative macro focus of gross national product (GNP), the term "development" has been expanded to refer to development along a human axis, sustainable development and human development.

The English-Chinese Lexicon on Women and the Law , coedited by Xin Chunying and myself, and that you all contributed to, is another example of an effort at discursive intervention. Instead of an authoritative text, our *Lexicon* attempted to name the cross-cultural and language translation issues presented by basic terms and concepts that are often taken for granted in English-centric international meetings, particularly at women's/human rights meetings, such as gender, sexuality, feminism, and reproductive rights. At the same time we tried to encourage sensitivity to multiple cultural contexts and engaged in the critical tasks of contributing to the creation of some new "Chinese" terms. Although we struggled with the overdetermined theorizing of Western-based feminist scholars and English-centric discursive paradigms, we also drew upon the contributions and insights from these debates.

These international human rights advances demonstrate the significance of discursive and feminist political interventions over the past two decades, and the viability of coalition strategies based upon commonalty and difference. At the same time, some Third World feminists criticize First World feminists for their inadequate analysis and strategic attention to the intersection of race, class, ethnicity, sexual orientation, religion, culture, and gender. Third World women's writings on feminism have consistently focused on the simultaneity of oppressions, the grounding of feminist politics in the histories of racism and imperialism; the differences, conflicts, and internal contradictions in Third World Women's organizations and their communities, and the significance of memory and writing as a source of oppositional agency (Mohanty, Russo, and Torres, p. 10). As Chinese women who work across national, cultural, and linguistic terrain, we have useful insights that contribute to a productive engagement with and development of these critiques.

CHINA WELCOMES THE WORLD AND THE OPENING OF DOMESTIC SPACES

Wang Zheng: As a Chinese woman returning home to China from abroad, I was eager to learn how Chinese women would respond to the FWCW and the NGO Forum and how this historic event would affect the women's movement in China. When the leaders of the Chinese government made a bid in early 1991 for hosting the FWCW, I believe they were trying to use the opportunity to change their international image created by the brutal crackdown of June 4, 1989. Their assumption that hosting a women's conference would help change their image reflects one of the Marxist principles guiding the official view on women (as stated by the French socialist Fourier), "the degree of women's emancipation is a natural measure of the general emancipation." As the Chinese leaders believe that the degree of Chinese women's liberation is higher than the degree of women's liberation in the West (a myth created since the Mao era), displaying the great achievements of women's liberation in socialist China would therefore demonstrate to the world the high degree of universal liberation in China. Viewed in this light, the FWCW was the best showcase that China's top leaders could ever dream of.

However, the decision to host the FWCW also affected Chinese women positively in some respects right away. In its effort to present the best face to the world, the Chinese government began to support women's projects. For example, a project called "Welcoming the FWCW, Millions of Loving Hearts Devoted to Spring Buds" coordinated the resources from both the government and the public to help thousands of girls in the poor regions begin schooling. Officials at different administrative levels understood that they had to do something special to "welcome the FWCW." As a result, the National Women's Federation got a huge new office building in downtown Beijing; local women's federations got funds to conduct special activities; more women's studies centers appeared in universities; publishers began to look for monographs on women's issues, including feminist texts; editors of journals and newspapers organized special issues to either display women's achievements or discuss issues related to women; and special television programs were produced to spread information about the FWCW and NGO Forum.

Actually, the preparation for the conference, involving the efforts of many Chinese women inside and outside of the government, also served as a process of consciousness-raising. For many Chinese men and women, this was the first time they had ever heard of the term "NGO." For those women involved in preparation, especially those who had the opportunity to attend international preparatory meetings, seeing how NGOs functioned and what issues they raised was an eye-opening and empowering experience. Inspired by global feminism, many women quickly began to popularize the idea of NGOs, the concepts of women empowering women, sustainable human-centered development, and other major issues raised by women all over the world. Presenting global feminist activities to a Chinese audience, women scholars and cadres of women's federations changed their former reservation toward feminism. The new slogan was to "connect the rails" (*jiegui*, "to merge") with international women's movements. The word "feminism" not only appeared frequently in official women's journals and newspapers but also became a positive word.

The preparation for the FWCW and NGO Forum thus both circulated global feminism and generated much more women's activism in China. Women working in the Chinese official preparatory committee, local women's federations, and women activists in society made concerted efforts to increase Chinese women's participation in the NGO Forum. Originally, the Chinese government decided to organize thirty panels by government branches and the National Women's Federation. With the increasing knowledge of what the NGO Forum was really about, women in the Chinese preparatory committee maneuvered to expand the number of panels and to include the participation of nongovernmental organizations. In the end, there were forty-seven panels presented by Chinese women. Moreover, in order to "connect the rails" with global women's movements, the organizers of Chinese panels also included topics that had not been discussed in public previously, such as women and human rights, women and environment, and violence against women. As a result, the final list of topics presented by Chinese panels looked very close to the major issues raised in the Platform for Action. Many women participants saw the FWCW and the NGO Forum as the greatest opportunity of the century for them to break China's intellectual isolation and to push the boundaries of women's activism in China. They were also excited by what they perceived as the new openness expressed by the government.[2]

Ma Yuanxi: On the one hand the government wanted to present to the world a nice picture of Chinese women's status; and on the other hand people who are really concerned about women seized this excellent opportunity to create more space for research on women's issues and women's activities or activities good to women and have women's voices heard. Over the past couple of years a number of women have been promoted to leading administrative or professional posts at different levels in the Communist Party and in government and state-owned companies. In addition to the projects and activities that Wang Zheng mentioned, more official green lights were given for publications on women and women's issues. A number of provinces published books on the situation of women in their own provinces; a set of twenty-two literary books by twenty-two women writers entitled "The Red Poppies" (edited by Wang Men, a prominent male writer and former Cultural Minister of China before 1989) came out as a Chinese contribution to the FWCW. Many other books, articles, and critical essays were published too. Although many were assigned to be written mostly in praise of China's great achievements in improving women's status over the decades, a group of women seized this opportunity to translate and try to publish the translation of *The New Our Body, Our Selves*, a project in collaboration with the book's editor, the Boston Health Collective group. Although the authorities had earlier denied approval for the project, the project was approved during the preparatory phase of the FWCW. However, the Chinese translators were still told to delete particular sections on sexuality and lesbians. When I left Beijing after the FWCW, the negotiations were still going on between the publishing bureau, the editors, and the translators.

Another result of the preparatory work was that people became more aware of women's issues and problems, such as the problem of women workers (mostly in state-owned factories or enterprises) stepping down from their posts, and developed immediate responses. For example, in Shanghai, for women age thirty-one to forty, 52 percent stepped down or lost or quit their jobs; for women over forty-five, 80 percent. A group of activists from the women's cadres school decided to do something about this serious problem. They solicited donations from big companies, started training classes for these women to acquire a skill such as cooking, baking, tailoring, and repairing bicycles, and advocated with the labor department to award licenses, so that these women could at least support themselves or help support their families.

Sharon Hom: I heard there were also negative local reactions to the hosting of conference. Also, there were some negative consequences for Chinese women during the preparatory process and afterward.

Tan Dali: Yes, when I was in Beijing, local residents also complained a lot about the preparations for the conference. I heard that many people thought the Chinese government paid all the expenses for all the foreign women who came to China. They felt that the government wasted so much money in building up Huairou just for the conference. Factory and company workers had to "volunteer" their time to clean up the major streets. I asked one taxi driver about it, and he told me that even though those workers were not "forced" to do the cleanup, many companies or factories were assigned a portion of the street to clean. In his words, it was the task (*ren wu*) that they had to do, or they would get into serious trouble. Some people saw the conference as the government's effort to curry favor from the foreigners (*tao hao yang ren*).

Sharon Hom: What about the impact of the Conference specifically for Chinese women scholars and activists?

Wang Zheng: Although the official line of welcoming the FWCW in 1993 and 1994 did create a focus on women that contrasted sharply with the state withdrawal from women's causes in the previous years, the government's new attention to women was not viewed as necessarily beneficial to women. Many women scholars and activists found that the state's interest in presenting a glamorous image of Chinese women interfered with their effort to name and study women's problems in contemporary society. This effort, research on women (*fun* *yanjiu*) has been carried out by women since the mid-1980s and is aimed at both theoretical research and social practice. Now Chinese women researchers found the focus on women dubious. The problem was not only that much energy and resources were diverted from solving women's problems to praising women's achievements, but more seriously, the exposing of women's problems was becoming politically incorrect in the context of the official imperative to display the high degree of Chinese women's liberation.

Some women researchers also began to worry about another possible negative consequence of the FWCW: drawing the state attention to the movement of research on women that had been largely overlooked by the state previously. If women's issues, or representation of women's issues, became connected with the political interests of the government, then research on women could be defined as political. In the PRC, "political" means something relating to the interest, position, and power of the government. Anything that is seen as political automatically invites regulation or surveillance by the government. Politicizing research on women, therefore, could lead to the end of women's activism that had been pretty much left alone in the reform era. For example, when global feminists demanded loudly for treating women's rights as human rights, Chinese women researchers were very cautious and would rather deploy the officially approved phrases like "improving women's status" and "protect women's rights and interests" than use the language of human rights. In the tremendous political tension that developed around the human rights issue prior to the conference, an open identification with human rights could put one right in the official category of antigovernment political dissident. However, up to the end of 1994 many women activists were still hopeful that the FWCW, especially the NGO Forum, would provide an impetus to the growth of a nongovernment-controlled women's activism in China.

Ma Yuanxi: "Are there any genuine women's NGO's in China?" From knowledge and information I had gathered by attending the panels and talking to Chinese participants at preparatory meetings and at the NGO Forum, I think there are different types of organizations that are referred to as an NGO (here I limit my comments to women's NGO) in China. The first type is the Chinese Women's Federation at all levels, whose tasks are basically to carry out Communist Party and government policies and assignments. Most Chinese view it as similar in nature to the Communist Youth League and the Trade Union, all three of which were established by the Communist Party as its "assistants" early in the liberated areas prior to 1949. Some people call them "GONGOs" (government-organized NGOs). Since the country reopened to the outside world in the early 1980s, organizations such as women's studies centers and women's research groups were set up, totaling about seventy (that were registered) throughout the country till the preparatory phase of the FWCW. These centers or groups may constitute the second type. A number of them were formed by their respective provincial or municipal women's federation and are under their auspices and supervision. For the FWCW, many new centers or research groups were set up, such as the Women's Center set up under the Shanghai Academy of Social Sciences in April 1995 and a few others in provinces that previously had no women's studies centers. Though they were set up with official support and had been assigned projects by their leadership, these centers have been doing some very good work within the framework and beyond, such as the Shanghai project I mentioned. An example of going beyond the framework of work "assigned" is the research on lesbians conducted by a group of people from one of the centers. It is of course "underground," as it is still a taboo topic and Chinese lesbians hide their identities. They knew this topic would be discussed at the forum, so they wanted to compare Chinese lesbians with those from foreign countries. I think it's very hard to define whether these kind of centers or groups were NGOs. Their nature and roles shift from time to time. But no matter what name we give them, they are contributing to work on women's issues.

There is a third kind of Chinese organization, and perhaps we can call it a genuine NGO. These are women's studies institutes, centers, or research groups, many of them located in universities, formed by members on their own initiative. Among the most prominent are the Women's Research Institute of China Academy of Management Science set up in 1988 and the Office of the Journal *"Rural Women Knowing All"* set up in 1993. The funds to establish both organizations came from the personal savings of the initiators. At the beginning the Women's Research Institute could afford an office of only six square meters, where they conducted research on such topics as women's employment, the revival of prostitution in China, women in politics, and women scientists. It was not until 1992 that they set up the first Hot Line for Women, funded by the Global Fund for Women, and the Specialists' Hot Line for Women in 1993, funded by the Ford

Foundation. The hot lines became very popular. They get dozens of calls every day from Beijing and outside Beijing, from women and a number of men as well.

CHINESE OFFICIAL DAMAGE CONTROL RESPONSES

Wang Zheng: A suddenly changed political climate in early 1995 dispelled women's initial sense of empowerment in the process of preparing for the FWCW. Chinese government leaders, encountering challenges and protests by human rights organizations at international meetings, began to see the risks lying ahead: What if those organizations put up a demonstration right in the middle of Tiananmen Square? This revelation hit them like lightening, and they responded swiftly to prevent the political nightmare from coming true. The site of the NGO Forum was moved far away from Beijing. Chinese women activists at home and abroad were stunned when they heard the decision of the Chinese government. The implication was clear. An international honor to China had now become an international threat to China's political stability or, rather, to state control of power, in the eyes of the nation's top leaders. The decision to isolate the NGO Forum expressed not only the leaders' determination not to let this event disturb China's political status quo but also the state's suspicion and hostility toward women's spontaneous activities. The ramifications of this decision quickly and adversely affected Chinese women activists.

The government, as a matter of fact, wasted no time in tightening control over every aspect related to the women's conference. Forty-seven panels presented by Chinese women were closely screened through "rehearsals." Talks were geared more to displaying Chinese women's achievements rather than discussing problems. All the delegates to the NGO Forum had to go through official training sessions that warned them against the would-be international hostility toward China. Nationalism was fanned so that each delegate would consciously defend China's honor in front of foreigners even without presence of security personnel. Rumors were spread through official channels to taint the image of the NGO Forum, to create a psychological gap between Chinese and foreign women, and to justify the tight security measures. Local Chinese newspapers were not allowed to send their journalists to report on the conference. Western scholars who wanted to do research on Chinese women were not welcomed. Meetings held jointly by women in China and women from abroad on the topic of Chinese women could no longer get official approval. And those women who had attended conferences abroad were visited and questioned by public security personnel. In short, the situation in China was ironic: The country was about to host the largest international conference in world history, as the Chinese state, meanwhile, was taking the most severe security measures in the reform era to keep Chinese people isolated from the outside world.

To many Chinese women scholars and activists, the drastically changed political situation threatened to close up the social space that they had created in the past decade. To serve the best interests of their cause, they had to keep a low profile so as not to attract unwanted attention from the security system. Their strategy was to further depoliticize research on women. This included a conscious effort to keep research on women away from politically sensitive issues, such as human rights, and to engage in some projects purely nonpolitical for the time being. The strategy had its cost, as it meant that women participants could not expect to have an open exchange on all the issues with foreign women at the NGO Forum. Instead, they had to perform within the political boundary drawn by the government in this historic event. In other words, they had to treat the NGO Forum more or less like a showcase, as the government stipulated.

Yet even in this kind of situation, Chinese women tried to maximize whatever opportunities they could. Keenly aware of their limited options in the repressive political atmosphere prior to the conference, women in Shanxi Fulian began a huge project—a gigantic silk wall hanging embroidered by over a thousand women from grassroots. The collective embroidery project was a way to inform rural women of the approaching women's conference, since the piece was to be displayed at the site of the NGO Forum. This masterpiece of women's art was sold after the conference, and the funds were used to support Shanxi rural women's development.

Ma Yuanxi: The Chinese social and political system reflects a kind of animosity toward people who have different views or use different methods from officially approved ones. For a world conference to be held in China, because the government was afraid that things would happen that would affect its stability especially at a time when some leaders wanted to consolidate and strengthen their political power, it had to adopt a defensive posture. It made every effort to control the situation. First they tried to control their own people. No newspapers could carry their own articles about the Forum or conference except repeat the news from the Xinhua News Agency (the official organ). When I saw my relatives and friends in Beijing and talked about the conference the first question they would ask was "Is there really going to be a nude parade or demonstration of prostitutes?" They told me that they heard that many policewomen were prepared with blankets to cover the nude paraders and to break up the demonstrations. They were also were warned "for their own safety" against "bad" people and not to talk to foreigners on the street. Tiananmen Square was heavily guarded, as the government was most afraid of the demonstrations that might be held there. There was heavy surveillance and control by the Chinese government over the Forum and participants. But the surveillance had started quite some time before the forum and conference.

About fifty women were selected from each province as representatives to attend the NGO Forum. They had to go through a training class from three days to a week varying from province to province. They were briefed on how to answer questions about such "sensitive" issues as human rights, Tibet, abortion/birth control, female infanticide, and trafficking of women. The general stand that women representing China should take was that we women of China have a higher social status than women of most countries; that China's internal affairs allow no outsiders to interfere, such as on the human rights issue; and that Participants should avoid as much as possible discussing sensitive questions with foreigners. The Chinese NGO preparatory committee had prepared some forty panels or workshops to present at the forum. These were rehearsed three or four times before the presentation, and at these sessions panelists were told to avoid answering "difficult" questions. Some Chinese women delegates walked out of the training class feeling angry that they were treated as tools. Because of this a few of them were "disqualified" to be delegates and were replaced. One said she'd rather not go than be a mouthpiece of the government.

As for dealing with people coming from outside, the government tried to prevent perceived troublemakers from getting into China through bureaucratic tactics like delaying visa approvals. In Beijing, the government placed "their people" around the hotels, and in Huairou, at the meeting sites. In each panel or workshop, security people tailed their "suspects." And among them were some of my former students, who were assigned to each panel or workshop to collect information and then report to the preparatory committee. Things did loosen up a little after protests by NGOs supported by some official foreign delegates and a meeting with the Chinese Organizing Committee. Some of the guards were criticized for their untactful behavior in following some "suspects," such as their use of force in taking away some people's videotapes and materials.

There were also designated taxis. If you got in one of those taxis, the doorman would ask you where you were going and would actually write it down, and he would even ask you where you would go after that. Later we knew better, we just went out without asking for a taxi at the hotel, and would get one on the street some distance away from the hotel. As Chinese, it was sometimes easier for us to circumvent these controls, but not always. On each floor of the hotel there was an attendant always standing outside the elevators. Some were actually friendly, one of them on my floor later asked me to teach him some English. The first day, as I hadn't registered yet, I had no pass, so I was stopped at the door of the hotel. I had to produce all my papers. Then in the evening, a friend of our Chinese women's group came to see us. She was actually one of the leaders of the preparatory committee for the Chinese NGO and a member of the government delegation. Somehow she got upstairs and knocked on the door of our room. Just as one of us opened the door, four guys surrounded her and rudely asked, "Who are you?" "How come you got upstairs?" "You must go down immediately." Finally she had to show her identity papers before they let her go.

Sharon Hom: When I lost my badge, I had to go in for another one, and because I recognized one of the young women working behind the desks, I was able to get another one fairly quickly. Doing things in China or anywhere is easier if you know people! But later I discovered that the replacement badge was the open "B" identification given to *guonei* (internal/Chinese domestic) delegates! And so this may have accounted for some of the confusion when Chinese people were interacting with me. They thought my English was very good, and commented that I must have been abroad for a long time, or they asked me what *danwei* (work unit) I was from.

Ma Yuanxi: There was also another side of the picture. A former student of mine happened to be one of the plainclothesmen (*bianyi*). We've known each other for years and we trust each other. He said to me, "What can you expect? Have you forgotten what kind of country we are and what kind of system we are in? We have to be here, but we don't have to do or report much. Not many of us are doing our jobs seriously. I see little threat from the women here. The demonstrations are against nuclear war, against their own government for its exploitation of women, or for basic women's rights, and human rights. Why should I interrupt or interfere with them? And what harm are they doing to China?" I also met some other students who were assigned to different panels or workshops to oversee and report if there was any "slander" against China. Their attitude was more or less the same. The interesting thing was that instead of supervising and reporting to their leaders, they themselves became interested in and had learned things from the sessions to which they were assigned.

HUAIROU EXPERIENCES AND REFLECTIONS

Ma Yuanxi: We lived in a hotel in the city and had to leave every morning at seven to go to Huairou. All of a sudden Beijing hotels and streets and the town of Huairou were filled with women of different colors and costumes, each having a tag around her neck to show her identity (different categories had different signs on the tags) pass for access to hotels, conference buses, and meeting places. It took about an hour and a half to get to Huairou from the center of the city. As there were so many buses carrying people from the city to the Forum, the buses were often lined up at the edge of the town. It was the first time for me to attend a conference in a place like this. In fact, the physical look was quite unique. Huairou is in the countryside. The place was quite beautiful, with trees alongside the roads, lakes, and ponds. The splendid new hotels built just to accommodate the Forum participants, the scaffolds on the still incomplete hotels, and the village houses in the side streets seemed such a juxtaposition. The biggest meeting place was a converted cinema which holds about 1,500 people, where keynote speakers gave their speeches and larger meetings took place. Most panels and workshops (the schedule listed about 2,000 from various countries and in different languages) were held in tents, and some in middle school classrooms and meeting rooms in hotels.

Unfortunately it rained most of the time during the ten days of the Forum and there was often mud or puddles everywhere. If you slipped off the narrow paths connecting the tents, you stepped into the muddy ground or sometimes puddles. My shoes and socks got soaked most of the time, which brought me back to the old days when we worked in the countryside during the Cultural Revolution. Alongside the paths there were vendors (mostly Chinese, but there were people from other countries too) selling all kinds of things: t-shirts, pins, bags, mugs, caps, and stamps, with the conference logo of various designs, handicrafts, films, umbrellas, and food. Even McDonalds had a stand there! The whole place was crowded and chaotic. Very often you could see a sea of umbrellas, which made the place seem even more crowded, and people rushed from place to place trying to find the panel or workshop to which they wanted to go.

Tan Dali: There is a joke that I told my colleagues about the terrible wet weather in Huairou during the *she fu hui* (women's conference). They loved it. Usually, it is sunny and seldom rains in Beijing in the fall. Some Chinese women suggested that it rained most of the time because there were so many women around in such a little place. According to the theory of yin and yang, there is too much yin (female energy) around (*yin qi tai zhong*). My whole China trip felt like a real homecoming, until I went to pick up my registration identification card with my Chinese passport and an organization letter from the American Association of University Women. The woman stared at me a little and went behind the screen. About half an hour later, I was given my registration tag. My "homecoming" was also marred by a sense of between-the-worlds uneasiness. On my train from Shanghai to Wuhan, I noticed that I could not turn off the water tap. When I informed one of the train conductors, she just stared at me and did not bother to reply. Another incident occurred when we approached Wuhan. The conductors were cleaning up, and they simply threw trash out of the train windows. But in general, it was an empowering experience to be able to meet and talk to so many women and to see women networking. I saw people crying in each other's arms—they really need that kind of support. I realize that together we can make a difference, but by ourselves it is very hard to change things. A woman from South Africa said that "women are like tea bags—the longer they are under the hot water, the stronger they get."

Ma Yuanxi: You did hear complaints, complaints of all sorts, yet despite all the inconveniences and difficulties, there was a kind of enthusiasm and spirit in the air, a kind of eagerness to share experiences or to discuss issues and try to solve problems, and friendliness to help. Once without an umbrella, I was rushing to another panel, and suddenly an umbrella appeared over my head held by a woman from Italy, and I felt the warmth of this gesture of friendship. Another time I was attending a panel with some of my friends when one of the inflatable tents collapsed after a technician tried to respond to complaints about the noise from the machine keeping the tents up. For a few moments there was chaos. The chair said, "Let's open up our umbrellas and go on with our discussion." So the discussion went on under the umbrellas with no less zeal on the part of both the panelists and the participants.

I remember the day Hillary Clinton came to Huairou to deliver her speech to the NGO Forum. She had talked at the government session the previous day and touched upon almost all those sensitive questions: human rights, forced abortion, and female infanticide, among others. The Chinese government was not happy about it at all. They gave her only one line in the newspaper at the end of reporting the day's activity: "Mrs. Clinton also spoke at the session." People were curious about what she was going to say at the NGO Forum. Her speech at the NGO Forum was much toned down, and that eased the tension a little on the part of the Chinese government.

Another reason that Chinese women were curious and would like to have seen and heard Hillary Clinton was that she was considered a "superwoman" (not necessarily in a good sense). But it rained quite hard that day, and the meeting was moved inside to the cinema hall, which could hold only 1,500 (compared to the 10,000 capacity of the sports ground, the original site for her talk). When we arrived at about half past seven in the morning, there were already thousands of people in front of the cinema. We were told the cinema was already packed. Mrs. Clinton had her own guards, and with the Chinese guards, most of whom were quite big, she was so lost behind this wall of human protection, nobody could see her even if they were right on the side of the street. There were many, many more guards and policemen on the streets, and guards both inside and outside the gates, the doors, and all possible entrances to the cinema, forming a human wall with arms. I just left and went to panels. Unfortunately most people tried to hear Hillary Clinton, so many tents or meeting rooms were empty.

A group of sixteen of us from the Chinese Society of Women's Studies in the United States (CSWS) attended the NGO Forum. Five of us (four Chinese and one American professor) did a panel entitled "Women's Studies in China and in the West." The presentations included topics such as the formation of the feminist discourse in China during the period of the May 4th Movement, the women's studies program in a university in the United States and its impact on women on and off the school campus, the contested feminist discourses in the United States centered around identity politics, the development of a women's movement in twentieth-century China, a comparison of women's movements in China and in the United States, and issues concerning the practical and strategic gender interests in pursuing the goal of feminism.

The CSWS panel was held during a rainstorm, and the rain poured and thunder clapped outside while the panelists were delivering their talks. Despite the adverse conditions, over 150 people (more than half were Chinese and others were from different countries) attended. The response was enthusiastic and positive. One of the CSWS members served as an interpreter, as many questions arose from the audience. Issues raised and discussed at and after the panel were differences in women's position based on nationalities and other identities; the impact of economic and political situations on women and their lives in China and the United States; the discrimination against Chinese women in employment, higher education, and skill training; further development of women's studies not only in universities but also in smaller cities and towns and the countryside; and the gap between Chinese women scholars and local women.

Someone took a picture of me standing in front of the audience after the panel. Above me is a banner reading "NGO Forum on Women '95; Aug. 30–Sept. 8, 1996, Beijing" in both English and Chinese. Looking at myself in the tent, I realized suddenly what a long way I've come to reach this moment and to have my voice heard alongside my comrades of the same panel and of the same group (CSWS). Trying to stand up straight alone by myself there, I felt actually I am never alone. It's such a vivid image of a part and the whole and a whole composed of the parts. In that photo, my comrades are smiling at me, and I am smiling back.

Tan Dali: However, I still feel that the spirit of sisterhood was marred by a kind of territorialism and stratification. For example, because we could not do our workshop during the slotted time for us, since the tents were blown down, I tried to distribute copies of our American Association of University Women (AAWU) reports on the dropout issue of Chinese girls. I went to a tent to see if I could leave some reports at their counter and was told that their tent is on women's rights issues, so I couldn't leave the reports, as if girls' right to education is not a part of women's rights.

Our AAUW workshop also could not take place during the scheduled time because the tent was blown down and there was water everywhere. Before the workshop, we had gone to a warehouse to get seven boxes of materials that we had shipped from the United States. When we got to our tent, we realized that we could not unload our materials. We tried to call the Chinese Organizing Committee, but it was hard to find a phone and to get through to the committee. In the end we had to pay the company for shipping the material back and forth from the warehouse and pay extra for more storage time. We filled out a request for rescheduling, but we never heard anything from them. Fortunately, one of the other professors offered us some time to present our research results in one of her sessions. Although we had to give a shortened presentation, it went very well. I heard from other women that their disrupted presentations were also worked out among the other women.

Sharon Hom: I think that the incident Dali described about the women's rights tent may have reflected a territorial assertion of space and authority, but I think it also reflects a substantive perception of the distance and difference between women's rights and particular issues. Or perhaps seeing a Chinese face, they may have misinterpreted who you were and what the reports were.

Tan Dali: I also felt this kind of territorialization among Chinese women representatives from China. When I tried to distribute copies of our AAUW report, "Keeping Chinese Girls in School: Effective Strategies from Hubei Province," to some women representatives from China, one of them glanced at the well-printed and bound reports and said, "Oh, Hubei's so Lavish (kuo qi)." And then she realized that it was the AAUW in the United States that did the report and suddenly felt more distanced from me. I also had the B type badge.

My experience with foreign/Western delegates was a mixed one. They also first thought that I was a Chinese representative but realized later that I was from an American organization. But I think most of their interest in Chinese women is genuine and well intentioned, but some of them were unjustifiably critical of the whole event in China. Even though I speak Chinese, I was also very frustrated by the conference logistics and the lack of organization at the NGO Forum, so

I can imagine how hard it must have been for others. However, I still think that the effort of the Chinese Organizing Committee should be recognized. Another between-the-worlds dilemma for me.

I was also angry about the number of Chinese men wearing representative badges. I don't mean that men should not participate in discussions about the women's issues. But when Chinese people like my sister and another woman I got to know in Nanjing who worked on women's issues could not go because of the limited domestic Chinese slots, I feel that my indignation is justified. My sister was the main researcher for our American Association of University Women report. When she applied to go to the NGO Forum to present our report, she was told that only seventy-two women from Hubei Province were selected to go. There were not enough slots for women from the provincial women's federation. She was told, "You are an ordinary university teacher, how could we give you a slot?"

It was also ironic that we came all the way to China to attend the conference and the folks back in the States knew much more about the conference and the NGO Forum than those of us attending. I tried to read Chinese newspapers and watch Chinese television news, but there was very little coverage about the NGO Forum. The only coverage related to the conference was about the conference volunteers. One Chinese student I met said that he got a telegram from his school during his summer vacation to return to school earlier so that they could help out at the conference. I did not see any of the issues discussed at the forum covered in the Chinese news during the time of the NGO meeting.

Sharon Hom: Given a meeting of this scope and complexity, the logistical nightmares and problems were inevitable, although much more sensitive prior planning could have better addressed the difficulties for disabled women in wheelchairs. The presence of those ominous Chinese people with cameras, whatever "journalist" credentials they had, was a chilling sight for me. I was really aware of the impact on Chinese women who knew that there were cameras present. In these circumstances, often they were speaking for the camera, creating a record that they said the right thing. Of course we should acknowledge that there were very many people who came away feeling that it was a wonderful meeting and didn't experience any of the security or repression. There were clearly target groups, those working on human rights and Tibet especially. Not all of the Chinese groups experienced the same degree of pressure and surveillance either. Those groups that had more contact with people abroad or received foreign money were more carefully watched.

The workshop on human rights sponsored by the Law Institute of Chinese Academy of Social Science was very carefully prepared, and dealing with sensitive and sticky points, it had been to some extent rehearsed like many other panels prior to the forum. Compared to other workshops the surveillance there appeared very, very light. The title of the workshop, "Women and Human Rights," is significant, as it represents a conscious, strategic decision not to link the two concepts more closely together by the use of the "and" (*yu*), to denote two distinct categories (rather than saying "women's rights are human rights"), thus creating some political and ideological space to continue to work on the human rights aspects of women's work while avoiding the government's allergic reaction to human rights. This is another example of what Wang Zheng meant in terms of a strategy to "depoliticize" the issues within careful labeling. For me personally, two very different aspects of my China work, law/human rights and women's studies, were suddenly coming together, and I was trying to figure out the relationship between them. The hard thing was that although they must be related, maybe for China internally there needs to be a bit of distance. It was as if I had spent the past ten years of my life trying to bring law and the gender issues into one room, both strategically and theoretically, and then had to recognize the strategic use for the women in China of having them distanced to avoid political interference.

The reaction of Chinese participants to Human Rights in China's two reports on Chinese women was very instructive about the levels of exchanges possible. Although the workshop focused on strategy very concretely, as a way of identifying a range of human rights implementation strategies, and presented two case studies, the United States and China, the reaction of Chinese respondents afterward was very defensive and focused only on the China case study. They loudly defended China's record and challenged the factual basis of the China presentation, which they said did not reflect Chinese realities (of course the video cameras were rolling). The Human Rights in China (HRIC) reports were not claiming to speak for women in China, but were ironically using primarily official Chinese sources to come up with an analysis that was not within the official discourse, to come up with observations, recommendations, and an analysis from Chinese human rights scholars and activists who by and large are not inside China, but not claiming to speak for anyone inside. The Chinese official regime often acts as if the minute you mention China in the context of human rights, you're already being critical. Given the leadership's sensitivity to human rights, there is a very, very small space in which outsiders—and for certain Chinese, an even smaller space—can talk critically about the problems. That line-drawing is being done by the Communist Party, and it cannot tolerate criticism. The official worldview is that on every single issue, including human rights, there is a correct analysis, and that the official analysis is the correct one. I believe this view is doomed to fail because of the partial nature of each person's understanding. The danger is in any one of the parts claiming the legitimacy to speak for an other's experience or the whole. This is essentially what I tried to point out when I intervened in that workshop. Afterward, some of the same critics of the HRIC reports came up to me to ask me what *danwei* I was from and to say quietly that they agreed with what I said.

This underscores what a Chinese scholar or cadre working on women's issues can say in public when directed only at a Chinese reader or Chinese audience, that is, *neibu* (internal), not for foreigners. Speaking internally, of course all the problems can be aired and people can be quite critical to a point. But once these Chinese delegates were at the conference, in a public forum, they could not speak outside their role as Chinese citizens in an international arena, because anything they said would be construed as a reflection of China and of their individual position vis-à-vis their government. The Chinese delegates were constrained by what had been set as the permissible boundaries for the debate.

Afterward, the official acknowledgment of the contributions made by each Chinese delegate suggests that the official assessment of the conference was positive, that is, that everyone stayed within the permissible bounds of exchange. But one prominent Chinese women's studies scholar and activist wrote an open letter stating the reasons she had refused to participate in the NGO Forum. Not one of her extensive publications on Chinese women was included in the exhibition of books published on women. She also said the political performance of herself and other NGOs were being investigated, and she herself had been criticized as a proponent of bourgeois feminist movements. For those reasons she refused to participate, and her case reminds us that there were many missing Chinese women's voices at the conference and the NGO Forum.

IMPACT ON CHINESE WOMEN

Sharon Hom: One of the rationales of many NGOs for having the conference in China was that it would provide opportunities for advancing human rights work and women's issues inside China, despite the concessions needed to achieve it. From that perspective it is very important to assess the impact of the FWCW and the NGO Forum on Chinese women. For certain aspects of women's studies in China, the situation was very tense at various times. But it is difficult to assess whether the impact in the long run will be empowering to women and democracy movements within China. The repression before, during, and after the conference should make us wonder who actually benefited from the negotiated concessions and trade-offs? It should make us take a long, hard look at the sometimes uneasy and certainly complex relationship between international NGOs and domestic strategies.

In some private conversations during the forum Chinese friends and colleagues tried to share with me their perspectives on what would be an acceptable speed for reform, on what could be said, and on who should say it. They also suggested that I was saying certain things that many Chinese people could not accept. But while respecting their analysis of what could be attempted from within China, I also see the appropriate strategy outside of China as a related but different question. It is very important for those of us outside to understand that our strategy could have negative consequences for people inside. There is nothing wrong with pressure and critiques from outside, as a complement to these slower, incremental internal strategies. It would be a major achievement if people could understand and appreciate the value of multiple, simultaneous, and different kinds of interventions undertaken by diverse actors.

Wang Zheng: When I met my friends at the NGO Forum, everyone said, "Just keep a low profile and wait for the paranoia to pass." They sounded like seasoned farmers who know very well how to deal with bad weather. In this kind of unfavorable political climate, one should just do some fixing and repair work, preparing well for a warmer, more productive season. The political weather in China has always changed frequently. Before the adjournment of the official conference, the

Chinese government leaders' paranoia had already faded. First of all, the NGO Forum ended without any incident. There was no demonstration against the Chinese government. Instead, there were some demonstrations against American imperialists! China was obviously not the target of attack, much to the relief of Chinese leaders. Actually, they realized that most women from abroad were not coming to discuss China's problems at all. On the side of Chinese participants, no one acted as a troublemaker either. Everyone in the forty-seven panels read their lines according to the script that had been rehearsed many times. With their skillful performances, Chinese participants showed the state that women were not an oppositional force against the government. The end of the NGO Forum brought tremendous relief to the government leaders, and they were further thrilled by the gratitude and praise expressed by foreign government officials at the UN conference. It seemed to them, hosting the conference had gained them honor after all . Their nervousness was thus suddenly replaced by a smugness when the FWCW adjourned. Officials at different government branches quickly staged celebrations to blow their own horn. Each of them had contributed a lot to winning honor for China in their different capacities of working for the conference. The Chinese preparatory committee also had a grand celebration, issuing award certificates to each participant in the NGO Forum (there were five thousand of them nationwide) to acknowledge their great contribution to the nation. This national farce amused many women participants. They understood that celebrations signified an official lift of the curse on the conference.

After the Platform for Action was solemnly signed by government officials from all over the world, the All China Women's Federation was quick to use the pledge of the Chinese government and launched a nationwide campaign on fulfilling the Platform for Action and the Beijing Declaration. This campaign is creating legitimacy for expanding Chinese women's activism under the guidance of the two official international documents. In the congenial climate of post-FWCW China, the impact of the conference on women is openly discussed by Chinese women themselves. The official newspaper of the National Women's Federation, *Zhongguo funbao* (Chinese women's newspaper), has become the chief vehicle to promulgate the spirit of the conference. In order to "let every one share the treasure left by the conference," the chief editor invited a group of participants of the NGO Forum to a discussion meeting in October 1995. The newspaper printed the abstracts of each participant's talk with the title "Look at the World Through Women's Eyes." The concentrated topic was the concept of gender. A woman scholar expressed succinctly the major point of the discussion: "The greatest inspiration the women's conference gave to people is: we should look at things with a gender perspective." A woman writer described how her heightened gender consciousness enabled her to discern blatant sexism in the media. She emphasized, "Raising gender consciousness, you will notice all those things you have never been aware of before." Several women stressed the urgency of promulgating a gender perspective in China. They strongly asserted, "Our newspapers should develop the achievements of the conference to influence the society and decision makers so that they will consider the gender issue. We should use our pens, our mouths and our minds to spread out gender consciousness."

Not only has the largest official women's newspaper in China been openly promoting a feminist gender consciousness, but women's periodicals run by the national or local women's federations all over China have also joined the expanding feminist discourse by printing excerpts of the two documents of the conference and articles discussing plans for fulfilling the Platform for Action. All these suggest that the Women's Federation, the largest and official women's organization in China, is moving from its former reservation and isolation from feminism to an open enthusiastic embrace of feminism. This significant change, virtually a sign of the state sanction to merge with global feminism, promises a thriving growth of a women's movement with feminist gender consciousness and feminist agenda in post-FWCW China.

Tan Dali: The impact of the conference seems to have been very positive from what I know. Many Chinese women realized that women in other parts of the world dared to speak out. Chinese people also gained insight about foreigners. When I was in Beijing this past February, our tour guide told me that people in Beijing realized that not every foreigner that attended the conference was rich. He told me that during the conference, a bus driver took a group of delegates from a Beijing hotel to Huairou. When those women left the bus to attend the conference, he decided to clean up the bus a bit. He saw what looked like a half a piece of bread left on a seat and threw it away without thinking. When the delegates came back, he saw one of the women looking for something on the bus. Even though the driver did not speak

English, he was able to communicate with the woman through gestures. When he realized that the woman was looking for that piece of bread he gestured that he had thrown it away. The woman was very angry and told him that that was her dinner. Shocked, the driver bought the woman a sandwich. The tour guide also told me about a taxi driver who drove a foreign delegate to various places for a whole day but was told that she could not pay him because she did not have money.

Ma Yuanxi: We spent some time, mostly in the evenings, talking and having discussions with Chinese women scholars, professors, journalists, lawyers, writers, workers, and our own relatives. I also learned quite a lot more about the situation of Chinese women. The more than fifteen years of reforms have brought about great changes, such as the physical look of many places (especially cities), the way of life, and the economic prosperity (business has not been affected much). As I was told by my former students working in Chinese companies, transactions are still going on with other countries and the United States even though the relationship between the countries seems strained at moments. Of course there are still numerous problems—autocracy, corruption, and laws that are not followed. There are also many, many problems existing for women—unemployment, lack of education, trafficking of women, prostitution, illiteracy, violence against women—especially in the countryside, where the feudal, traditional mores and values are still very strong.

At the same time, women are often still treated as objects, mostly sex objects of men. There is a current Chinese saying about how some young women are "eating out of their bowl of youth." Some of these women are prostitutes and "accompanying ladies" (a new term for girls who sit, drink, and dance with businessmen, Chinese or foreign, in hotels, restaurants, or dance halls), and their presence is increasing in big cities, especially in coastal cities and the economic zones. Some women serve as mistresses for wealthy men, which is considered prostitution of a higher level. These women lead a more stable life, at least for a while. Their "clients" are mostly businessmen who frequently come to China and would rather keep a mistress than take any girl at random. The usual practice is that the businessman rents a room in a hotel for his mistress and provides for her livelihood. He comes once or twice a month when business requires his presence. People call this kind of woman "a canary," or a "plaything" in a cage.

Tan Dali: When I was in China in March, I heard from our tour guides that some women college students, teachers, and even nurses from the army hospitals are prostitutes. Those women are called "military flowers" (*jun hua* , in Chinese), and that even the policemen are afraid to arrest them. In Guilin, my colleague and I were so exhausted from chaperoning fifteen teenagers, that we decided to have a massage in the hotel. I was shocked as to what I saw. In the dimly lit and smoke filled parlor, about twenty young women with heavy makeup in highly revealing dresses were waiting. One man there had his hand between a woman's legs. The masseuses told us that they have mostly male clients. Their monthly salary is 220 yuan, so they depend chiefly on tips.

Ma Yuanxi: However, I think that people, though still a small number now, are working to solve these problems. I think the overall impact of the forum and conference on Chinese women was great. The forum opened the world, at least part of the women's world, to Chinese women. A number of Chinese participants were greatly interested in what was going on in the world about women. Although the schedule for the NGO Forum was only in English, Chinese women got people to translate the postings for relevant panels and workshops and help them talk to foreigners. During the forum after our panel, some teachers and students came to us asking for syllabi and course descriptions of women's studies programs in the United States. A member from a Taiwan women's group asked to establish contact with CSWS and exchange ideas with us on a regular basis. Two women activists working in a county women's federation from Shanxi Province invited us to give talks to their local women. Two journalists, one from France and the other from Belgium, expressed great interest in CSWS and asked to know more about it and its members.

People who went to Beijing for the conference have different reactions or experiences. On the whole I had a good and pleasant experience. I see and feel the impact of the conference and the impact of the changes over the past fifteen years on Chinese women. I see the changes (good and bad) in them, and in Chinese people. I think what matters ultimately is the change is in people's minds, their attitude, mentality, and behavior. The system seems to be, and is bound to be gradually, changing from within. Some one summed up the women's situation as:

1919 was the liberation of the feet.

1949 was the liberation of the hands.
1990s is the liberation of the minds.
I left Beijing with hope in my heart for Chinese women and for my country.

Sharon Hom: For people who've been working on Chinese human rights issues, our central focus was hopefully to bring an international focus to the domestic human rights situation. Of course this was not a "China" conference, so for other people it is understandably more peripheral. Trying to find out what was going on in China was not their main objective, and they didn't want to divert energy from their work on the international agenda. I understand that kind of strategic push, but this raises serious questions about what it means to make the international agenda a priority and marginalize domestic human rights abuses. Those trade-offs have consequences. By not raising questions about issues such as the crackdown that was going on while we were there, we have contributed, in part, to allowing that to happen. So that trade-off, while understandable, is not a cost-free strategy.

I think Western human rights feminists talking about the human rights situation in China are often almost too careful in their efforts to avoid being "imperialistic" and say things like, "let 'the Chinese' articulate their own problems." But this collapses "the Chinese'' into one monolithic identity, erasing the differences between Chinese official voices and the complex voices of Chinese people, situated in different classes, and different geographic or political locations. If the Chinese government claims the sole right to speak about human rights authoritatively, failure to challenge this in part stems from a dangerous nativism, an assertion that "Chinese" speaking are automatically more legitimate that anyone else speaking. And the problem with this legitimation claim is that it does not take adequately into account how difficult it is to speak within China, and secondly, that some "Chinese" speaking can take positions that are absolutely disastrous in terms of their consequences for other Chinese women and men.

Zhong Xueping: Two days before the Fourth World Conference on Women, I went to visit my aunt in Beijing. I had not seen her for more than twelve years. Since my father is originally from Beijing, I have many relatives there. To many of them, I am considered to be twice removed from their lives: as someone born and raised in Shanghai and as someone having lived abroad for over nine years. Like all my relatives in Beijing, my aunt knew that what brought me there was the conference. Shortly after I sat down, she told me that she was doing something in relation to the conference. When I asked what she was supposed to do, she replied (not without feeling somewhat amused herself) that she was to wear a red arm-band and sit around the street corner to be on watch (*zhiqing*). But what she (and her daughter and her family who happened to be visiting there as well) wanted to know was why I was participating in the conference. In my efforts to answer her question, I quickly realized there was no simple way (or no way) for me to explain. For her and the others present, according to the officially circulated rumors, it was an international event that would bring dangerous elements into China. According to a popular stereotypical view, at the same time, the Fourth World Conference on Women, though translated in Chinese as *shi fu hui* (literally: "world women meeting"), was not that different from the *fu dai hui* (literally: "women delegates meeting") meetings where women discuss women's (and therefore trivial) matters. From their perspective, it was hard to associate me, an academic in the United States, with either the dangerous international elements or the *funu daibiao* (woman delegate) who deals with "trivial matters."

In my efforts to be a good niece, I tried to explain the importance of women's issues. I could tell while explaining that they were puzzled by whatever I was trying to say, as if I did not get my geography straight. My aunt, still trying to figure out who I was, said: "*zhongguo funu yijing hen jiefang le*" ("Chinese women are already quite liberated").

One afternoon before the conference, I decided to take a trip to downtown Beijing to check out some bookstores. Walking along the Wangfujing Avenue, I stopped at the table of a book vendor to look at some magazines. While I was standing there, I felt someone tug me from behind. I turned around and saw two (Asian) women. They asked if I spoke English and if I could help them find the way back to Huairou, where they were staying. One of them was quite pregnant. Other people were eager to help too. Among various conflicting directions given, I finally figured out two possible ways for them to get back.

After they left (and I hope the directions helped them get back to Huairou), something interesting happened. The owner of the bookstall asked me in a rather puzzled way: "Are they delegates to the conference?" "Yes," I replied. "But they looked very decent," she wondered aloud. "What do you mean?" I asked. "Didn't they say that the delegates are all like prostitutes?" "Who said so?" I asked. "Well, everybody did." Once again, I felt at a loss for words. The only thing that I could say was that "these people are here to have a conference, not for anything else." Of course, I did not want to tell her and the other people around that I was a daibiao (delegate) as well. How could I begin to explain any of it when in real life no one seemed to know what the conference was really about, and seemed only to be curious about the "delegates?"

In both cases, I wondered about my loss for words. Maybe feeling speechless is a normal reaction in these situations. Why should I have felt the impulse to explain? Should I have tried harder? Do I necessarily know any better? If it is a matter of consciousness, isn't the amused reaction my aunt had toward her duty a demonstration of a discrepancy between her performing the duty and her detachment from the idea behind the duty? Didn't the people around the bookstall perform their civility by actively offering help to the two delegates? And isn't the book vendor's wondering aloud also a form of questioning? I may have more access to information than these people, but do I know better simply because I have access to certain knowledge? These may be rhetorical questions echoing some of the debate familiar to us in the United States, but my wondering did keep my mouth shut and my ears open when in China and continues to keep me "sober" when I do speak. Also, on a different level, given my experience at the conference, I do not think these are mere rhetorical questions: Do we really know what to do under political pressure and do we know that we may be playing into the hands of the very authority and power structure that we challenge and question?

POSTSCRIPT:

Following the 1995 Fourth World Conference on Women, NGOs such as WEDO, the InterAction's Commission on the Advancement of Women, and the International Women's Tribune Center (IWTC) sponsors and reports on follow up on the progress of implementation via multilingual publications, a global fax network, and the internet. In addition to the pressure and monitoring of NGOs, the UN has also urged UN member states to deliver national plans for action as set forth in the Platform of Action. Yet by October 1996, only 19 of the 185 member states had filed plans of action with the UN. Clearly, much work remains to be done to implement the paper commitments of governments and to make a wider range of actors, including transnational corporations, responsible and accountable for the impact of their "private" corporate policies. In the context of international human rights work, more attention to a matrix of multiple actors and interrelationships between state and non-state actors would contribute to approaches for recentering individual and collective human agency and institutional accountability beyond polar discourses of victims/oppressors asserting competing rights-based claims. Towards the work of developing and building multiple simultaneous human rights strategies, this move away from polar and state-centric models might be conceptualized as a project of affirmative justice (Hom forthcoming 1998).

NOTES

1. Chandra Mohanty, Ann Russo and Lourdes Torres, eds., *Third World Women and the Politics of Feminism* (Bloomington: Indiana University Press, 1991), p.21

2. Portions of Wang Zheng's discussion are drawn from her report "A Historic Turning Point for the Women's Movement in China," *Signs: Journal of Women in Culture and Society* 22 (Autumn 1996).

Bibliography

Alford, William P. "Law, Law, What Law? Why Western Scholars of Chinese History and Society Have Not Had More to Say about Its Law," *Modern China* 21, no. 4 (October 1997):398–419.

Amnesty International. *Women in China: Imprisoned and Abused for Dissent.* (Amnesty International: London, June 28, 1995).

Aoki, Keith. "Forgiveness and Asian American Identities: Yellowface, Propaganda and Bifurcated Racial Stereotypes and World War II Propaganda." *UCLA Asian Pacific American Law Journal* 4 (forthcomong 1998).

————. "Colloquy: The Scholarship of Reconstruction and the Politics of Backlash." *Iowa Law Review* 81 (1996). Participants: Keith Aoki, Margaret Chon, Garrett Epps, Neil Gotanda, Frederick Dennis Grenne, Natsu Saito Jenga, Peter Kwan, and Alfred Yen.

Best Chinese Idioms. Hong Kong: Hai Feng Publishing Company, 1989.

Bow, Leslie. "For Every Gesture of Loyalty, There Doesn't Have to Be a Betrayal: Asian American Criticism and the Politics of Locality." In *Who Can Speak,* edited by Judith Roof and Robyn Wiegman. Chicago: University of Illinois Press, 1995.

Brooks, Peter, and Paul Gewirtz, eds. *Law's Stories: Narrative and Rhetoric in the Law.* New Haven: Yale University Press, 1996.

Bryant, Susan. "Collaboration in Law Practice: A Satisfying and Productive Process for a Diverse Profession." *Vermont Law Review* 17, no.2 (Winter 1993): 459–531.

Bunch, Charlotte, Mallika Dutt, and Susannah Fried. "Beijing '95: A Global Referendum on Human Rights of Women." Center for Women's Global Leadership on the Internet at: cwgl@igc.org

Cao, Guilin. "Beijing Natives in New York (Beijing zai niuyue)." *Shiyue* (October) 4 (1991).

Chang, Robert S. "A Meditation on Borders." In *Immigrants Out! The New Nativism and the Anti Immigrant Impulse in the United States*, edited by Juan Perea. New York: New York University Press, 1996.

———. "Passion and the Asian American Legal Scholar." Keynote address: Asian Law Journal Spring Banquet (April 19, 1997).

———. "Toward an Asian American Legal Scholarship: Critical Race Theory, Post- Structuralism, and Narrative Space." *California Law Review* 81, no. 5 (October 1993): 1241–1323.

Charlesworth, Hillary, et al. "Feminist Approaches to International Law." *American Journal of International Law* 85 (1991): 613–645.

Chatterjee, Partha. "The Nationalist Resolution of the Women's Question." In *Recasting Women: Essays in Colonial History*, edited by Kumkum Sangari and Sudesh Vaid. New Brunswick, N.J.: Rutgers University Press, 1990.

Cheung, King-Kwok . *Articulate Silences: Hisaye Yamamoto, Maxine Hong Kingston, Joy Kogawa*. Ithaca: Cornell University Press, 1993.

Chon, Margaret (H.R.). "On the Need for Asian American Narratives in Law: Ethnic Specimens, Native Informants, Storytelling and Silences." *Asian Law Journal* 3, no. 1 (1996):4–32.

Chopin, Kate. *The Awakening*. New York: Dover Press, 1993.

Chow, Rey. "Against the Lures of Diaspora." In *Gender and Sexuality in Twentieth- Century Chinese Literature and Society*, edited by Tonglin Lu. Albany: SUNY Press, 1993.

———. *Primitive Passions: Visuality, Sexuality, Ethnography, and Contemporary Chinese Cinema* . New York: Columbia University Press, 1995.

———. [Keynote address:] "Sex, Gender and Public Space in Contemporary China." Tufts University, Medford, Mass., April 5, 1996.

———. "Things, Common/Places, Passages of the Port City: On Hong Kong and Hong Kong Author Leung Ping-kwan." *Differences: A Journal of Feminist Cultural Studies* 5, no.3 (1993): 179–204.

———. *Women and Chinese Modernity: The Politics of Reading Between East and West* . Minneapolis: University of Minnesota Press, 1991.

———. *Writing Diaspora: Tactics of Intervention in Contemporary Cultural Studies* . Bloomington: Indiana University Press, 1993.

Chrenshaw, Kimberle Williams. "Demarginalizing the Intersection of Race and Sex: A Black Feminist." *Legal Forum: Feminism in the Law: Theory, Practice, and Criticism (*Chicago: University of Chicago Press): 139–167.

Cixous, Helene. *Three Steps on the Ladder of Writing*. Translated by Sarah Cornell and Susan Sellers. New York: Columbia University Press, 1993.

de Groot, Joanna. "Conceptions and Misconceptions: The Historical and Cultural Context of Discussion on Women and Development." In *Women, Development and Survival in the Third World*, edited by Haleh Afshar. New York: Longman Press, 1991.

Dirlik, Arif. "The Postcolonial Aura: Third World Criticism in the Age of Global Capitalism." *Critical Inquiry* 20 (Winter 1994): 328–356.

———. "Reversals, Ironies, Hegemonies: Notes on the Contemporary Historiography of Modern China." *Modern China* 22, no.3 (July 1996): 243–284.

Earth Negotiations Bulletin. 14, no.21. (September 18, 1995).

Espiritu, Yen Le. *Asian American Women and Men: Labor, Laws, and Love.* London: Sage, 1997.

Field, Norma. *In the Realm of a Dying Emperor: A Portrait of Japan at the Century's End.* New York: Pantheon, 1991.

Fong Yue Ting v. U.S., 149 U.S. 698, 717 (1893).

Ford Foundation. *Reflections and Resonances: Stories of Women Involved in International Preparatory Activities for the 1995 NGO Forum on Women* (in Chinese and English). Beijing: Ford Foundation, March 1995.

Frost, Robert. "The Road Not Taken." In *The Top 500 Poems*, edited by William Harmon. New York: Columbia University Press, 1992.

Ghosh, Bishnupriya, and Brinda Bose, eds. *Interventions: Feminist Dialogues on Third World Women's Literature and Film* . New York and London: Garland, 1997.

Ginsberg, Elaine K. "Introduction: The Politics of Passing." In *Passing and the Fictions of Identity*, edited by Elaine K. Ginsberg. Durham: Duke University Press, 1996.

Gotanda, Neil. "Asian American Rights and the Miss Saigon Syndrome." In *Asian Americans and the Supreme Court: A Documentary History*, edited by Kim Hyung-chan. Seattle: University of Washington Press, 1992.

Greenhouse, Linda. "Justice to Review Arizona's Law Making English Its Official Language." *New York Times* (March 26, 1996): A10.

Grewal, Interpal, and Caren Kaplan, eds. *Scattered Hegemonies: Postmodernity and Transnational Feminist Practices* . Minneapolis: University of Minnesota Press, 1994.

Haberstam, Judith. "F2M: The Making of Female Masculinity." In *The Lesbian Postmodern*, edited by Laura Doan. New York: Columbia University Press, 1994.

Hall, Stuart. "Cultural Identity and Diaspora. " In *Discourse and Post-Colonial Theory: A Reader*, edited by Patrick Williams and Laura Chrisman. New York: Columbia University Press, 1994.

Hing, Bill Ong. *Making and Remaking Asian America Through Immigration Policy, 1850-1990* . Stanford: Stanford University Press, 1994.

Hochschild, Arlie, and Anne Machung. *The Second Shift: Working Parents and the Revolution at Home* . New York: Viking Press, 1989.

Hoffman, Eva. *Lost in Translation: A Life in a New Language* , New York: Penguin Books, 1990.

Hom, Sharon K "Cross-Discipline Trafficking: What's Justice Got to Do With It?" In *Disciplining Asia: Theorizing Studies in the Asian Diaspora*, edited by Kandice Chuh and Karen Shimakawa (Durham:Duke University Press, forthcoming).

———. "Re-positioning 'Human' Rights Discourse on 'Asian' Perspectives: Beyond Dead(ly) Paradigms and State-Centered Narrative." *Buffalo Journal of International Law* 3, no. 1 (Summer 1996): 209–234.

———,with Robin Paul Malloy. "China's Market Economy: A Semiosis of Cross Boundary Discourse Between Law and Economics and Feminist Jurisprudence." *Syracuse Law Review* 45, no.2 (1994): 815–851.

———, with Sophia Woodman. "Representations of Chinese Women: International and Domestic Strategies Meet at the Women's Conference." *China Rights Forum* (Winter 1995): 24–27.

———, with Xin Chunying, eds. *English-Chinese Lexicon of Women and Law (Yinghan funnu yu falu cehuishiyi)* . China Translation and Publishing Corp. and UNESCO, 1995.

hooks, bell, *Ain't I a Woman: Black Women and Feminism.* Boston: South End Press, 1981.

———. "Choosing the Margin as a Space of Radical Openness." In *Yearning: Race, Gender and Cultural Politics* . Boston: South End Press, 1990.

Hsu, Cho-yun. "A Reflection on Marginality." In *The Living Tree: The Changing Meaning of Being Chinese Today*, edited by Tu Wei-ming. Stanford: Stanford University Press, 1994.

Human Rights in China. *Caught Between Tradition and the State.* New York: HRIC, 1995.

———. *Fighting for Their Rights: Chinese Women's Experiences Under Political Persecution.* New York: HRIC, 1995.

Hune, Shirley. " Rethinking Race: Paradigms and Policy Formation." *Amerasia Journal* 21, nos.1 and 2 (1995): 29–40.

Kao, Hsin-sheng C., ed. *Nativism Overseas.* Albany: SUNY Press, 1993.

Kastely, Amy H., Deborah Waire Post, and Sharon Hom, eds. *Contracting Law.* Durham: Carolina Academic Press, 1996.

Lai, Him Mark, Genny Lim, and Judy Yung, eds. *Island: Poetry and History of Chinese Immigrants on Angel Island, 1910–1940* . Seattle: University of Washington Press, 1980.

Lâm, Maivân Clech. "Feeling Foreign in Feminism." *SIGNS: Journal of Women in Culture and Society* 19, no.4 (Summer 1994): 865–893.

Lee, Tahirih. "Risky Business: Courts, Culture and the Marketplace." *University of Miami Law Review* 47 (1993): 1335–1414.

Lesnick, Howard. "Infinity in a Grain of Sand: The World of Law and Lawyering as Portrayed in the Clinical Teaching Implicit in the Law School Curriculum." *UCLA Law Review* 37, no.6 (1990): 1157–1197.

Li, Victor Hao. "From Qiao to Qiao." In *The Living Tree: The Changing Meaning of Being Chinese Today*, edited by Tu Wei-ming. Stanford: Stanford University Press, 1994.

Lowe, Lisa. "Heterogeneity, Hybridity, Multiplicity: Making Asian American Differences." *Diaspora* 1, no.1 (Spring 1991): 22–44.

Lubman, Stanley. "Studying Contemporary Chinese Law: Limits, Possibilities and Strategy." *American Journal of Comparative Law* 39 (1991): 293-341.

Lukacs, Georg. *Soul and Form*. Translated by Anna Bostock. Cambridge, Mass.: MIT Press, 1974.

Mazumdar, Sucheta. "Asian American Studies and Asian Studies: Rethinking Roots." In *Asian Americans: Comparative and Global Perspectives*, edited by Shirley Hune et al. Pullman: Washington State University Press, 1991.

Miyoshi, Masao. "A Borderless World? From Colonialism to Transnationalism and the Decline of the Nation-State." *Critical Inquiry* 19 (Summer 1993): 726–751.

Mohanty, Chandra Talpade. *Third World Women and the Politics of Feminism,*" edited by Chandra Talpade Mohanty, Ann Russo, and Lourdes Torres. Bloomington: Indiana University Press, 1991.

Moy, James S. *Marginal Sights: Staging the Chinese in America* . Iowa City: Iowa University Press, 1993.

Mukherjee, Bharati. *Jasmine.* New York: Fawcett Press, 1989.

Myers, Ken. "Deans Disagree on the Usefulness of Magazine's Annual Ranking." *National Law Journal* 18, no.34 (April 8, 1996): A19.

Okihiro, Gary Y. *Margins and Mainstreams: Asians in American History and Culture* . Seattle: University of Washington Press, 1994.

Ong, Aihwa, and Nonini, Donald. *Ungrounded Empires: The Cultural Politics of Modern Chinese Transnationalism.* New York: Routledge, 1997.

People v. Hall, 4 Cal. 399, 409 (Oct. 1854).

Radhakrishnan, R. *Diasporic Meditations: Between Home and Location* . Minneapolis: University of Minnesota Press, 1996.

————. "Nationalism, Gender, and the Narrative of Identity." In *Nationality and Sexualities*, edited by Andrew Parker et al. New York: Routledge, 1992.

————. "Post Modernism and the Rest of the World." *International Journal of Organizational Analysis* 1, no.2 (1994): 305–340.

Rong, Shen. *At Middle Age* . Beijing: Foreign Languages Press, 1987.

Said, Edward. "The Mind of Winter: Reflections of Life in Exile." *Harper's Magazine* (1984): 49–55.

Schwartz, Benjamin I. *The World of Thought in Ancient China* . Cambridge: Harvard University Press, 1994.

Södergran, Edith. *Complete Poems: Edith Sodergran*. Translated by David McDuff. London: Bloodaxe, 1984.

————. *Samlade Dikter*. Stockholm: Wahlstrom & Widstrand, 1977.

Spivak, Gayatri Chakravorty. *In Other Worlds: Essays in Cultural Politics*. New York: Methuen, 1987.

Stephens, Thomas B. *Order and Discipline in China: The Shanghai Mixed Court , 1911– 1927*. Seattle: University of Washington Press, 1992.

Sullivan, Donna. "Envisioning Women's Rights: What Was Achieved in Beijing?" *China Rights Forum* (Winter 1995): 19–23.

Takagi, Dana Y. "Maiden Voyage: Excursion into Sexuality and Identity Politics in Asian America." *Amerasia Journal* 20, no.1 (1994): 1–17.

Tyler, Patrick E. "China's Campus Model for the 90's: Earnest Patriot." *New York Times* (April 23, 1996): A4.

United States v. Wong Kim Ark, 169 U.S. 649, (1898).

Wang, Jing. 'Who Am I?'—Questions of Voluntarism in the Paradigm of 'Socialist Alienation.' *Positions: East Asia Cultures Critique* 3, no.2 (1995): 448–480.

Wang, L. Ling-Chi. "The Structure of Dual Domination: Towards a Paradigm for the Study of the Chinese Diaspora in the United States." *Amerasia Journal* 21, no.1 and 2 (1995): 149–169.

Weber, Max, G. Roth, and P. Wittich, eds. *Economy and Society,* vol. 3. New York: Bedminster Press, 1968.

Wei-ming, Tu. "Cultural China: The Periphery as Center." In *The Living Tree: The Changing Meaning of Being Chinese Today*, edited by Tu Wei-ming. Stanford: Stanford University Press, 1994.

Williams, Patricia. *The Alchemy of Race and Rights: Diary of a Law Professor* . Cambridge: Harvard University Press, 1991.

Wing, Adrienne K., ed. *Critical Race Feminism* . New York: New York University Press, 1997.

Wong, Sau-Ling C. "Denationalization Reconsidered: Asian American Cultural Criticism at a Theoretical Crossroad." *Amerasia Journal* 21, nos.1 and 2 (1995): 1–27. (Special theme issue: "Thinking Theory in Asian American Studies").

Woo, Margaret Y.K. "Chinese Women Workers: A Delicate Balance Between Biology and Equality." In *Engendering China*, edited by C. Gilmartin. Cambridge: Harvard University Press, 1994.

Wu, David Yen-ho. "Chinese and Non-Chinese Identities." In *The Living Tree: The Changing Meaning of Being Chinese Today*, edited by Tu Wei-ming. Stanford: Stanford University Press, 1994.

Xu, Zhimu. "Leaving Behind." In *Selected Poems of Xu Zhimu* . People's Literature Press, 1994.

Yoo, David, guest ed. Special theme issue of "Racial Spirits: Religion and Race in Asian American Communities." *Amerasia Journal* 22, no.1 (1996).

Zhang, Xinxin. "On the Same Horizon." *Harvest* 6 (1981).

Zizek, Slavoj. *The Sublime Object of Ideology* . New York: Verso, 1989.

Contributors

Ying Chan received a B.A. in sociology and economics from Hong Kong University. She was a 1993 recipient of the George Polk Award for Local Reporting and a Nieman fellow at Harvard University (1995-1996). She is presently the consultant for Hong Kong University for the development of a media studies program for mid-career professionals. Until 1997, Ying Chan was an immigration reporter for the *New York Daily News*. Her *Daily News* work included the first extensive report on the people-smuggling trade between the United States and China, based on a month of investigation in Asia in 1990. She also reported extensively on the smuggling of immigrants, on U.S. immigration policy, and on immigration issues generally. From 1976 to 1989, she covered immigration and Asian-American communities for New York-based Chinese-language dailies. In 1989, Ying was the U.S. correspondent for *Yazhou Zhoukan* (Asiaweek), a Time-Warner Chinese-language news weekly published in Hong Kong. As a freelance reporter for the *Village Voice* in New York , she worked on a special report on Chinatown's economic growth and changing political scene. Ying was born and raised in Hong Kong, and speaks three Chinese dialects (Cantonese, Mandarin, and Toisanese).

Tan Dali was born in Shenyang, China. She received her master's degree in American literature from Liaoning University in Shenyang, China, in 1985. She is an ABD in the Comparative Literature Program at the University of Maryland, College Park. Her dissertation, is entitled "Exploring the Intersection Between Gender and Culture—Rereading Li Qingzhao and Emily Dickinson from a Comparative Perspective."

Sharon K. Hom is professor of law at City University of New York School of Law. She was a Root-Tilden scholar and received her J.D. from New York University of School of Law in 1980. From 1986 to 1988, she was a Fulbright professor of law in residence at the China University of Politics and Law. Since returning to the United States in 1988, she has been active in U.S.-China legal education and women's studies training programs and exchanges. She serves on the Board of Governors for the Society of American Law Teachers (SALT), the Special Asian Committee of the Association of the Bar of the City of New York, the advisory board of Human Rights Watch/Asia, the Asian Advisory Board of *The New Press*, and the editorial board of *Amerasia Journal*. Her publications include the *English-Chinese Lexicon on Women and Law (Yinghan funu yu falu cihuishiyi)* (1995), co-edited with Xin Chunying; *Contracting Law* (1996), co-edited with Amy Kastely and Deborah Waire Post; and articles on Chinese law and legal reform, human rights, and feminist theory. Her prose writings and poetry appear in *IKON* #9 (1988), *Without Ceremony,* an anthology of the work of Asian-American women artists, writers, and activists. Sharon was born in Hong Kong, and immigrated to the Unted States when she was five. She is a single parent of a teenage son, James.

Vivien Ng is chair of the Department of Women's Studies at State University of New York at Albany. Prior to her relocation to Albany, she taught Chinese history and women's studies for thirteen years at the University of Oklahoma. While in Oklahoma, she wrote a column for the *Herland Voice*, a newsletter published by Herland Sister Resources, a lesbian feminist collective in Oklahoma. She was president of the National Women's Studies Association in 1993-1994. She was a member of the board of directors, Center for Lesbian and Gay Studies, City University of New York Graduate Center from 1991 to 1994. She is series editor of the new Lesbian Studies series for Garland Publishing. Her primary research focus is Chinese lesbian and gay history and she has published articles on the subject. She has also published a short story, "Bus Stop," in the summer 1995 issue of *Common Lives/Lesbian Lives*. Although she sees a promising future in creative writing, she plans to keep her day job for a while longer. She grew up in Kowloon, Hong Kong, and attended Maryknoll Convent School. She credits the Maryknoll sisters for instilling in her at a very young age a strong sense of personal and social responsibility.

Mary Ting is a visual artist, educator, and Chinese folk art scholar. Mary's sculptures, drawings, and artists' books have been exhibited extensively in the U.S. and abroad. She has lectured and taught at the Cooper Hewitt Museum, Metropolitan Museum of Art, Parsons School of Design, University of Massachusetts at Amherst, and the Henry Street Settlement. She has received grants from the Pollack Krasner Foundation, New York State Council on the Arts, Dieu Donne Papermill, and the Lower Eastside Print Shop. Ting has a BFA from Parsons School of Design and an advanced studies degree in Chinese folk art from the Central Academy of Fine Arts, Beijing.

Margaret Y. K. Woo is professor of law at Northeastern University School of Law. In 1990, she was a fellow at the Bunting Institute of Radcliffe College. She is also an associate in research at the East Asian Legal Studies Center at Harvard Law School and at the Fairbanks Center for East Asian Studies at Harvard College. She holds a visiting professorship at the South Central Institute of Politics and Law in the People's Republic of China. Her publications and research areas include the Chinese court system, human rights, legal institutions, and issues involving Chinese women and labor equality. Margaret was born in Hong Kong and immigrated to the United States when she was seven years old.

Zhong Xueping is assistant professor of Chinese language and Chinese literature at Tufts University. She received her Ph.D. in comparative literature from the University of Iowa. Xueping was born and grew up in Shanghai as a *Beijingren* (Beijing person). Although she was too young to experience the Cultural Revolution as a red guard, or *laosanjie*, she managed to see most of it. Xueping was sent to a state farm at age fifteen and went to college after the Cultural Revolution. She came to the United States in 1986 and went directly to the "heartland" of America—the University of Iowa. She studied British and American literature and switched to comparative literature, where she found an intellectual "home." She has published articles in collections of essays and academic journals. Currently, she is working on a book project examining male Chinese intellectuals through representations of men in contemporary Chinese literature.

Ma Yuanxi is director of translation at the law firm Baker & McKenzie. She received her M.A. and Ph.D. degrees in American literature and comparative literature (with a focus on women's literature) from the State University of New York at Buffalo, and B.A. and M.A. degrees in English and English literature from the Beijing Foreign Studies University in China. She has taught English and English and American literature for thirty years at the Beijing Foreign Studies University, Chinese literature and Chinese language at New York University and the New School for Social Research, and English writing and Asian women courses at the State University of New York at Buffalo. Her projects include English textbooks for Chinese college and university English departments and Chinese television English-language programs. She has published essays and articles on Chinese women's literature, Chinese women's social status, teaching strategies, and translations of novels, short stories, and essays (both from English into Chinese and from Chinese into English).

Eleanor S. Yung founded the New York Asian American Dance Theatre (Asian American Arts Centre) in 1974, and was its artistic and executive director until 1990. She remains the artistic director of the dance component, and continues an active administrative and artistic role in the organization. Born in China and raised in the British colony of Hong Kong, Eleanor has trained in both Chinese classical dance and ballet. She received a bachelor of arts degree in sociology from the University of California at Berkeley and studied dance education at Columbia University Teachers College in New York. Eleanor was also awarded a National Endowment for the Arts choreography fellowship. As an artist instrumental in bringing national attention to traditional and contemporary Asian dance, Eleanor developed a unique modern dance repertoire containing Asian structural influences. Her work has received critical national and local acclaim within the dance field. She began to study chigung in 1987, and in 1994, she began teaching t'ai chi chuan at the Asian American Arts Centre and at the Brooklyn Women's Centre.

Zhang Zhen is a Ph.D. candidate in Chinese literature and film studies at the Department of East Asian Languages and Civilizations at the University of Chicago. She received her master's degree in comparative literature from the University of Iowa. Zhang Zhen was born and raised in the turbulent 1960s and 1970s in Shanghai. During her third-year major in journalism at the prestigious Fu Dan University, she decided to withdraw and subsequently immigrated to Sweden in 1983. During her two years in Sweden she studied languages and film. In the mid-1980s, she returned to China to live and work in Beijing. She continued to write poetry, and was involved in literary and artistic activities such as poetry salons, art exhibitions, and underground publications. Zhang Zhen subsequently lived in Japan for three years. She has written three books of poetry, and has published poems and essays in numerous literary journals and anthologies both in China and overseas, including the literary journal *Jintian (Today),* a key publication for Chinese diaspora writing today.

Wang Zheng is a founding member of the Chinese Society for Women Studies. She received her Ph.D. in history from the University of California at Davis in 1995. She is the author of *Nuxing de jueqi* (a history of the second wave feminism in the U.S.) (Beijing: Dangdai Zhongguo chubanshe, 1995) and coauthor with Gary Hamilton of *From the Soil: The Foundations of Chinese Society* (Berkeley: University of California Press, 1992).